The Working Class in European History

Editorial Advisers
Standish Meacham
Joan W. Scott
Reginald Zelnik

The Road to Revolution in Spain

The Road to Revolution in Spain

The Coal Miners of Asturias
1860–1934

Adrian Shubert

University of Illinois Press
Urbana and Chicago

The publication of this book is made possible by grants from the Program for Cultural Cooperation between Spain's Ministry of Culture and North American Universities and the Isobel Thornby Bequest, University of London.

A Spanish edition of this book was published as *Hacia la revolución. Orígenes sociales del movimiento obrero en Asturias, 1860–1934*, by Editorial Crítica of Barcelona in 1984.

This book is printed on acid-free paper.

Library of Congress Cataloging-in-Publication Data

Shubert, Adrian, 1953–
  The road to revolution in Spain.

  (The Working class in European history)
  Revision of thesis (Ph.D.)—Queen Mary College,
University of London, 1982.
  Bibliography: p.
  Includes index.
  1. Coal miners—Spain—Asturias—History—20th century.
2. Strikes and lockouts—Coal mining—Spain—Asturias—
History—20th century. 3. Trade-unions—Coal miners—
Spain—Asturias—History—20th century. 4. Coal trade—
Spain—Asturias—History—20th century. I. Title.
II. Series.
HD8039.M62S68 1987   331.7'622334'094615   86–24998
ISBN 0–252–01368–9 (alk. paper)

To my parents,
by way of thanks

Contents

Tables

Acknowledgments

In the course of preparing this study I accumulated a number of debts which I would now like to repay. A doctoral fellowship from the Social Science and Humanities Research Council of Canada from 1978 to 1981, and a Vicente Cañada Blanch fellowship from 1981 to 1982, permitted me the luxury of devoting four years to research and writing. As Visiting Post-Doctoral Fellow at the Calgary Institute for the Humanities, and Andrew W. Mellon Post-Doctoral Fellow at Stanford University, I was able to revise my dissertation for publication.

The staffs of a number of archives and libraries in Spain: the Biblioteca Nacional, Hemeroteca Municipal, Escuela Superior de Ingenieros de Minas, Fundación Pablo Iglesias, Fundación Francisco Largo Caballero, and Fundación de Investigaciones Marxistas, all in Madrid, the Archivo Histórico Nacional, Sección de la Guerra Civil, in Salamanca, the Archivo Histórico Provincial in Oviedo, and the Hemeroteca Municipal in Gijón were always sympathetic and helpful. The mayors of Mieres and Pola de Laviana gave me free run of the municipal archives. Father Patac, S.J., of Gijón let me use his impressive collection of materials about Asturias.

A number of Spanish colleagues were generous in providing me with suggestions and material. I want to mention two who became friends in the process, Germán Ojeda of the University of Oviedo, and Francisco Martín Angulo of HUNOSA. Joan C. Ullman of the University of Washington has provided much appreciated moral support and invaluable comments on various versions of my work.

Paul Preston of Queen Mary College, London, was the ideal dissertation supervisor. His vast knowledge of Spain and its recent history is matched only by his willingness to share it with others, and by his concern for his students.

The unflagging support and encouragement of my wife, Agueda, who has followed this book through many stages and to many places, has been invaluable.

Finally, I want to thank my parents, to whom I owe so much and to whom I dedicate this book.

Abbreviations

AHE	Archivo de la Hullera Española, Ujo
AHN	Archivo Histórico Nacional
AHN-GC	Archivo Histórico Nacional—Sección de la Guerra Civil
AMM	Archivo Municipal Mieres
AMPL	Archivo Municipal Pola de Laviana
AS	*Aurora Social* (Oviedo)
AV	*Avance* (Oviedo)
CNT	Confederación Nacional del Trabajo
DGM	Dirección General de Minas
EMME	*Estadística Minera y Metalúrgica de España* (Madrid)
ES	*El Socialista* (Madrid)
FIM	Fundación de Investigaciones Marxistas
FLC	Fundación Francisco Largo Caballero
FPI	Fundación Pablo Iglesias
MH	*El Minero de la Hulla* (Mieres)
NO	*El Noroeste* (Gijón)
PCE	Partido Comunista de España
PSOE	Partido Socialista Obrero Español
RIMA	*Revista Industrial Minera Asturiana* (Oviedo)
RM	*Revista Minera* (Madrid)
RNE	*Revista Nacional de Economía* (Madrid)
SMA	Sindicato de Obreros Mineros de Asturias
SUM	Sindicato Unico de Mineros
UGT	Unión General de Trabajadores

Introduction

On the afternoon of October 4, 1934, Teodomiro Menéndez arrived in Oviedo on the train from Madrid. One of the most moderate leaders of the Socialist party (PSOE), Menéndez was not happy about this trip to his native Asturias, for in his hatband he carried the password that was to initiate the long-planned insurrection against the right-wing government of the Second Republic.

The idea for such a rising had emerged immediately after the elections of November 1933, in which an alliance of parties of the Right, led by the CEDA of José María Gil Robles, had defeated the parties of the Center and the Left that had governed during the first two years of the Republic. The Socialists feared that the victory of the Right meant that the achievements of those two years would be undone and that Spain would be led toward fascism. Only three days after the election the Socialist National Committee was discussing the possibility of an armed insurrection, and four days later it had set up a liaison committee with the Socialist trade union confederation, UGT, to discuss the matter.[1]

On February 3 a liaison committee among the party, UGT, and Socialist Youth (FJS) was set up "to deal with whatever is necessary to confront fascism."[2] The committee set to work in a deliberate and careful manner to organize the rising throughout the country. Juan Simeon Vidarte, vice-president of the PSOE and secretary of this committee, described the planning of the insurrection:

[Carlos] Hernández and [Felipe] Pretel took charge of the instructions for the unions which were to declare the general strike at the precise moment; [Santiago] Carrillo, president of the Youth, of structuring the shock troops and of selecting young men to serve as liaisons and carry out special missions; while we, the

1

party representatives, prepared our commanders who would lead the insurrection in the provinces.

First we sent a circular to our provincial federations and to the groups in places where there was a military garrison, important police detachments, railway centers, naval bases, etc., in which we asked a number of questions intended to determine our real strength in the area as well as that of parties sympathetic to us and that of our opponents, as well as the contacts our people had with members of the Army, Civil Guard, or Assault Guard. We also had them prepare strategic studies for the occupation of radio transmitters, post offices, airfields, railway stations, etc.[3]

Indalecio Prieto and Francisco Largo Caballero maintained contacts with military figures, including a number of generals, whom they hoped to convince to participate in the rising. In Asturias, Ramón González Peña, Amador Fernández, and Belarmino Tomás were convinced that the military governor, Colonel Antonio Aranda, would support them. Amaro del Rosal, president of the National Federation of Bank Employees, was in touch with members of the Civil Guard and Assault Guard who were to participate in the movement in Madrid.[4] Prieto and del Rosal were in charge of the finances for the movement, and Prieto, who had a vast network of contacts in the bureaucracy and the business world, played a key role in the acquisition of arms.[5] The Basque country was a principal source of weapons. There Enrique de Francisco, president of the UGT and a founder of an important cooperative in Eibar, was able to use his influence among the gunsmiths, who smuggled weapons out of the factories and set up clandestine workshops where they produced guns for the insurrection. In Asturias, as del Rosal learned from a friend, Socialist workers were smuggling seven guns per week, in pieces, out of the state small arms factory in Oviedo.[6]

While the Socialists' careful plans were being made through the spring and summer of 1934, the political situation became ever more brittle, as Largo Caballero answered with threats of revolution Gil Robles's ominous declarations about his intentions.[7] The moment for the Socialists to deliver on their rhetoric finally came in October. Gil Robles set off a cabinet crisis on September 26 by demanding that his party, which was the largest in the Cortes, have three portfolios in return for its continued support of the government. The Samper cabinet resigned on October 1, and after three days of indecision, during which the Socialists called for new elections, President Niceto Alcalá Zamora called on the veteran leader of the Radicals, Alejandro Lerroux, to form a ministry that included the three CEDA members demanded by Gil Robles. The news found the Socialist revolutionary committee at the party's headquarters in central Madrid, and took the members, who had not believed that Alcalá Zamora would take such a step, totally by surprise. Del Rosal described the scene:

Caballero, Prieto, Zugazagoitia, de Francisco, Carrillo, and a soldier whose name I forget were there, among others. . . . The news was followed by a tremendous silence. Caballero and Prieto were on their feet, ready to leave when the two messengers arrived. Hats in hand they looked at each other as if to ask "What do we do?" Someone broke the silence by saying that they had to give the word to launch the strike and begin the movement. Silence followed. Largo spoke. . . . With considerable dignity he said, "I won't believe it until I see it in the *Gazette*." [8]

When more people arrived to confirm the news of the president's decision, the orders were given.

The rising that the Socialists had designed was a total failure. None of the plans had been completed, and the Socialists were caught off guard: "Who coordinates? Who leads? Who gives orders? No one. Everything is expectations, confusion, vacillation." [9] The leaders in Madrid were arrested immediately or forced into hiding (Largo Caballero) or exile (Prieto). The hoped-for participation of military figures did not materialize. Nor did that of the police. After a few days of desultory street fighting led by the Socialist militias, the members of the committee still at liberty called an end to the strike. In Catalonia, Luís Companys, president of the Generalitat (autonomous regional government), proclaimed the independent Catalan republic, but the radical nationalists who had encouraged him to do so refused to arm the workers, and the rebels were forced to surrender once it became apparent that the military garrison had remained loyal to Madrid. Only in the northern coal mining region of Asturias did the movement get off the ground, but there the outcome was far different from what the Socialists had anticipated.

The regional revolutionary committee had drawn up a precise military plan, which called for the miners to quickly take control of the coalfields and launch a surprise attack on the capital Oviedo, which would be supported by a rising of the workers inside the city and, it was hoped, by the military governor, Aranda. The first step, the assault on the posts of the paramilitary Civil Guard in the coalfields, was accomplished successfully but took much longer than anticipated. In Sama de Langreo the battle lasted a full thirty-six hours, and thirty-eight Civil Guards were killed. In all, ninety-two died in the attacks on their posts.

In the Aller Valley the Civil Guard posts were all subdued by the afternoon of October 5, but the revolutionaries were then confronted by another enemy. Twenty-seven militants of the Sindicato Católico took refuge in the union's headquarters, which was then besieged by 400 miners. The occupants fled after a bomb partially destroyed the building. Only in Mieres was the initial victory swift. At 8:30 on the morning of the 5th, Manuel Grossi, a militant of the dissident Communist group the Bloque Obrero y Campesino, and a member of the committee of the Alianza Obrera (Workers' Alliance), proclaimed

3

the Socialist Republic from the balcony of the town hall. He was answered by "cries of long live the revolution and the Socialist Republic." [10]

The delays and the lack of coordination among the three columns of armed miners that advanced on Oviedo (one from Ablaña commanded by Ramón González Peña, president of the Socialist Sindicato de Obreros Mineros Asturianos (SMA); one from Mieres; and one from Langreo) eliminated the element of surprise and allowed the military authorities to prepare their defenses. González Peña's group spent all of the 5th on the outskirts of the city waiting for the provincial revolutionary committee to give the order to attack. Due to confusion, the order did not arrive until the next day, and in the interval the workers in the city did nothing.

The battle for Oviedo had some 1,400 soldiers and 300 Civil Guards defending the capital against an initial force of 1,200 workers, which was later supplemented by 700 reinforcements. After the first day, the revolutionaries controlled a large part of the city, but they had to endure four days of street fighting before they were able to take the center and reduce the defenders to a few isolated pockets—the barracks, the jail, the Civil Government building, and the cathedral. At the same time the workers scored a number of victories around the capital. On the 6th, a small group staged a surprise attack on the cannon factory at Trubia during which the workers inside were able to disarm the soldiers. Twenty-seven cannon were captured, but they proved to be much less useful than had been hoped, as the detonators had been removed from all the shells, which meant that the shells did not explode after hitting the target. The explosives factory at La Manjoya surrendered on the 7th. Finally, on the 9th, the workers captured the state small arms factory in Oviedo itself after a battle that lasted three days. This gave the revolutionaries 24,000 weapons, but this windfall was immediately neutralized by a shortage of ammunition. Production of bullets was organized, but never surpassed the figure of 3,000 per day, not nearly enough to supply between ten and twelve thousand men in arms. [11]

The obsession with Oviedo meant that the other major Asturian city, Gijón, with its large and combative working class composed predominantly of anarchosyndicalist metal workers, dockers, and fishermen, was neglected. Oviedo was of course politically symbolic, but Gijón and its port, El Musel, were strategically more important. The workers of the city, short of arms, fought bravely behind barricades but were unable to hold the port or prevent Colonel Juan Yagüe, commanding the African troops of the Spanish Foreign Legion— the same forces at whose head Francisco Franco would initiate the Civil War—from landing.

Meanwhile, at the southern end of the coalfields, at what was called the "southern front," General Carlos Bosch's column, advancing along the main highway from Leon, was encircled at Vega del Rey by between two and three thousand miners. These amateur fighters made skillful use of the mountainous terrain to trap professional soldiers who had badly underestimated their adversary. The miners set up field kitchens, medical assistance, and even telephone links to the local committees in Pola de Lena and Mieres. On the 7th, representatives of these two committees and those of Oviedo, Olloniego, and Sama met in Mieres to discuss taking the offensive in the south: "organizing an invading army to occupy Campomanes and begin the march on Madrid." [12] This idea was finally rejected after a long debate on the grounds that it would be dangerous to turn attention away from Oviedo, which had not yet been totally subdued.

Bosch's troops remained trapped for six days before the arrival of reinforcements under General Balmes allowed them to break out and retreat. On the 15th, almost totally out of ammunition, the miners began to withdraw, but the efforts of a small guerrilla force—and the concern of General Balmes not to fall into another trap—meant that his troops advanced cautiously and never reached their objective, Mieres.

The workers' forces were organized in small militia groups of thirty men, which acted autonomously at the front. In spite of the obstacle to coordinated action that this represented, the military achievement of the workers was considerable, for they were facing a well-armed, professional enemy of 26,000 men: General Eduardo López Ochoa advancing on Oviedo from Galicia, Colonel Yagüe moving south after landing at Gijón, and General José Solchaga's force marching on the Nalón valley from the east, in addition to the Bosch-Balmes column trapped at Vega del Rey. The government also made liberal use of aerial bombardments, which had an incalculable demoralizing effect. "Aviation was a terrible weapon . . . against which there was no other defense than hiding. The bombs which were dropped so accurately on Oviedo, Campomanes, and Mieres dampened the revolutionary spirit much more than did the news of the defeat of the revolution elsewhere in the country. But you can be sure that the terror which the planes and their bombs infused in the civilian population, and which sometimes spread to the revolutionaries, was much greater than the real damage they did." [13]

The real importance of the Asturian revolution, however, lies not in its military aspects but in the social organization that began to emerge in the zones dominated by the workers. The insurrection was theoretically under the control of the provincial committee in Oviedo, which was composed of five Socialists, two Communists, and an anarchosyndicalist. This was the Asturian arm of the national committee based in Madrid, which was in charge of overall organization. In contrast to the precisely planned military operation, there was no predetermined revolutionary blueprint beyond "a concrete program for taking the physical centers of power by military action, which would allow the workers' leaders to take administrative control of the region." [14] With a victorious rising throughout Spain, the Socialists would presumably implement the program of reforms that Prieto had presented.

However, the writ of the provincial committee did not run into the coalfields, where the revolutionary impetus of the miners almost immediately exceeded the official objectives of the rising. During the brief two-week life of the Asturian Commune the workers controlled about one-third of the region and 80 percent of its population. Within this territory, with the coalfields at its heart, all established authority disappeared with the subjugation of the Guardia Civil. On the 5th and 6th numerous local committees appeared. These were composed of representatives of the relevant working-class organizations, although not necessarily in strict relation to the local balance of forces. In Sama the committee included the PSOE, the Communists, and the CNT, while in Turón only the Socialists and Communists participated. In Mieres the committee was appointed by Grossi and included Socialists, anarchists, and "official" Communists as well as himself. In La Felguera, where the CNT was dominated by the ultrarevolutionary FAI, the anarchists were in charge by themselves.

These local committees were the organizational heart of the revolution. The most pressing matter was military organization. In Mieres and Pola de Lena, headquarters and recruiting offices were set up in the Casa del Pueblo. The Lena office was run by Sergeant Diego Vázquez, a soldier who had joined the movement. In Langreo the committee issued an order on the 7th calling for volunteers for its "Red Army." On the 8th a special war committee was created to relieve the local committee from some of its burden. A central motor pool of 600 vehicles was set up in Sama, with smaller ones in Mieres and Turón. In all, about 1,000 vehicles were requisitioned to carry troops around the coalfield. Trains were also used for this purpose.

The production of military equipment was organized. A bomb factory was set up in the Mieres Casa del Pueblo, and the foundry of the Fábrica de Mieres was used to manufacture bomb throwers. Armored vehicles were produced in Turón, while in La Felguera the FAI kept the Duro-Felguera foundry going, turning out armored vehicles in three eight-hour shifts per day.

The committees took charge of a wide range of other activities, in fact of all aspects of social organization incumbent on a government. These committees considered themselves revolutionary organs, not merely stand-ins for a public authority that had temporarily disappeared. They styled themselves "revolutionary committees" in their decrees, which generally ended with "long live the social revolution!" The Grado committee flatly announced that "we are creating a new society," and the Communist-controlled Turón committee used the radio of the Central Eléctrica de Hulleras to proclaim the "Republic of Asturian Workers and Peasants." [15]

Money was abolished and replaced by vouchers issued to each family. In Mieres "the Supply Committee acted with complete autonomy . . . and decided that the workers would be issued with vouchers. . . . The bourgeoisie would have to pay in cash and the money would go into a fund created by the Committee." [16] In La Felguera, on the other hand, the anarchists did not impose rationing. [17]

In Oviedo, Sama, and Mieres hospitals were organized where the wounded of both sides were treated. Both nuns and doctors worked in these hospitals, although the latter often had to be forcibly recruited. Work committees organized the conservation of the mines and the operation of essential public services such as water and electricity. Sama even had its streets washed every day. [18] Public order was maintained by armed police forces, generally called the Red Guard, and in Oviedo, where the revolutionaries controlled the bourgeois residential and commercial districts, special attempts were made to prevent looting by what Grossi called the "canaille." [19]

Jails were improvised where necessary, and in general terms the prisoners were well treated. There were some executions, mostly in the latter stages of the insurrection when defeat was imminent and word of the brutal military repression began to spread. In Turón eight Hermanos de la Doctrina Cristiana and a priest were killed on the orders of the local committee and later the director of Hulleras del Turón, Rafael de Riego, was also shot, although this was probably an act of personal vengeance. While the revolution did have its excesses, it was far less bloodthirsty than the repression. At least sixty-one innocent civilians were killed in the outer districts of Oviedo as the army occupied the city and between twenty-five and fifty others summarily executed in the Pelayo barracks.

The Socialist-dominated provincial committee began to consider abandoning the movement as early as the 9th, when it was clear that only Asturias had risen. González Peña favored a withdrawal into the stronghold of the coalfields, a move vigorously opposed by the Communists, who considered it cowardly and claimed that the Soviet Union was sending aircraft to help the revolution. [20] On the 11th, with López Ochoa's troops on the outskirts of the capital, the committee fled, and González Peña, the so-called generalissimo of the revolution, was not seen again until he was arrested long after the movement had been put down. [21] The Mieres committee also agreed to flee, and on the night of the 11th all but the Communist members, who said they would follow shortly afterward, left. When the Communists did not follow, Grossi and the others returned to the city to find that "despite the committee's unanimous decision to abandon Mieres, the comrades of the official Communist party were trying to turn the workers against us, making us responsible for the desertion of all the committees in Asturias." [22]

The precipitous, unannounced flight of the provincial committee caused a temporary panic—in Sama the Red Guard left its weapons in the street—but the local committees remained in place. The committees in Sama, Mieres, Quirós, and Pola de Lena continued to put together new militia units and send them out to fight as late as the 17th. On the 14th, Sergeant Vázquez led 1,000 men from Langreo to Oviedo and kept them in action for three days in spite of a pressing shortage of arms.

On the 12th, the day following the flight of the provincial committee, a second committee, composed of five Communists, an anarchosyndicalist, and two members of the Socialist Youth, was chosen at a meeting in the main square of Oviedo. It lasted only a day, launching counterattacks against the troops entering the city. It also tried to replace the workers' militias with a "Red Army" based on the conscription of all workers between the ages of eighteen and thirty-five. Grossi tried to convince the committee to abandon the capital, which was under heavy aerial bombardment, but without success.

During the course of the 12th some of the Socialist members of the first committee, including its president, Belarmino Tomás, returned to Oviedo, and a third, and final, provincial committee was formed with six Socialists and three Communists. Representatives of the CNT attended the meetings but refused to serve as members. The next day the committee moved to Sama, where it was closely watched by the workers who suspected another escape attempt. The Communist members stayed in Oviedo to mount a last defense.

The Socialists' main concern was to find a way to wind up a struggle they knew was lost. Negotiations with López Ochoa began on the 17th, but his initial terms—that all weapons be laid down immediately and that a quarter of the members of the provincial committee and those of Mieres and Trubia surrender themselves as hostages—were rejected by the workers at a mass meeting in the main square of Sama. Tomás then went to negotiate with the general and agreed to surrender all arms in return for the general's word that the African troops would not enter the coalfields and that there would be no reprisals, a promise that was not kept. Tomás then returned to Sama to announce the terms but had great difficulty in convincing the workers to accept them. That night both the provincial committee and the CNT issued their final communiqués calling on the workers to lay down their weapons. The Asturian revolution was over.

The October revolution of 1934 was one of the few occasions in European history in which an industrial working class threw itself into a total frontal and armed assault on the state and the organization of society. Although the events of those epic two weeks have been reconstructed, the most important question—why did they happen?—has not been adequately addressed. Up to now there have been two schools of thought to account for the revolutionary outbreak of October 4 to 18, 1934. The first, shared by historians of various political persuasions, sees the Asturian revolution as the work of the Socialist party and its trade union affiliate, the UGT, and in particular the SMA. Thus David Ruiz, in his pioneering study of the labor movement in Asturias, ends his narrative with the coming of the Second Republic and concludes that "the SMA revived during the first three years of the Republic and was the motor which drove the other working class organizations to carry out, under its direction, the great revolutionary experiment of October, 1934." [23]

Even such a fierce contemporary critic of Socialist reformism as Juan Andrade pointed to the resuscitation of militant attitudes among the Socialist leadership as an explanation. "Anguished by what might happen to the proletariat with neo-fascists in power, a part of the social-democratic and UGT bureaucracy recalled its proletarian origins and its solidarity with the working class reappeared. It decided to stand or fall with its own kind, with those who had raised them politically. This was the cause of the October revolution." [24] On the other side, the conservative Sánchez Garcia-Sauco agrees that the SMA was the focus of the movement. Using police and judicial records unavailable to Ruiz, he allows himself to be seduced by his sources and their determination to establish the guilt for the events. The Socialist leaders are portrayed as being completely culpable for the revolution, and the police perspective that permeates his work is reflected in his initial questions: "How was the proletariat organized? What was its political orientation? What were its goals and who set them?" [25]

The second school of thought, generally favored by those on the far left, replaces the organizational role of the Socialists with the intense radicalization of a working class that despaired of its leadership and took matters into its own hands. Anarchist Manuel Villar claimed that the militance of the coal miners determined the conduct of the Socialist leadership: "The openly revolutionary temperament of the miners was crucial in shaping their behavior. Just contrast the conduct of the Asturian Socialists with that of Socialists elsewhere in Spain." [26] Trotskyist journalist Narcís Molíns i Fábrega wrote at the time that an inverse relationship existed between the strength of the Socialist bureaucracy and the force of the revolution. Grandizo Munis, of the Izquierda Comunista, agreed: "The dispersion of the working class in a number of small centers and its isolation from the main political centers, which is usually an important handicap for a revolutionary movement, was instead an advantage in Asturias and was the principal reason the movement succeeded in becoming an insurrection. Because the miners were well removed from the bureaucratic brake of the major cities they were able to act on their account and present the leadership with the *fait accompli* of the revolution." [27]

Two of the Socialists most involved in the organization of the insurrection straddle these two interpretations. Francisco Largo Caballero, in his memoirs, "Notas históricas de la Guerra en España, 1917–1940," provides a detailed account of the Socialist preparations but then attributes the virulence of the movement in Asturias to "the special psychology of the miners created by a special life and atmosphere" and to "the proximity of the tools of struggle: the arms factory, cannon factory, dynamite factory." [28] In his recently published account of the events of 1934 Amaro del Rosal repeats and adds to Largo's description of the detailed planning of the insurrection, but is adamant that "October was not the movement which was being planned: it was an abortion of that movement in a preliminary phase of its development." [29] Planning had not been completed in Asturias either, but there the accessibility of weapons made action possible, "a factor which was present only in Asturias." [30]

There is no doubt that both elements—the organizational framework and capacity offered by the Socialists and the massive upsurge of militancy among the workers, especially the coal miners—were important. There is, however, considerable ambiguity surrounding the intentions of the Socialist leadership, at both the national and regional levels.

This ambiguity stemmed from two causes. The first was the division of the Socialists into three main currents: the Kautskian orthodoxy of the right wing headed by Julián Besteiro, president of the UGT until January 1934; the center group headed by Indalecio Prieto, which favored collaboration with the Republicans; and the increasingly revolutionary left wing led by Francisco Largo Caballero, who after February 1934 was both president of the PSOE and secretary-general of the UGT.

The divisions had emerged in the 1920s over the question of what position the Socialists should assume toward the military dictatorship of General Miguel Primo de Rivera; they deepened in 1930 when they were faced with a decision over whether to form part of the Republican conspiracy against the monarchy. [31] Prieto and his followers wanted the Socialists to take part in the conspiracy, but Besteiro, who controlled the party executive, did not—his rigid Marxism required that such a "bourgeois revolution" be made by the bourgeoisie itself, not by the working class. Largo Caballero tipped the balance, responding to a growing restlessness in the rank and file that indicated support for a republic, as well as to the offer of three cabinet posts for the PSOE, including the ministry of labor from which Largo could control the institutions of labor relations to favor the UGT at the expense of the rival CNT. The enmity between the Besteiro and Largo Caballero factions increased following the dispute over who was to blame for the failure of the general strike in Madrid, which was to have accompanied the military rising planned for December 15, 1930.

Largo Caballero's advocacy of the Republic was not, as in the case of Prieto, based on any principled belief in the value of republican democracy. Once the advantages that collaboration with the Republicans seemed to hold out did not materialize as planned, and once the dashed hopes of the Socialist grass roots in Republican reform began to manifest themselves, he began to reconsider his position. Largo Callabero's second thoughts were furthered by the political fallout from the brutal repression of an attempted anarchist rising in the Andalusian village of Casas Viejas in January 1933,[32] and culminated in September when President Alcalá Zamora dismissed the cabinet of Manuel Azaña and called on Alejandro Lerroux, a corrupt old demagogue and leader of the Radical party, to form a government. In his younger days Lerroux had advocated the use of violence against the monarchy and had been involved with anarchist attempts to assassinate Alfonso XIII, but by 1933 he had moved far to the right. His government allowed the social legislation written while Azaña was prime minister—much of it by Largo Caballero's own labor ministry—to go unenforced. As a result whatever confidence Largo Caballero had had in the Republic evaporated.

The Socialists broke their alliance with the Republicans and went into the election of November 1933 alone. While Largo Caballero had good reason for his disillusionment, this decision was a major error. The electoral law, written while three Socialists were in the cabinet, had been designed to prevent parliamentary fragmentation by favoring coalitions, and as a result the PSOE was heavily penalized. Their 1.6 million votes won them fifty-eight seats while the Radicals, with about half as many votes, took 104 seats as part of a right-wing alliance. The Socialists were fairly, and predictably, defeated, but many felt that they had been illegitimately expelled from power. In this context they began to discuss the possibility of an insurrection against the Right.

But as the Socialists debated this question, the enmity between Largo Caballero, who controlled the party, and Besteiro, who controlled the UGT, surfaced once again. There was no fundamental disagreement about whether or not to plan some kind of insurrection—the question was "when," and as we will see in a minute, "why." On November 21 the UGT Executive met to discuss the results of the election and voted to create a joint committee with the Socialist party. The UGT National Committee[33] met on November 24 and heard a report on the two meetings between members of the UGT and PSOE Executives, where it had been decided that the two organizations "must count on the possibility of an anti-Republican or fascist movement and be prepared to confront it and if possible destroy or contain it. . . . The goal was the preservation of the democratic Republic . . . in which we can count on the support of other elements."[34] The committee then voted to appoint a liaison committee with the party. The two Executives met on November 25, and Largo Caballero proposed that a revolutionary movement be planned. A note stating their decision to resist any attempt at a coup against the Republic was drafted and sent to *El Socialista*. The two Executives met again on December 18, and the differences began to emerge, as they could not agree on whether to plan for an immediate action or to wait until the Right took the initiative. Prieto, for the PSOE, argued that Socialist supporters were already suffering under the Right and that delay would mean loss of support, especially in the countryside, "because they are being tortured there. If we delay we will lose the game."[35] Besteiro, president of the UGT, argued that the Right was still acting legally and that action against the government could not be justified. It was necessary to wait on events and then decide what to do.[36]

This division over when to act led to the cessation of the activities of the joint committee and the temporary breaking of relations between the two organizations. On December 31 the UGT National Committee met to discuss a letter from Largo Caballero that suggested that Socialists be prepared to act immediately should the Right move. Andrés Saborit stated the position of the UGT Executive, that "such events would be the signal for us to meet and decide whether to act, but we do not accept, in advance, that such conditions mean that we must act."[37] The National Committee met again nine days later and voted that the two Executives resume their meetings to see if they could come to some agreement.

On January 12 the Socialist Executive met, and Prieto presented what he called "six points of view on what might be a program for unified action against the forces of the right."[38] The main points of his proposed program were the collectivization of the large landed estates, educational reform, dissolution of the religious orders, the reorganization of the armed forces and the purge of all officers hostile to the Republic, the dissolution of the Civil Guard and its replacement by a popular militia, more advanced labor legislation, fiscal reform, and the dismissal of the president of the Republic.[39] In short, it was a step or two beyond the liberal revolutions of the nineteenth century and a program that Republicans could have accepted without much difficulty. Yet when Besteiro met with Prieto to resume the contacts between the two Executives, they were unable to overcome their differences about the need for immediate action. Besteiro was left "perplexed and stunned" by Prieto's program and told him that further meetings would be "useless."[40]

Yet when Besteiro reported on these meetings to the UGT National Committee on January 27, he found that an overwhelming majority was in favor of accepting the party's draft program. He and the rest of the Executive resigned and were replaced two days later by a new team, which included Largo Caballero as secretary-general. At its first meeting, on February 3, the new Executive named a delegation to a joint revolutionary planning committee with the party and the Socialist Youth. Preparations for the insurrection were underway.[41]

The second ambiguity, complicated by and complicating the first, was the looseness and imprecision with which the Socialists used the word "revolution." During the discussions within the PSOE and UGT leaderships over whether to plan what they called the "movement" there was absolutely no precision, and certainly no consensus, about what its objective was. Here the alignments were different from what they were over the tactical question of when to act. The principal division was between Prieto and Besteiro, who wanted to defend the Republic from the threat of a right-wing coup, and Largo Caballero, who appeared to favor a social revolution.

Besteiro's position was clear. There was, he said, no way the Socialists could take power, either to implant Socialism or "to govern in a bourgeois way on our own." [42] He supported the original declaration of the two Executives to resist any attempt by the Right to abandon constitutional methods, but by the same token he saw the Socialists' best means of defense as "the guarantees offered to us by the democratic state." [43]

But Besteiro was losing influence, and after his resignation of January 27, 1934, he and his supporters counted for little in Socialist councils. Prieto was another matter. He was the author of what was accepted as the program for the movement, even though it was not made public until January 1936, and he played a central role in securing weapons and making contacts with the military. And his position was also clear: in presenting his program to the Socialist Executive on January 12 he announced that "it is essential to radicalize the Republic." [44] At a meeting of the PSOE and UGT Executives on July 2 he, along with Fernando de los Ríos and Enrique de Francisco, demanded an alliance with the Republicans if the Socialists did not act on rumors that President Alcalá Zamora was going to resign. [45]

The confusion arises from those who most strongly supported what they called revolution, and especially from Largo Caballero. In his memoirs Largo Caballero states that the position of the Socialist Executive, of which he was president, in the discussions with the UGT was that the goal of the movement was "to impose Socialist postulates" and not merely to defend democracy. [46] Yet he also said that the movement was to be against fascism and his response to Prieto's proposal was that it was "simply a program to be realized the day after the revolution has triumphed. . . . the bourgeois elements will never stand for it." [47] At the same time he stated that he was opposed to setting any program for the rising: "I do not believe in programs prior to a revolutionary movement such as the one we want to organize: History has shown without exception, that the realities of the struggle force all such programs to be changed." [48] And during a meeting of the revolutionary committee in early March he talked of the "need to organize a revolutionary movement . . . which would rescue the Republic and permit its democratic and social development." [49] Amaro del Rosal, a fervent defender of Largo Caballero as a revolutionary leader, confirms this vagueness and cites it as a major cause for the defeat of the insurrection:

Caballero and Prieto embodied the vacillations. They did not believe that the president would bring the enemies of the Republic into the government. When this did happen it had to be asked, what is the character and objective of the movement? Was it solely a threat, a means of coercion to prevent the CEDA from entering the government? If the CEDA did enter the government, which no one thought likely, then the revolutionary movement would be unleashed, in desperation. This policy of doubt, of vacillation, this lack of firmness and decision at the top, determined the weakness and coherence of the movement at the bottom.[50]

But Largo was not the only Socialist unclear about the objectives of the movement. The minutes of the UGT National Committee meetings of December 1933 and January 1934, which culminated with the resignation of the Besteiro leadership, reveal a startling inability among the advocates of "revolution" to define, in an unambiguous way, what the goals and purpose of the revolution were supposed to be.

The question was certainly asked. On December 31 José Castro of the National Agricultural Workers' Federation (FNTT) expressed the "confusion" of his members over the "reach" of the movement.[51] Later the same day, Andrés Saborit, a member of the Executive, asked the authors of a resolution defining the UGT's position whether its purpose was to defend the Constitution or for the working class to seize power. The answer was less than unequivocal. Carlos Hernández of the Urban Transport Workers, an advocate of social revolution, replied that there was no need to make such a delineation beforehand: "We cannot judge in advance of the movement what the reach of that movement is going to be because that will depend on the objective conditions which will structure the beginning and development of the movement."[52] In an earlier intervention in the debate he had voiced a similar vagueness: "the time has come to organize as perfectly as possible a system which will permit the organization to move into the street in an offensive or defensive manner."[53] Trifón Gómez, a member of the Executive who on the morning of December 31 strongly criticized the excessive "revolutionism" of some members of the National Committee and called for the defense of the Republic, declared that as far as the nature of the movement was concerned "we will see once it starts."[54] Pascual Tomás of the Metalworkers' Federation called for a revolutionary movement to defeat the Right, but a movement that would be "defensive and offensive" at the same time.[55]

The most consistent defender of social revolution within the National Committee was del Rosal. On December 13 he responded to Saborit's demands for clarity about the goals of the movement by saying that "we must answer the bourgeois front and take power: once in power we are not going to automatically impose Socialism . . . but to begin the trip toward the implantation of Socialism, which is not the same thing."[56] In his introduction to the minutes of the afternoon session on that day he writes that the supporters of revolution had no alternative to "a revolutionary movement to save democratic institutions and the social process begun by the Republic," and during that session he proposed that "we agree to a revolutionary movement to defend the interests of the working class which are threatened." [57] At the meeting of December 31 he stated within the first few minutes that "he wanted an immediate movement to seize power for the working class" and that "the first thing to decide is whether to have a movement or not and then, later, we can discuss whether . . . we are going to make a democratic revolution and after that has been achieved whether we are going to go further because, of course, a social revolution would have to be very thoroughly studied." [58] The confusion over the purpose of the movement created by del Rosal is only thickened when he concludes his memoir by stating that the defeat of October 1934 led to the "tremendous victory of February 16, 1936." [59] Is he implying that the revolution he so fervently demanded would have led to the establishment of a reformist government coalition dominated by Republicans who refused to allow any Socialist content in their program?

Whatever the real goals of the Socialist leaders were (and it seems quite clear that the most important figures, Largo Caballero and Prieto, were not planning a social revolution), their intentions had little in common with what took place in Asturias between October 4 and 20. As Andrés Saborit told the prisoners in the Model Prison after the events, "Nobody ordered you to make the revolution. The order was for a strike." [60] Yet from the moment the signal was passed on by the national leadership in Madrid, only in Asturias was there a massive working-class response, and there "the revolutionary impulse of the workers was well beyond the ability of the successive revolutionary committees to control." [61] This brings us back to the existence of such a high degree of radicalization among the miners. It is not enough merely to claim that this existed without asking how and why it came to exist.

The answer is not that the Socialist miners' union (SMA) was wealthier or better organized than other unions or that it exercised stronger control over its membership. Instead, the miners came to their readiness to rebel out of their own immediate experience in the years between 1919 and 1934. The following five developments were particularly significant: the ongoing crisis of the coal industry in these years; the inability of the miners' unions, and especially the SMA, to protect their members from the direct, severe social and economic consequences of the crisis; the failure of the Second Republic to provide a remedy for the situation; the pessimism and the fear created by the rise of fascism in Europe; and the ending of the ideological rivalry among Socialists, anarchosyndicalists, and Communists and the creation of the Alianza Obrera (Workers' Alliance) in April 1934.

Within this set of causes, the disillusion resulting from the failure of the Republic to deal successfully with the miners' problems is central, for it is here that strictly economic grievances became directed at a larger, political target and thus became revolutionary, or at least potentially so. The expression of mundane economic demands does not automatically lead to the politicization of a working-class movement; the bridge must come from elsewhere. As Richard Geary has argued, this often comes in response to the rigidity of employers and the hostility of the state: "To a large extent labor protest remained purely industrial where it could satisfy its needs through the application of industrial muscle. The absence of such muscle, however, or its thwarting by laws and the intransigence of employers, transformed attitudes and the arena of conflict." [62]

Ever since the onset of the postwar crisis of the mining industry, the Asturian miners had been accustomed to look to the state for solutions to their problems. During the Primo de Rivera dictatorship (1923–30) the policy of the SMA was based on appealing to the government to defend the miners from the layoffs and wage cuts imposed by the mine owners. The declaration of the Second Republic in April 1931 created a new hope and optimism that the state, now in friendly hands, would act to resolve the mining crisis, but the governments of the Republic quickly showed that this would not be the case. In Asturias the shattering of the republican illusion during the *bienio negro*, the two-year period of Center-Right government from November 1933 to December 1935, provided the link between the economic and the political. The political regime was made responsible for the miners' economic fortunes, and when it showed itself at first incapable, and then overtly hostile, the conclusion the miners drew was that it would have to be replaced. [63] This conclusion was reinforced by the newly revolutionary rhetoric of the Socialist leadership following the victory of the Right in the election of November 1933.

In this way the Asturian revolution stands as a clear foreshadowing of the Spanish Civil War, which was less than two years in the future. It also signaled the failure of the Second Republic to resolve its central dilemma: the threat of social conflict if it did not provide meaningful social reform.

The radicalization of the Asturian miners can be fully appreciated only against the background of the highly fragmented working class from which it emerged. This gives it an importance that transcends the borders of Spain and of Spanish historiography. Miners, and especially coal miners, have long been considered the most militant segment of the working class, and there is substantial debate about why this should be the case.

The first and most durable explanation was the theory of the "isolated mass" developed by C. Kerr and A. Siegel in 1954. Based on an analysis of strike statistics for eleven countries, the authors discovered that miners together with sailors and dockers have a high propensity to strike. To explain this tendency they put forward two hypotheses. The first states that "the location of the worker in society is heavily influenced by the industrial environment." Thus miners "form isolated masses, almost a race apart." They are specialized workers with little opportunity to move either up or out. In these circumstances, with few contacts with outside society, the union replaces that society or even the government in the miners' lives, and the strike becomes an irrational outburst of anger, "a colonial revolt against far removed society." [64]

The second hypothesis states that "the inherent nature of the job determines by selection and conditioning, the kinds of workers employed and their attitudes, and these workers, in turn, cause conflict or peace." The harshness and danger of mining as an occupation are said to attract tough workers who are more likely to strike. Put together, the isolated mass theory states that industries that segregate large numbers of workers who have relatively unpleasant jobs are most likely to be strike prone. [65]

Kerr and Siegel in many ways set the pattern for those theorists who followed: Rimlinger, Blaumer, Lockwood, and Bulmer, all of whom start from the premise that workers' behavior is determined by their social conditions. Kerr and Siegel have a highly simplistic image of the miners' world; in the isolated mass all are equally isolated and equally "massified." There are no intermediate cases. Logically this means that there should be no differences in strike activity from one company or country to another. This is clearly untrue, and the authors are content to write these differences off to "the industrial mix of each nation" and "the general integration of workers and their institutions into society." [66] No sooner have they established the notion of isolation than Kerr and Siegel are forced to admit that this comes in varying degrees. They do not, however, consider the possibility that this means that miners are not isolated in any meaningful sense.

Also, in the Kerr and Siegel approach social conditions are mechanically translated into labor unrest, which itself is seen as a more or less mindless protest. As we have mentioned, the authors attribute a fundamental role to the union as the vehicle for this unrest. They seem to imagine that a union is another automatic by-product of the social conditions of mining, that it will play a major role in the miner's life, and that, indeed, there will be only one union.

Subsequent writers have attempted to develop more sophisticated and flexible models, but even those who have rejected the concept of the isolated mass have retained the foundation on which it stands and which is, at the same time, its weakest point. All these theorists view the miners as a group apart from the rest of society sharing "certain universal characteristics." [67]

For G. V. Rimlinger, the environmental circumstances of mining, of which miners' existence as a socially distinct group is the most important, do create solidarity, but this does not necessarily mean that frequent strikes will be the result. Rather, the translation of solidarity into labor unrest depends on what he calls nonenvironmental factors. He emphasizes the case of the miners of the Saar, who had a high degree of solidarity without this leading to numerous strikes. Rimlinger finds a number of "historical factors" that help explain this: the support of the state for the miners, traditional organization, the absence of geographical and social isolation, and the continuing ties of the miners to the land. The product was a group of workers who wished to preserve their social position and who used their group identity to prevent strikes.[68]

Rimlinger calls his image of the mining community the "separatist group." This may or may not be integrated into larger society, but is based on a set of characteristics shared by all miners. R. Blaumer extends Rimlinger's argument, introducing the concept of "occupational community," in which the key factor in miner solidarity is after-work socializing. This is produced by a mining community that is its own little world, spatially isolated and socially homogeneous.[69] David Lockwood uses a similar idea. He argues that the images people hold of their society are determined by their social environment. Thus, the various environments in which different sectors of the working class were situated produced different images. The miner becomes a "traditional proletarian worker," a product of "the isolated and endogamous nature of the community, its predominantly one-class population and low rates of geographical and social mobility all tend to make it an inward looking society and to accentuate the sense of cohesion that springs from shared work experiences."[70]

Martin Bulmer develops a more flexible approach, an "ideal type" of mining community comprising a number of characteristics: physical isolation; the nature of the work; the social consequences of occupational homogeneity and isolation; leisure activities; the family; economic and political conflict; and "the whole." This model allows for a number of factors left out by its predecessors, or at least is more explicit about them, and even admits that departures from the ideal type are bound to occur. However, this greater flexibility is more apparent than real, and the model suffers from the same fundamental problems as the others. As all the others do, it emphasizes, and indeed insists, that all miners share certain characteristics and that the mining community is static and immutable. Bulmer retains the idea of a "general sociological model of the mining community," provided that it expands beyond purely industrial factors to include "the neglected problem of industry-community linkages." He explicitly rejects the approach of the historian—"historical particularist" is his somewhat deprecatory expression—who chooses to emphasize the differences among historically concrete mining communities.[71]

This is the shared underlying weakness of all these theories. The connection between social conditions and workers' behavior is important, but to assume that the social conditions of mining are always the same for all miners is to take a giant step away from reality. By establishing "community" as a central explanatory factor of workers' behavior, the distinctiveness that characterizes each mining experience is lost, as are the possible divisions within each.

Moreover, these sociological interpretations of miner militancy all present the mining experience as essentially static. The mining community is seen as a finished product, or perhaps as the necessary accompaniment to the economic activity in question. Even Rimlinger, who devotes some attention to "historical factors," does not recognize the contradiction between his acceptance of the role of specific historical circumstances and his insistence upon the universal characteristics of the mining world. For example, the close ties of the miners of the Saar to the land, which he cites as one of the reasons for their reticence to go on strike,[72] is itself a feature of their social environment radically different from the picture of the miner as archetypal proletarian that he and the others describe, but this goes unacknowledged. As regards Bulmer, he admits the possibility of deviant cases without concerning himself with how these came about.

What these theories do is to recognize the importance of the labor process and social environment in determining workers' behavior, only to neutralize them as an explanatory factor by insisting that there is a single mining experience. Yet when historians have looked at individual mining communities they have found these bear little resemblance to the static, homogeneous worlds prescribed in the theories. After analyzing the actual experience of actual miners, they have found few generalizations that retain their validity. Perhaps the only one is that mining is always a hard and dangerous profession. For the rest—isolation and homogeneity, the lack of geographical and social mobility, the role of unions, and even the idea of solidarity—the variations are so great as to make the construction and application of ideal types illusory.

In order to arrive at an understanding of the behavior of miners, we must appreciate one basic point: that there is not, nor has there been, a single experience shared by miners at all times and in all places. The work and social environments vary substantially from place to place and over time, and it is here, in these differences, and not in any presumed universal characteristics, that the sources of the behavior of different groups of miners may be found. Royden Harrison makes this point in his introduction to *The Independent Collier*:

> The tautology that a mining village is distinguished by "isolation and concentration upon one type of employment" conceals the fact that many miners did not live in villages and that those who did might be more or less isolated from Ireland or from Glasgow, more or less dependent upon a number of masters producing sale coal or upon one or two great proprietors of great vertically integrated concerns in which coal was subordinated to iron. The reference to the "extraordinary cohesion" of such villages masks the contrast and tension which might characterize their relationship with each other.[73]

We must approach the study of the mining world accepting each community as a unique historical process in which a number of variables combine in different ways. A checklist of these variables could include the following: the nature of the pits, seams, and technology; the nature of ownership and management of the mines; methods of payment and variability of earnings; demographic mix; prospects for geographic or social mobility; proximity to other populations and their occupational and class structure; the nature and control of social provision; and the dominance of particular religious or political beliefs.[74]

The second objective of this study is to contribute to this discussion of miner militancy, to show through an examination of the development of the Asturian mining industry and the society to which it gave rise that behind the term "mining community," and even for the same community at different times in its history, there hide varying and dynamic historical experiences.

The book is divided into two sections. Chapters 1 through 4 analyze the development of the mining industry in Asturias, of the working class that sprang from it, and the conditions within which it lived and worked. Chapters 5 through 8 offer a narrative of the course of labor protest in the Asturian coalfields, beginning with the first miners' strike in 1873, through which a heterogeneous and fragmented group of workers coalesced and traveled the road to revolution.

NOTES

1. Actas de las Reuniones del Comité Nacional, 26.XI.1933, Archivo Histórico del PSOE, 24-1, FPI.

2. Actas de la Comisión Ejecutiva de la UGT, 3.II.1934, FPI.

3. J. S. Vidarte, *El Bienio Negro y la Insurrección de Asturias* (Barcelona, 1979), 185–87. See also Amaro del Rosal, *1934: El Movimiento Revolucionario de Octubre* (Madrid, 1984), 210–11.

4. Ibid., 212–28.

5. The most notorious, and confusing, of these acquisitions was the *Turquesa* affair. According to del Rosal, Prieto's close friend, the Basque businessman Horacio Echevarrieta had ordered a large number of weapons from the government's Military Industries Consortium for export. When he could not make the payments, the order was embargoed by military authorities in Cádiz. Prieto arranged for a contact claiming to be an agent for the government of Ethiopia to acquire the order and make all the outstanding payments. He then arranged for a former leader of the Socialist Youth to purchase a boat that a right-wing member of parliament had up for sale. The boat, christened the *Turquesa*, was loaded and set sail eastward in the Mediterranean, but then reversed course for the Atlantic and toward the north coast. It arrived off the Asturian port of San Estebán de Pravia in September 1934, but the nighttime unloading operation was discovered by the police, who were able to capture a large part of the shipment. del Rosal, *1934*, 235–36.

6. Ibid., 233–34.

7. For details see P. Preston, *The Coming of the Spanish Civil War* (London, 1983), 96–124.

8. del Rosal, *1934*, 260.

9. Ibid., 259.

10. This description of the October revolution is based on contemporary accounts by M. Grossi, *La insurrección de Asturias* (Gijón, 1978), and by N. Molíns i Fábrega, UHP: *La insurrección proletaria de Asturias* (Gijón, 1977), and on historical accounts by B. Díaz Nosty, *La Comuna Asturiana* (Bilbao, 1974), and in *Historia de Asturias*, 7 (Gijón, 1979).

11. Díaz Nosty, *La Comuna*, 254.

12. Grossi, *La Insurrección*, 42.

13. Molíns i Fábrega, *UHP*, 118.

14. Díaz Nosty, *La Comuna*, 159.

15. Grossi, *La Insurrección*, 70–71; Díaz Nosty, *La Comuna*, 283.

16. Grossi, *La Insurrección*, 75.

17. Molíns i Fábrega, *UHP*.

18. Díaz Nosty, *La Comuna*, 279.

19. Grossi, *La Insurrección*, 40.

20. Díaz Nosty, *La Comuna*, 288–90.

21. González Peña was tortured while in prison. When he was brought before a military court and tried for his role in the insurrection, he assumed responsibility for it, whereas other Socialist leaders, and especially Largo Caballero, in accordance with an agreement made earlier, denied their role. After October González Peña sided with Prieto's position of resuming the alliance with the Republicans in the dispute over the direction the party should take.

22. Grossi, *La Insurrección*, 87.

23. D. Ruiz, *El Movimiento obrero en Asturias* (Gijón, 1980), 167.

24. J. Andrade, *La burocracia reformista en el movimiento obrero* (Madrid, 1935), 250–51.

25. J. A. Sánchez García-Sauco, *La revolución de 1934 en Asturias* (Madrid, 1974), 31, 39.

26. M. Villar, *El anarquismo en la insurrección de Asturias* (Buenos Aires, 1936), 73.

27. Molíns i Fábrega, *UHP*, 81; G. Munis, *Jalones de Derrota: Promesa de Victoria* (Bilbao, 1977), 185–86.

28. Largo Caballero, "Notas históricas de la guerra en España, 1917–1940," 160, manuscript, FPI. These memoirs have recently been published with an introduction by Santos Juliá, under the title *Escritos de la República* (Madrid, 1985).

29. del Rosal, *1934*, 317.

30. Ibid., 320.

31. The following discussion is based on Preston, *Coming*, 20–25.

32. On Casas Viejas see J. Mintz, *The Anarchists of Casas Viejas* (Chicago, 1982).

33. The National Committee was made up of the Executive Committee plus representatives of the member industrial federations.

34. del Rosal, *1934*, 29.

35. Largo Caballero, "Notas históricas," 42.

36. del Rosal, *1934*, 190.

37. Ibid., 129.

38. Actas de las Reuniones del Comité Ejecutivo, 12.I.1934, Archivo Histórico del PSOE, 20–3, FPI.

39. Largo Caballero, "Notas históricas," 46.

40. del Rosal, *1934*, 190–91.

41. Ibid., 188–200.

42. Ibid., 79.

43. Ibid., 73.

44. Largo Caballero, "Notas históricas," 45.

45. Ibid., 90.

46. Ibid., 28.

47. Actas de las Reuniones del Comité Ejecutivo, 12.I.1934, Archivo Histórico del PSOE, 20–3, FPI.

48. Largo Caballero, "Notas históricas," 44.

49. del Rosal, *1934*, 202.

50. Ibid., 257.

51. Ibid., 105.

52. Ibid., 137.

53. Ibid., 127.

54. Ibid., 143.

55. Ibid., 103–4.

56. Ibid., 50.

57. Ibid., 76.

58. Ibid., 135, 133.

59. Ibid., 320.

60. F. Solano Palacio, *La Revolución de Octubre* (Barcelona, 1936), 17.

61. M. Bizcarrondo, *Octubre del '34* (Madrid, 1977), 46.

62. R. Geary, *European Labor Protest* (London, 1981), 180, 54–62.

63. In contrast, for the workers of Madrid 1934 was not a "black year," as the government sought to resolve long-standing labor disputes, often to the displeasure and frustration of their putative supporters among the employers. See S. Juliá, *Madrid, 1931–1934* (Madrid, 1984), 409.

64. C. Kerr and A. Siegel, "The Inter-Industry Propensity to Strike: An International Comparison," in A. Kornhauser, ed., *Roots of Industrial Conflict* (New York, 1954), 191–93.

65. Ibid., 195–96.

66. Ibid., 202.

67. G. V. Rimlinger, "International Differences in the Strike Propensity of Coal Miners in Four Countries," *Industrial and Labor Relations Review*, 1959, 390–405.

68. Ibid., 396–97, 405.

69. R. Blaumer, "Work Satisfaction and Industrial Trends in Modern Society," in W. Galenson and S. M. Lipset, eds., *Labor and Trade Unionism* (New York, 1960), 351.

70. D. Lockwood, "Sources of Variations in Working Class Images of Society," *Sociological Review*, 1966, 250–51.

71. M. Bulmer, "Sociological Models of the Mining Community," *Sociological Review*, 1975, 74–76.

72. Rimlinger, "International Differences," 393–95.

73. R. Harrison, ed., *The Independent Collier* (Hassocks, 1978), 2, 7–8.

74. Ibid., 3, 13.

1

Rural Society, Migration, and the Mixed Worker

Mining and the Social Origins
of the Mine Workers

The Asturian coalfield covers some 1,450 square kilometers in the center of the province in the *concejos* (municipal districts) of Mieres, Langreo, Laviana, San Martín del Rey Aurelio, Siero, Lena, Aller, Quirós, Teverga, and Morcín. The valleys are of great natural beauty, disguising the tortured geology that lies beneath.

> The seams are always narrow and twisted, and almost always vertical. They run capriciously from one mountain to another, forming incredible folds in the valleys. There are no coal deposits in Europe as irregular as those in Asturias. The rocks which cover them vary in constitution and cohesion, not only from one vein to another but also between points in the same vein. The seams being mined likewise vary in their basic composition and width. Their only common feature is their irregularity and narrowness. . . . This confused situation is worsened by numerous faults which increase the irregularity of the seams.[1]

Nevertheless, these characteristics represented an initial advantage for the Asturian mining industry, "as if in this privileged country Providence wanted to save us the costs of exploitation," exulted the *Revista Minera* in 1855.[2] But this initial advantage would almost immediately become a major handicap. As Lucas Aldana foresaw in 1862, once the surface seams were exhausted extraction would require "more powerful means."[3] In the long run, the inability of mine owners and managers to overcome this difficult geology by technical means would prove to be the fundamental obstacle to the growth of the industry.

Mining was underway in Asturias in the mid-eighteenth century, but by the 1840s it was still small in scale and haphazard. The Polish traveler Alexander Holynski found that the Real Compañía Asturiana de Minas, a Belgian firm, was "the only company with any real activity to be found in the province,"[4]

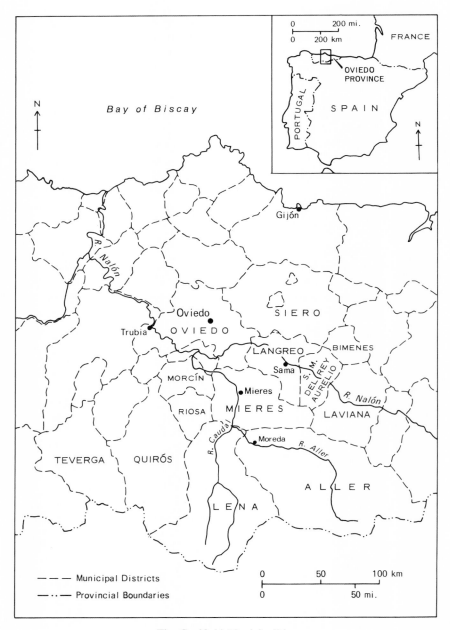

The Coalfield Municipalities

and Richard Ford noted that the rich deposits of the Nalón valley were ignored "except by peasants who used to scrape out a little here and there, digging at their own rude caprice." [5] The coal was then taken to the coast in carts—"the poor used their shoulders"—or sold to muleteers who resold it to merchants in Gijón. [6]

Coal mining began to take off only in the 1860s, "due to a demand which had not previously existed," a demand generated by the railways and the nascent iron industry in both Asturias and the Basque provinces. [7] Although the creation of this demand was a development of the utmost importance, it was not sufficient to guarantee the success of the Asturian mining industry, which faced a number of serious problems: confused and inadequate legislation, fragmentation of concessions, inadequate and expensive means of transportation, tariffs that were too low and taxes that were too high, and a lack of capital and cooperation among investors. [8]

Despite all these obstacles the industry did achieve a gradual long-term increase in production (table 1).

The increase in production was particularly marked after 1885, coinciding with the emergence of three important large companies: Unión Hullera y Metalúrgica Asturiana in 1885, Hulleras del Turón in 1891, and Hullera Española

Table 1. Coal Production in Asturias, 1872–1933   (in metric tons)

Year	Tons	Year	Tons	Year	Tons
1872	424,499	1901	1,671,913	1917	2,828,911
1882	483,041	1902	1,441,441	1918	3,409,676
1883	469,622	1903	1,418,423	1919	2,925,631
1884	445,225	1904	1,748,428	1920	2,974,503
1885	434,871	1905	1,915,285	1921	2,993,099
1886–87	474,588	1906	1,867,076	1922	2,502,183
1887–88	519,410	1907	2,194,123	1923	3,783,169
1889	563,681	1908	2,375,613	1924	3,978,497
1890	620,704	1909	2,395,074	1925	3,934,149
1891	675,384	1910	2,329,515	1926	4,195,870
1895	1,008,769	1911	2,266,036	1927	4,040,788
1896	1,227,144	1912	2,373,403	1928	4,286,209
1897	1,445,936	1913	2,413,509	1929	4,814,167
1898	1,606,725	1914	2,457,613	1930	4,786,256
1899	1,791,596	1915	2,697,939	1931	4,688,035
1900	1,564,664	1916	2,888,259	1932	4,474,759
				1933	3,790,416

Source: *Estadística Minera y Metalúrgica de España* (Madrid, 1865–1933), an official publication of the Ministry of Development.

in 1892. As G. Chastagnaret has remarked, "After 1888/9 a new division of the production appeared and only the strong units appear to play a part in the progress of production . . . which is not at all surprising as this is a phenomenon common to all industrialization." [9] Even so, the atomization of the industry, which had always been one of its hallmarks, was not brought to an end. In fact, in the years immediately before World War I "it was precisely the most lilliputian enterprises which showed the most vitality," [10] and these small producers continued to exist through the war and afterward (table 2).

The increase in production was achieved with little technical improvement, through the extension rather than the intensification of production, and as a result the number of mine workers also increased markedly (table 3).

However, the rapid growth of the industry between 1885 and 1908 did not mean that all was well. In fact, the boom triggered by the Spanish-American War was followed by a collapse of particular intensity between 1906 and 1909 as coal prices fell sharply. [11]

Despite the restoration of a high tariff in Spain in 1891, and especially after 1906, Asturian coal was not able to compete with imported British coal. (Between 1906 and 1922 the tariff on coal increased by 650 percent.) [12] This situation was due in large part to the high cost and unreliability of transportation from the coalfields to the main center of consumption, Vizcaya. In 1925 Luís Olariaga observed that for all its natural disadvantages, Asturian coal was only three or four *pesetas* per ton more expensive than British coal to produce and that it was the cost of transportation "which more than anything else makes Spanish coal uncompetitive with British coal." [13]

The problem of British competition was temporarily solved by World War I. The Asturian mines, producing some three-quarters of domestic coal, held the national market captive, and the industry entered a five-year boom of unprecedented dimensions. Production rose a modest 20 percent between 1914 and 1921, from 2.5 to 3 million tons, but soaring prices provided the

Table 2. Mining Companies in Asturias, 1890–1934

Year	No. of Cos.	Year	No. of Cos.	Year	No. of Cos.	Year	No. of Cos.	Year	No. of Cos.
1890	36	1905	42	1911	37	1917	137	1929	62
1900	57	1906	42	1912	45	1921	83	1930	62
1901	56	1907	37	1913	53	1923	69	1931	57
1902	49	1908	36	1914	62	1926	65	1932	59
1903	49	1909	37	1915	76	1927	63	1933	65
1904	47	1910	31	1916	121	1928	61	1934	73

Source: *Estadística Minera y Metalúrgica de España;* G. Chastagnaret, "Contributions," 603.

Table 3. Mine Workers in Asturias, 1865–1934

Year	No. of Workers	Year	No. of Workers	Year	No. of Workers
1865	4,226	1902	13,477	1919	34,177
1872	4,292	1903	13,565	1920	39,093
1875	3,785	1904	13,086	1921	34,031
1881	4,356	1905	14,427	1922	29,648
1882	4,508	1906	15,854	1923	29,834
1883	4,976	1907	14,435	1924	30,759
1884	4,976	1908	15,638	1925	31,023
1885	4,795	1909	15,182	1926	31,232
1886	5,581	1910	14,315	1927	28,244
1887	5,417	1911	15,410	1928	25,803
1888–89	4,432	1912	16,083	1929	27,074
1890	5,578	1913	17,796	1930	28,460
1897	10,063	1914	18,233	1931	29,280
1898	11,279	1915	19,952	1932	30,420
1899	11,154	1916	23,927	1933	27,755
1900	12,100	1917	28,606	1934	27,596
1901	12,185	1918	33,020		

Source: *EMME,* 1865–1934.

mine owners with a true bonanza. Freed from all competitive restraint, the price of coal rose astronomically. The index of coal prices jumped from a base of 100 in 1913 to 138 in 1915, 277 in 1916, and 563 in 1918. It then began to drop, to 376 in 1919 and 269 in 1921, but in 1924 it was still at 199.[14]

Profits kept pace with prices. Duro-Felguera more than trebled its profits between 1913 and 1916, and its profit in 1918 was more than eight times that of the first year of the war. Hulleras del Turón had profits of a half million *pesetas* in 1913 and almost two million in 1917. Hullera Española, which had paid dividends of 8 percent between 1906 and 1912, paid 11 percent in 1915 and 20 percent between 1917 and 1923. In 1916–17 its production fell by 65,000 tons, but profits increased by almost 50 percent. The profits of Fábrica de Mieres went from 500,000 *pesetas* in 1913 to 1.4 million in 1916, 4.4 million in 1917, and 9.3 million in both 1918 and 1919.[15]

Unfortunately, the opportunity offered by these highly favorable but fleeting conditions was not fully grasped, and the boom served only to exacerbate, not resolve, the industry's basic deficiencies. The large-scale producers were unable to respond to the challenge and substantially increase production. The percentage of total production held by the nine largest companies fell from 82 percent in 1915 to 71 percent in 1919.[16] Consequently the extra production came overwhelmingly from new and mostly marginal mines, which did not long survive the end of the war. The private business journal *Revista Nacional de Economía* called the state of the industry a fiction, "because it is a fiction to exploit uneconomic mines with inexperienced men to produce unusable coal." [17]

The end of the war brought a rapid return to reality. British coal exports resumed, throwing the industry into an immediate crisis. Hullera Española noted in its annual report for 1919 that "it is very difficult to compete with foreign coal which arrives with reduced costs and does not even pay duty, as this was suspended indefinitely at the beginning of the war." [18] As early as September 1919 the Socialist miners' leader Manuel Llaneza was announcing the effects of the situation on mine workers: 3,000 were without work, and many others were working a short week, four, three, and in some cases only two days. [19] The situation was becoming dire even for those fortunate enough to retain their jobs, as owners and managers sought to improve their competitive position at the expense of the workers, producing more coal with fewer miners receiving lower wages.

Table 4 demonstrates the reconversion of the industry that took place, particularly between 1921 and 1924. While the wage index fell 83 points in 1921 and 1922, the productivity index jumped 42 in the two succeeding years. Over the decade as a whole, wages fell from a weekly average of 78.12 to 53.75 *pesetas*. The wage increase registered by Asturian miners between 1914 and 1930 was the lowest of any miners in the country. [20] At the same time, the work force was cut by 8,300 between 1920 and 1924. Looking at this panorama, the immense labor strife of 1921–24, with four general strikes among the region's miners, comes as no surprise. [21]

Although conflict diminished after the 1924 general strike, this was not a sign that the crisis was being resolved. If anything, it only got worse. Despite the gains in productivity and the reductions in the work force and the wage cuts that had made it possible to cut costs, Asturian coal did not manage to achieve any significant increase in competitiveness. Ironically, these improvements only led to further problems, such as worrisome accumulations of stocks. [22] This situation was exacerbated by the onset of the general economic depression, which severely effected the iron and steel industry, the largest consumer of Asturian coal. Production fell from 1,793,500 tons in 1929 to 832,000 in 1934. By 1932 there was a buildup of half a million tons of coal. [23]

The Republic brought little relief. The reserve force of labor created during the twenties continued to exist, and the mining companies began to encounter problems in paying those workers they still employed. [24] By January 1934 the Industrial Asturiana was three months behind in meeting its wage bill, and in February Fábrica de Mieres declared bankruptcy. [25]

The response of the state to this crisis, and to the mine owners' demands for

Table 4. Index of Wages and Productivity, 1914–29

Year	Wages	Productivity	Year	Wages	Productivity
1914	100	100	1922	215	120
1915	107	110	1923	223	153
1916	132	117	1924	223	162
1917	154	115	1925	222	160
1918	211	136	1926	212	171
1919	245	93	1927	216	165
1920	298	121	1928	218	175
1921	265	120	1929	219	193

Source: Ministerio de Trabajo, *Estadística de Salarios y Jornadas de Trabajo, 1919–1930* (Madrid, 1931), LXII.

more protection and subsidies, was an increasing intervention in the life of the industry. This was more marked during the Primo de Rivera regime than during the Republic. In 1924 the Aldecoa Commission was sent to study the industry and its report, *Dictamen oficial sobre la industria hullera en Asturias*, laid the basis for "the direct intervention of the state in the control of the coal economy" embodied in the Consejo Nacional de Combustibles.[26]

The "new regime" provided for state subsidies to those companies that agreed to join. By offering special railway freight rates—the cost of rail transport had long been a major complaint—and relief from national and local taxes, the government hoped to be able to fuse holdings and reduce the atomization of the industry. The companies inside the system were able to bid on government contracts. A central office monitored all coal imports, and the National Coal Council was to mediate in labor disputes, plan production on a national basis, and establish prices.[27]

During the Republic two national conferences were held to discuss the problems of the mining industry, but they failed to develop any effective policy. In July 1934 the Samper government announced a project to reorganize the industry that was essentially the same as the "new coal regime" of the Dictadura. The draft bill provided for regional production quotas, intensified working of good mines, the closure of poor ones, state credits, the creation of a unified system of grades and prices, and an "invitation" to the workers to increase productivity.[28]

In the absence of any effective response to the industry's chronic plight several partial, sometimes unorthodox measures were tried, including collective contracts and early retirement for workers. Such stopgaps had no chance of resolving the problems of an industry whose everyday condition was crisis and that had prospered only when war had disrupted the normal patterns of international trade. For an industry whose existence had always depended on the state, that did not have a reliable motor for growth, and that had to overcome a difficult geological inheritance and a rachitic infrastructure, stronger measures were required. In the period before the revolution of October 1934 these were not forthcoming.

The initial requirement for any industry is to find and train workers. This was no problem in the Asturian coal mines so long as the industry remained in its peasant-mining phase. Until the mid-nineteenth century Asturian workers were constantly praised by observers. As late as 1858 the *Revista Minera* exulted in the province's "availability of manpower and the frugality and naturally peaceful and submissive character of its inhabitants."[29] However, once the industry began to expand and came under the control of capitalist mining companies that required large numbers of full-time miners, the recruitment of the labor force became a question of major importance. Operating in an agricultural region with very little excess population that could be drawn into the mines, how did mine owners overcome what Sydney Pollard has called "a problem even anterior to that of controlling the labor force," the problem of recruitment?[30]

The population of Asturias in the early nineteenth century was almost entirely rural. A. Moreau de Jonnes estimated that only 5 percent of the population lived in towns or cities, the lowest figure for any region of the country. To a considerable degree, the two disentailments of the nineteenth century allowed the farmers to become the owners of the land they worked. Although this helped create a new yeoman class, the subsistence polyculture, which remained the dominant form of agricultural practice, was unable to guarantee the subsistence of the Asturian farmer. In the late 1840s and 1850s the countryside entered a major crisis.[31]

The crisis relented a bit in succeeding decades, but the position of the farmer remained precarious. According to one report, taxes consumed onequarter of the farmer's total produce, leaving little to pay rent. As a result, the farmer had frequent recourse to money lenders. García Fernández is right when he concludes that "misery was the most deeply rooted institution in the Asturian countryside."[32] In the coalfields agriculture continued, even though large amounts of land were converted to industrial uses. In Mieres, the Fábrica de Mieres emerged as the largest landowner around the city and one of the largest in the entire Caudal valley, but immediately after the company came the Conde de Revillagigedo and the Marqués de Camposagrado. Their land was broken into numerous small plots and rented to farmers. As late as 1900 some 70 percent of the land in the Mieres plain was being used for agriculture, and market gardening was actually expanding under the stimulus of demand from the city.[33]

The Asturian countryside was never able to meet the needs of its population. The acute crises of the 1850s and of 1867–68 were perhaps exceptional, but poverty and hardship were endemic among the rural population. Given these conditions, it is not surprising that Asturias was, even late in the eighteenth century, one of the major sources of emigration from Spain. In his seventh letter to Ponz, written in the 1790s, Gaspar Melchor de Jovellanos, one of the outstanding figures of the Spanish Enlightenment, observed the existence of what can be called an ideology of emigration based on the possibility of rapid enrichment in the American colonies: "And even though not many fortunes are made there . . . every now and then a couple of *indianos* come back loaded with gold and perpetuate the evil with the unfortunate example of their wealth." [34] Alexander Laborde, who toured the region in the 1790s, noted that seasonal migration was a normal part of life for many Asturians. "Seasonal migrations show the relative overpopulation . . . because it is just at the time of greatest agricultural activity that . . . many workers went to Castile as harvesters." [35]

The crisis of the 1850s increased the flow of emigrants to Castile and Extremadura as well as to Madrid—where the Asturian water carrier was a well-known figure—and to America, and this trend continued into the 1860s, especially in the coastal villages. There were noneconomic aspects to this migration, such as the desire to avoid military service, but the most important, perhaps even more important than the basic desire for economic improvement, was the psychological aspect, the existence of a migratory tradition. [36] Long-distance migration had come to form an accepted, even expected, part of an Asturian's life, and the kernel that kept the custom alive was the possibility of coming back a wealthy man, an *indiano*. A century after Jovellanos, a social commentator could write that "it is enough that a few rich ones come back for them to throw themselves into the lottery." [37]

The mid-century subsistence crisis marked a new plateau, after which emigration continued to increase. This was often blamed on the inadequacy of the region's agriculture and the absence of alternative wage labor, yet emigration remained high even after the mining industry had begun to expand and was able to offer considerable numbers of jobs. In 1891–92 Oviedo was the sixth most important source of emigrants among Spanish provinces, trailing only Almería, Alicante, Canarias, Barcelona, and Pontevedra, and in 1891–95 it was seventh in terms of emigrants per 10,000 of population behind Almería, Canarias, Alicante, Pontevedra, Coruña, and Orense. [38]

The mining towns of Mieres and Sama de Langreo, along with Trubia, the site of the state cannon factory, produced the fewest emigrants. Some did go to the mining zones of Palencia where they were "sought as experienced and tough workers." [39] There was also some movement to America. The destination of these emigrants was similar to that of Asturians in general. Of the 217 in 1908–10 for whom data are available, 104 went to Argentina, 26 to Cuba, 25 to Mexico, 34 to Chile, 8 to Brazil, and 8 to the United States. Two went to

France and 43 to other parts of Spain. These emigrants were somewhat older than was usual; more people in their twenties and more couples. According to the mayor of Baíña, "The emigrants are young people, half under 21, thirty percent in their 20s . . . a migration of families and bachelors along the old road to America." [40]

This tradition of migration and the preference for the chance of wealth over the certainty of a hard-earned subsistence wage meant that from early on the spokesmen for mining interests began to criticize the inadequacy of the labor force. The native worker, who had been perfectly satisfactory in the first half of the century, did not meet the needs of the large companies that emerged in the second half. In 1861 Restituto Alvarez Buylla wrote that the creation of a numerous and disciplined work force was the most significant challenge facing the companies: "to attract, adapt, and organize . . . a numerous working population which is both docile and obedient." [41] The problem got worse as the century wore on and became particularly acute in the 1880s and 1890s. The shortage of labor was felt intensely as coal production nearly tripled while the work force grew by only two and a half times. The government summary of mining activity for 1892 commented on the problem: "The creation of a mine work force has everywhere been the product of a difficult struggle and much effort. Imagine what will be needed to achieve this here when we see that not only is there an important and active emigration from the coastal villages and eastern and western regions . . . and even from some villages in the coalfields, not in search of a living, which this province would provide if they only applied their energies to those industries which already exist, but in search of a fortune they hope to find in other countries." [42]

The labor shortage restricted the ability of the companies to increase output. It also affected the way managers could deal with their workers. The Hullera Española, which did not tolerate workers who did not adhere to the company line, was at times forced to adopt a less rigid posture. In 1887 the company's chief engineer complained that he was unable to fire a group of workers who had taken the day off without permission: "I cannot put them out into the street because I would be badly short of assistants and we are already functioning badly at times." [43] Even more galling, in May 1898 the company had to rehire some workers fired shortly before for having joined the local Socialist organization. [44]

The depression that hit the industry in 1905–6 temporarily reversed the situation and allowed managers the luxury of firing workers and even breaking the nascent trade union movement. However, when conditions began to improve after 1909 the labor shortage reappeared. A commission that investigated the state of the industry in 1909 found that Asturias was the only coalfield in the country in which there was a shortage of workers. [45] In 1912

Hulleras del Turón noted that a scarcity of workers was preventing it from increasing production, and the next year Hullera Española was forced to send a recruiting agent to find workers outside the province.[46]

The outbreak of World War I and the need to increase coal production rapidly to compensate for the cessation of imports from Britain led to concern over the availability of mine workers. A commission of inquiry included the lack of hewers as one of the factors that could prevent Spanish mines from meeting demand, but the commission's president, prominent Asturian industrialist Luís Adaro, put much more emphasis on this point, calling it the key element in the coal crisis, "of such great importance that it affects not only the productive capacity of the mines, which is dependent on the number of workers available, but also the cost of production, the most important element of which is productivity." [47]

The government responded to these warnings by giving hewers "military status . . . for the purpose of meeting their national service obligations," and by suspending the law that prohibited women and boys under eighteen from working inside the mines.[48] However, by this time the focus of the labor question had shifted from the shortage of workers per se to the shortage of experienced workers, especially hewers, who "were really indispensable because of the difficulty of their apprenticeship." [49] The high wages of the war years drew large numbers of impoverished Castilians, Galicians, and Portuguese into the Asturian mines, so that the quantity of men available ceased to be a problem even if quality did not.

Until this wartime influx the mine owners had had to depend on native Asturians for their workers. The population of the province had grown since the middle of the nineteenth century, from 525,529 in 1857 to 685,131 in 1910, but because the two disentailments had not deprived farmers of their land and forced them to become wage laborers, and because the lure of emigration continued to seduce any excess population away from the province, this population growth was not even. Rather, it was concentrated in the coalfields, while the coastal and rural regions remained more or less stagnant.[50]

The rapid growth of the coalfield municipalities—Mieres and Langreo were among the fastest growing municipalities in the country in the first two decades of the twentieth century—was a result of immigration from other parts of the province and from other provinces, but this movement did not get underway until 1914–15.[51] Until then the work force had to be drawn from the municipalities in which the collieries were located, what Ramon Pérez González has called "the intensive drainage zone." [52] For example, in the district of Siero, Bimenes and the southwestern corner served as a labor reservoir for companies operating in the municipality: Hulleras de Rosellón, Minas de Langreo y Siero, Solvay y Compañía, and Duro-Felguera.[53] When the

Montanesa company began operations in Aller, it looked forward to employing the local farmers, "workers used to the conditions and low wages of coal mining." [54]

The result was that until World War I the dominant figure in the mine work force was the mixed worker (*obrero mixto*). Even when available in sufficient quantities the mixed worker was deemed unsatisfactory by management, because he was not a purely industrial worker completely dependent on his wage and therefore amenable to the labor discipline that his employers tried to impose. In 1890 the *Estadística Minera y Metalúrgica* remarked that "despite the efforts made by the principal companies the feature which characterizes the Asturian miner is his continued attachment to agricultural work, to which he subordinates his work in the mines, and this is directly related to his low productivity." [55] Manuel Montaves, the chief engineer at Hullera Española, discovered in 1891 that it was much more difficult for the company to impose its will on those of its workers who were also tenant farmers because "they are more afraid of losing their land than losing the wage we pay them." [56]

There were several facets to the alleged inadequacy of the mixed worker. The first was his irregularity of attendance, particularly at harvest and other times when agricultural work was particularly intense. Francisco Gascue, the director of Duro-Felguera, added that workers took off more time than they really needed. The large number of religious holidays further reduced the working year to only 250 days: "The saint of the parish, the festival of the hermitage of one place, the patron of another, of the home, of the district. . . . If it were really devotion that moved them to so much religious activity the custom would be excusable, even respectable. The worst of it is that there is no such devotion. There is only the desire to do nothing." [57] At Hulleras del Turón, the management complained that workers "did not come to work on festival days," a practice that increased its production costs. [58]

Managers had difficulty understanding workers who did not appear to respond to monetary incentives. Gascue voiced their frustration when, during the boom of 1882–83, a shortage of workers and the refusal of available workers to do extra work for extra pay prevented them from taking full advantage of favorable market conditions. Haulers refused an offer of 20 *céntimos* to move another load after their shift ended at 3:30, preferring "to sit for two hours in the square, arms and legs crossed." [59]

This supposed lack of interest in money was closely related to the alleged indolence of the mixed worker. The *Estadística Minera* claimed that he was responsible for the low productivity of the Asturian mines, while other observers, who agreed that it was a good idea for miners to own land, insisted that this was so only when it was the miner who acquired property, not the farmer who came to the mine. In this latter case "he brings the indolence of the farmer of these mountains, who spends three quarters of his time doing nothing, while the miner brings to his plot the habits of working at a certain intensity." [60]

Of course, the Asturian farmer was not a layabout, nor was he uninterested in money. The agricultural cycle forced him to work as hard as, if not harder, than the miner, even if his work was differently organized and he retained a certain amount of control over it. The owners and managers who made these charges were frustrated by their inability to turn the mixed worker into an obedient, malleable proletarian. As Alvarez Buylla noted in 1861, mining could only expand "to the extent that the inhabitants of the working class get used to the subordination required by formal, permanent companies and come to prefer their own interest to their old independence and natural liberty, which is no advantage in this class of industry." [61]

The workers were not prepared to go along with this. Mining engineers who reported on the state of the industry in 1911 discerned a decline rather than a strengthening in the miners' discipline over the previous thirty years, [62] while in Langreo companies were struggling against "a spirit which is little amenable to work and industry which pervaded the customs of our ancestors and which is difficult to overcome because of its marked antagonism to everything which might upset their tranquil lives as farmers." [63] This resistance continued into World War I, especially in the more isolated corners of the coalfield such as Teverga, where the local mining company, Minas de Teverga, failed to impose even a minimum of control over its workers. A student mining engineer who did his practical work with the company in 1920 commented that "it was impossible to make them submit to the discipline that is so necessary in mining, such as the imposition of fines for absenteeism, which became ever more frequent, especially on Mondays and the days following festivals, when up to 75 percent of the work force would stay home." [64]

Considering the attention paid to the mixed worker by contemporaries, he is a difficult figure to pin down. Indirect evidence indicates that in the early days of mining, in the 1850s, full-time miners were few. Death Registers for Mieres list no miners as such, although a number of people who appear as farmers died in the mines. For a later period, the 1870s and 1880s, the electoral registers and censuses for Siero list few miners, even in the mining districts of Carbayín and Pumurabule. [65]

Gabriel Santullano claims that the increasing demand for coal after 1890 led to the appearance of an increasing number of proletarian miners, and that "for the first time the worker who depended solely on his work in the mine is predominant." [66] However, what evidence we have indicates the reverse. In 1892 and 1896 José María Suárez, the government mining engineer in Oviedo, estimated that 60 percent of the miners lived in farmhouses (*caseríos*). Health studies done on workers at Hullera Española in the 1890s show that the work force was predominantly local and rural. [67]

Paul Nicou, a Frenchman who studied the industry in 1905, found few purely industrial workers in Asturias. "The native worker generally adds work in the fields to that in the mines. . . . The division of land is very great. . . . Even in the industrial regions of Oviedo and Langreo it is rare to find workers, unless they are outsiders, who do not mix agricultural work with work in the mines."[68] An extensive study of the socio-economic circumstances of Spanish miners prepared by the Dirección General de Minas in 1911 put the figure for mixed workers at between 60 and 70 percent of the work force. It found that the majority of the miners at Fábrica de Mieres were "local farmers who have had their own homes for many years." In the major centers of Mieres and Langreo there were few non-local, full-time miners, and in places like Laviana, Saus, "and others further away from the major centers of population, all or almost all the workers are from the local area." Non-Asturians accounted for only 4 percent of the work force at the Mosquitera mine, 8 percent at Fábrica de Mieres, 10 percent at Cardiñueyo, and 20 percent in Aller.[69]

In the Villandio district of Mieres there were, according to the 1910 municipal census, eighty-five households in which there were miners. In fifty-three a miner was the head of the household, and in these there were six in which one of the members was a farmer. In thirty-one households headed by a farmer there was a member who worked in the mines, usually the sons or sons-in-law.[70] Thus, on the eve of the war, the ties between the mines and the land remained strong.

Indirect but very interesting testimony to the weight of the mixed worker in the mine work force in these years comes from the August 1914 issue of *El Minero de la Hulla*, the monthly magazine of the Sindicato Minero. The issue contains a story, "Velando al Muerto" (Mourning the Dead Man) by "Elminas" of Mieres, which describes the hatred of a young miner for the village money-lender who had been able to foreclose on the family land when the father died. The story itself illustrates the symbiosis of coal and land among the Asturian working class, while its publication in the journal of the Socialist miners' union shows the relevance of the theme for the readership. A year later the magazine estimated that 80 percent of Asturian miners were "sons of farmers."[71]

The position of the mixed worker began to recede during World War I. The mine work force exploded from some 18,000 in 1914 to over 39,000 in 1920, and for the first time the mine owners were able to realize their long-held goal of drawing large numbers of non-Asturians into the mines. In the 1880s Gascue and others were calling immigration a necessary precondition for Asturian industrialization and were urging mining companies to provide social services to lure workers from other parts of the country, but until 1915 few immigrants came. Low wages, scarce and costly housing, and the hostility of

Table 5. Geographic Origins of Miners in Langreo, 1890–1934

Company	Pre-1914			Post-1914		
	Cuenca	Asturias	Immigrants	Cuenca	Asturias	Immigrants
Minas Sta. Ana	88.7%	5.0%	6.3%	84.0%	4.1%	11.9%
Minas La Justa	95.0	2.9	2.1	84.6	8.0	17.4
Minas de Saus	90.3	9.7	—	71.1	15.3	13.6
Mosquitera	94.7	3.0	2.3	83.0	9.0	8.0
Coto Sama	—	—	—	44.0	15.0	41.0

Source: Registros de Personal, Archivo Pasivo de HUNOSA, Ciaño.

Note: *Cuenca* refers to those workers who gave their place of birth as one of the following municipal districts: Mieres, Langreo, Laviana, Aller, San Martín del Rey Aurelio, Teverga, Quirós, or Oviedo. *Asturias* refers to those from all other parts of the province, and *Immigrant* refers to those from outside the province.

locals to outsiders made the Asturian coalfields unattractive to potential immigrants.[72]

An analysis of the geographical origins of Asturian mine workers before and after 1914 makes clear the watershed that the war represented (table 5). The scarcity of immigrant miners, either from beyond the coalfield or outside the province, is confirmed by the 1910 municipal census for Mieres. Of 2,206 households headed by miners, 1,907 were natives of the coalfield municipalities and 73.4 percent were natives of Mieres itself. There were 137 (6.2 percent) from the other Asturian municipalities and 162 (7.4 percent) from outside the province.[73]

After 1914 the situation in Mieres was very different (table 6).

The immigrants did not come in equal numbers from all regions of the country (tables 7 and 8). The largest contingent of immigrants to Mieres

Table 6. Geographic Origins of Miners in Mieres, 1914–34

Company	Total Workers (No.)	Cuenca (%)	Asturias (%)	Immigrants (%)
Minas de Olloniego	610	68.9	14.5	16.6
Tres Amigos	1,165	39.8	8.6	51.6
Riquela	441	63	6.8	30.2
Baltasara	1,978	66	10.3	23.7
Hulleras de Riosa	2,364	78.2	4.3	17.5
Ortiz Sobrinos-Clavelina	1,428	51.2	11.2	37.6

Source: Registros de Personal, Archivo Pasivo de HUNOSA, Mieres.

Table 7. Place of Origin of Immigrant Miners, Mieres, 1914–34

Province	Number	Province	Number	Province	Number
Galicia		Guadalajara	2	Murcia	8
Lugo	542	Ciudad Real	1	Logroño	4
Orense	197	Extremadura		Alava-Guipuzcoa	4
Pontevedra	103	Cáceres	13	Zaragoza	3
La Coruña	33	Badajoz	1	Mallorca	2
León		Andalucía		Huesca	1
León	368	Almería	13	Castellón	1
Valladolid	207	Córdoba	13	Gerona	1
Zamora	120	Huelva	8	Barcelona	1
Palencia	70	Jaen	8	Soria	1
Salamanca	47	Sevilla	3	Vitoria	1
Castilla		Granada	1	Abroad	
Madrid	16	Cádiz	1	Portugal	256
Burgos	10	Others		France-Belgium	5
Avila	8	Santander	80	South America	14
Segovia	5	Vizcaya	16		
Toledo	3	Valencia	8		

Source: Registros de Personal, Archivo Pasivo de HUNOSA, Mieres.

came from Galicia, 875, with Lugo providing more than any other province in the country. León came next: the region provided 812 workers, the province, 368. Portugal was also a major source, an indication of the relaxed border regulations at that time. Surprisingly, Andalucía and Extremadura, the source of so many immigrants to Catalonia and the Basque country, sent very few to Asturias.

The origins of the immigration to Langreo were somewhat different (table 8). León replaced Galicia as the chief supplier, while the province of León tied Lugo as the most heavily represented province. There were many fewer Portuguese than in Mieres, but the major difference was the much larger number of immigrants from Andalucía.

The work force did undergo "an intense transformation" [74] during the war, as immigration created a new group of proletarian miners, but the mixed worker was not eliminated, and he retained a strong presence. José María Jové y Canella noted that there had been a shortage of agricultural workers in Langreo during the war, when "almost all our farmers have exchanged the plow for the pick," but this process was reversing itself during the postwar crisis as mine workers were using their wages to purchase land.[75] The mixed worker remained a characteristic figure of the coalfield in the 1920s. During a strike in July 1923, the civil governor wired the minister of the interior that

Table 8. Place of Origin of Immigrant Miners, Langreo, 1890–1934

Province	Number	Province	Number	Province	Number
Galicia		Soria	4	Others	
Lugo	235	Toledo	3	Santander	40
Orense	122	Cuidad Real	2	Murcia	12
Pontevedra	23	Teruel	1	Vizcaya	8
La Coruña	20	Cuenca	1	Alava	8
León		Extremadura		Guipúzcoa	3
León	235	Badajoz	6	Zaragoza	3
Valladolid	159	Cáceres	1	Lérida	1
Salamanca	95	Andalucía		Navarra	1
Zamora	78	Jaen	38	Valencia	1
Palencia	68	Almería	24	Alicante	1
Castilla		Córdoba	14	Logroño	1
Burgos	29	Huelva	6	Abroad	
Madrid	22	Sevilla	3	Portugal	59
Avila	19	Granada	1	America	10
Segovia	13			Europe	5

Source: Registros de Personal, Archivo Pasivo de HUNOSA, Ciaño.

"almost all the strikes called during the summer fit the convenience of the workers who want to do agricultural work. Once the crops are in they return to work." [76] Ten years later *Avance* reported that striking miners "are as firm as the first day of the struggle, involved in the chores of the fields." [77] This was even more the case in the more isolated areas such as Quirós, Riosa, and Teverga. According to the Aldecoa Commission of 1924, the majority of the mine workers in Quirós were "natives of this area, where they have animals or other agricultural interests, and for this reason it is difficult to count on them during active periods in the fields." [78]

In the second half of the nineteenth century and the first decades of the twentieth, the Asturian agricultural system was unable to sustain the rural population. The absence of any sort of agricultural revolution that might have freed labor for nonagricultural activities meant that all "surplus" population retained close ties to the land, and that the search for additional sources of income was very much conditioned by the workers' continuing status as agriculturalists. Those who lived on the fringes of the coalfields could combine mining with agriculture and became mixed workers. Those who came from coastal areas or the impoverished west, faced with the necessity of uprooting themselves, preferred transatlantic emigration, which had become almost a normal feature of life.

The expansion of coal mining in the last decades of the nineteenth century left mine owners and managers facing an acute labor shortage, which they tried to overcome by attracting workers from other parts of the country, although without success. Only the high wages prevailing during World War I succeeded in drawing countless poor farmers from Galicia and Castile into the mines. These immigrants supplemented but never supplanted the native mixed worker, who continued to be an important part of the work force into the 1930s.

Thus the Asturian coal mines had a dual, divided labor force: on the one hand Asturian and partly agricultural, on the other immigrant and full-time. This vertical split was crucial to relations within the mining community and would provide a significant obstacle to the development of class consciousness.

NOTES

1. J. Townsend, *Journey Through Spain in the Years 1786 and 1787* (London, 1792), 2:60.

2. *Revista Minera*, 1855, 309.

3. L. Aldana, *Consideraciones generales sobre la industria hullera de España* (Madrid, 1862), 56. See also L. Olariaga, *La crisis hullera en España* (Madrid, 1925), 15–16.

4. A. J. J. Holynski, *Un coup d'oeil sur les Asturies* (Paris, 1843), 22.

5. R. Ford, *A Handbook for Travellers in Spain* (London, 1837), 392.

6. M. M. Gutiérrez, "Carbón de Piedra," in *Cartas Españolas*, 1831, 291. See also "Descripción general del principado de Asturias," in *Mercurio de España*, 1821, 176, and S. E. Widdrington, *Sketches in Spain During the Years 1830, 1831 and 1832* (London, 1833), 1:83.

7. J. L. García Delgado, "La minería del carbón en España durante la Primera Guerra Mundial," in *Revista del Trabajo*, 1971, 41.

8. There are a number of books, generally with a polemical bent, which discuss the problems of the industry, especially whether it was worth the time and effort. For an attack on the industry see R. Perpiñá Grau, *Memorandum sobre la política del carbón* (Valencia, 1935).

9. G. Chastagnaret, "Contributions à l'étude de la production et des producteurs de houille des Asturies de 1861 à 1914," in *Mélanges de la Casa de Velásquez*, 1973, 601–2.

10. Ibid., 614, 621.

11. Instituto de Reformas Sociales, *Informe acerca de la Fábrica de Mieres y los obreros de Mieres* (Madrid, 1907), 9–10. See also S. A. Hulleras del Turón, *Memoria* (Madrid, 1907), 6.

12. S. Roldán and J. L. García Delgado, *La Formación de la Sociedad Capitalista en España, 1914–1920* (Madrid, 1973), 2:103.

13. Olariaga, *Crisis*, 66.

14. M. Aldecoa et al., *Dictamen oficial sobre la industria hullera en Asturias* (Madrid, 1926), 39.

15. Hulleras del Turón, *Memoria* (Madrid, 1913–20); D. Fernández González, *La Sociedad Hullera y yo* (Barcelona, 1933), 7–8; Roldán and García Delgado, *La Formación*, 2:138–39.

16. Instituto de Reformas Sociales, *Informes de los inspectores del trabajo* (Madrid, 1915–19), 2:157.

17. *Revista Nacional de Economía*, Jan. 1919, 161. For a harsh critique of the wartime practices of the mining companies, see IRS, *Informes de los inspectores*, 2:197.

18. *RM*, 1919, 283.

19. *Boletín Oficial de Minería y Metalurgia*, 1919, 47–48.

20. Perpiñá Grau, *Memorandum*, 30. The average salary increase in the other coalfields was León, 98 percent; Ciudad Real, 134 percent; Córdoba, 75 percent; and Palencia, 128 percent.

21. For the details of this conflict, see chapter 6 herein.

22. Fábrica de Mieres, *Memoria* (Oviedo, 1929), 3–4.

23. J. Vicens Vives, "Movimientos obreros en tiempo de depresión económica," in *Obra Dispersa*, 151; V. Castaño Sanjuan, *El estado actual económico-social de las industrias mineras de hulla de España* (Madrid, 1933), 18.

24. M. Tuñón de Lara, *El movimiento obrero en la historia de España* (Barcelona, 1977), 770; *El Socialista*, 1.VI.1933.

25. *Avance*, 16, 18, 21, 30.I.1934; S. Suárez, *El caso de Fábrica de Mieres* (Mieres, 1934); Fábrica de Mieres, *Memoria* (Oviedo, 1939), 3.

26. Perpiñá Grau, *Memorandum*, 22.

27. *Gaceta de Madrid*, 9.VIII.1927; *El Noroeste*, 10.VIII.1928.

28. *AV*, 5.IV, 25.VII.1934.

29. *RM*, 1858, 665.

30. S. Pollard, *The Genesis of Modern Management* (London, 1965), 160.

31. J. M. Moro, "La Desamortización en Asturias en el Siglo XIX" (Ph.D. diss., University of Oviedo, 1978), 430, 452.

32. A. Amador y Valdés, "Informe sobre la crisis agraria, 1887," Archivo Revillagigedo, Gijón; *Revista de Asturias*, 1879, 193; J. García Fernández, *Sociedad y Organización Tradicional del Espacio en Asturias* (Oviedo, 1976), 184–86.

33. R. Pérez González, "Industria, Población y Desarrollo Urbano en la Cuenca Central Hullera Asturiana" (Ph.D. diss., University of Oviedo, 1980), 870–81.

34. G. M. de Jovellanos, *Obras Escogidas* (Madrid, 1956) 3, 220–24.

35. A. Laborde, *A View of Spain* (London, 1809), 3:415–16.

36. E. Escalera, *Recuerdos de Asturias* (Madrid, 1886), 120; L. A. Martínez Cachero, "Historia económica de la emigración asturiana," in *Conferencias sobre economía asturiana* (Oviedo, 1959), 3:27.

37. F. García Arenal, *Datos para el estudio de la cuestión social* (Gijón, 1980), 122–23.

38. *Estadística de la emigración* (Madrid, 1905), 15–63, 75.

39. R. Becerro de Bengoa, *Una escuela práctica de minería*, 82–84.

40. Cited in Pérez González, "Cuenca Central," 270–72.

41. R. Alvarez Buylla, *Observaciones prácticas sobre la minería carbonera de Asturias* (Oviedo, 1861), 15.

42. *EMME*, 1892, 248.

43. Hulleras del Turón, *Memoria* (Bilbao, 1894), 22; Montaves to Parent, 14.IX.1887, Archive of the Hullera Española, Ujo, 56/1.

44. *ES*, 27.V.1898.

45. Comisión de Estudio de la Riqueza Nacional, *Información pública efectuada en 1906* (Madrid, 1909), 157.

46. Hulleras del Turón, *Memoria* (Bilbao, 1913), 7; López to Montaves, 8.X.1913, 13.VII.1914, AHE 12/3. See also *RM*, 1914, 164.

47. Comisión de Estudio de la Riqueza Hullera Nacional, *Información*, 37, 51. See also *Revista de Economía y Hacienda*, 1916, 534.

48. *RNE*, Oct. 1917, 333–34.

49. *RIMA*, 16.II.1916.

50. C. M. Criado Hernández, *La Población de Asturias, 1857–1970* (Oviedo, 1975), 12, 62; Pérez González, "Cuenca Central," 216–17.

51. Castaño Sanjuan, *El Estado*, 28; A. Fernández García, *Langreo: de la Industrialización a la Crisis Actual* (Gijón, 1983).

52. Pérez González, "Cuenca Central," 226.

53. Ibid., 219; *RM*, 1876, 110.

54. *RM*, 1860, 98.

55. *EMME*, 1889–90, 492–93.

56. Montaves to Parent, 28.III.1891, AHE 2/5.

57. *RM*, 1883, 388. See also Alvarez Buylla, *Observaciones*, 28.

58. Hulleras del Turón, *Memoria* (Bilbao, 1902), 8.

59. *RM*, 1883, 146, 388. At this time the average daily wage was 2.40 *pesetas.*

60. *EMME*, 1889–90, 493, 387.

61. Alvarez Buylla, *Observaciones*, 20.

62. Dirección General de Minas, *Informe relativo al estado económico y situación de los obreros de las minas de España* (Madrid, 1911), 21.

63. J. G. Muniz, *La industria hullera* (Sama de Langreo, n.d.), 44.

64. L. Torón y Villegas, "Memoria de las Minas de Teverga" (Thesis, Escuela Superior de Ingenieros de Minas, Madrid, 1920), 41.

65. Pérez González, "Cuenca Central," 268; Archivo Municipal de Pola de Siero, Listas Electorales, Censos.

66. G. Santullano, *Historia de la Minería Asturiana* (Salinas, 1978), 125–26.

67. *EMME*, 1892, 241; J. M. Suárez, *El problema social minero* (Oviedo, 1896), 11; "Estado del sanatorio del Coto Minero de Aller en 1896," AHE 57/2.

68. P. Nicou, "L'industrie minière et metallurgique dans les Asturies," in *Annales des Mines, Memoires*, 1905, 218, 206.

69. DGM, *Informe*, 19, 36, 41.

70. Archivo Municipal de Mieres, Padrón Municipal, 1910.

71. *El Minero de la Hulla*, Aug. 1914, 5–9; Aug. 1915, 12.

72. *RM*, 1883, 372; Criado Hernández, *Población*, 42–43.

73. AMM, Padrón Municipal, 1910. At Minas de Aller, 83.6 percent of the workers in 1884 were from the coalfields, 8.4 percent from other parts of Asturias, and 8 percent from elsewhere. AHE 3/2.

74. Muniz, *Industria*, 151.

75. J. M. Jové y Canella, *Topografía médica de Langreo* (Madrid, 1925), 142, 123.

76. Civil Governor to Ministry of the Interior, 4.VII.1923, Gobernación, Legajo 58A, Expediente 16, Archivo Histórico Nacional.

77. *AV*, 22.IX.1933. See also Castaño, *El Estado*, 29.

78. Aldecoa, *Dictamen*, 66. In August 1930 the president of Hulleras de Riosa claimed that "all workers here are farmers and they usually all take three months off at this time to tend to their fields." *Aurora Social*, 22.VIII.1930.

2

The Working Life

The mine is not only a place of work. It is also a place of conflict, the scene of a daily struggle between worker and manager. Changes such as new technology, altered job categories, extended work days, increased productivity, and tighter discipline are introduced to increase or maintain profits. The worker has to fight back to defend his working conditions, his income, and even his job. In this way the changing work place can become a cradle of class consciousness. Were there changes in the conditions of work in the Asturian coal mines that pitted worker against management? Did a miner's working life teach him where his interests and those of the mine owner came into conflict? Did work generate solidarity?

In the middle decades of the nineteenth century, when mining in Asturias was still characterized by small-scale peasant exploitation, it was carried out on a casual basis without much, if any, attention being paid to the technical aspects. Only the seams at or near the surface were mined, and these were abandoned when the inflow of water made pumping necessary or when timbering was required. Costs were minimal, production limited, and much coal was lost.[1]

The large enterprises that increasingly came to dominate the industry after 1860 used more rational methods of exploitation. There were eighteen methods of extraction known in Spain in the 1860s, their use being dictated by the width and inclination of the seams. Where these were narrow and at sharp angles—less than three meters wide and more than 45 degrees—three methods were suitable: *testeros, tajos rectos,* and *desplazamiento.* In Asturias the first of these was used almost exclusively, and it came to be known as the *testero asturiano.*[2]

This was a straightforward method requiring little preparatory work and therefore allowing initial savings on fixed costs.[3] There were few cases of alternative methods of exploitation before the introduction of pits during World War I. The few local variations were due more to "the character and conditions of the work force" than to any geological or technical imperative. There were also some mines, such as Duro-Felguera's La Justa, where the gentler slope of the seams allowed the use of the slightly different *macizo corto* method.[4]

This uncomplicated method of exploitation was the basis for a simple and essentially static division of labor. The extractive process had six basic stages, to each of which corresponded a category of mine workers. The first stage, the opening of tunnels and galleries, was largely the work of the blasters (*barrenistas*). This was a skilled and highly paid job requiring a great amount of experience. Blasters also assisted in cutting the coal where its hardness demanded the use of dynamite or powder.[5]

At the heart of the mining operation were the hewers (*picadores*). They participated in opening the tunnels and cutting the coal at the face, generally using a pick. Because the seams were often sharply inclined, hewers were frequently unable to work standing up and had to attack the coal while lying on their backs.[6] Hewing was basically an individual activity. Hewers had assistants (*pinches*) to help them with timbering and removing cut coal and waste from the stall, but rarely did they work in organized teams (*cuadrillas*). Each worker was paid separately, hewers according to the amount of coal cut or the distance advanced in the tunnel, assistants on a set wage. The stall was the hewer's domain, an autonomous unit of production of which the miner with his pick was the core.[7]

As the tunnels and galleries were excavated, they had to be fortified with wooden supports. Initially this, too, was the responsibility of the hewers, but by the 1870s a new category, the timberer (*entibador*), had been created to do the job. Hewers remained responsible for timbering their own stalls, but were assisted by timberers. After the hewer this was the best paid and most prestigious category. Only hewers and timberers could enter the highest category of all, the mine worker (*obrero minero*).[8]

Auxiliary jobs such as carrying wood into the mine, putting up the wooden partitions between stalls, separating the cut coal from the waste, and moving both to the chutes were left to the youngest and most poorly paid interior workers, variously known as *pinches, ramperos, guajes*, and *arrastradores*. When the chutes were at an angle of more than 25 degrees, the coal slid down by itself, but when the angle was less "it is necessary to help it, which the boys do, pushing with their feet." Boys started in the mine as young as ten or eleven, and even when the legal minimum age of sixteen was established, it was common to find assistants who were younger.[9]

As the coal, and the waste not needed as refill, arrived at the bottom of the chutes, it fell into wagons that then had to be moved from the pithead to the sorting area. Until the 1880s these wagons were pushed by men. As each weighed over 500 kilos and had to be pulled upward of half a mile, the prime requirement for this job was physical strength. In the 1880s, however, these haulers began to be replaced by animals as labor costs rose sharply.[10]

The final stage of the process was sorting. This was done by hand, generally by women using a "shifting screen with a fixed grille and lateral piston. Two girls operate each one; one moves the piston and the other moves the coal inside the box."[11] This was effective only because of the lack of sophistication in the marketing of Asturian coal, which was sorted into only two or three grades, and because of the terribly low wages paid to these women, the most poorly paid of all mine workers.[12]

Women had never been numerous within the mine itself, working almost exclusively on the outside. The number of women employed was 534 in 1872 and 651 in 1934, and fluctuated between a low of 454 in 1910 and a high of 1,001 in 1901. However, their relative presence underwent a steady decline, from 1 in 8 in 1872 to 1 in 49 in 1934. At Hullera Española there were 43 women workers in 1895: 22 in the sorter, 16 in the coke factory, and 5 who served as crossing guards. All but 5, of whom 4 were widows, were unmarried, and of these 38, 33 were younger than twenty-two. Thus it would seem that women worked to supplement the family income, but that this job was left to unmarried daughters, not to the wife.[13]

Before 1914 the only major change in the nature of mine work was the replacement of haulers (*wagoneros*) by horsemen (*caballistas*) as animal power began to be used for haulage after 1880. This was a response to rising labor costs, but also reflected a desire to eliminate a particularly troublesome group of workers. Haulers were known as "unruly and rebellious; they make you pay and then attempt to lay down the law"; they were a group whose disappearance was "what we fervently desire."[14]

Did this division of labor make possible a career as opposed to a working life? Did the Asturian coal miner have much scope for advancement within his profession? In general terms, coal mining is a line of work that does not hold out much hope for advancement. As David Crew has written of the miners in Bochum, in the Ruhr, "The structure of working in the mining industry did not present the same scope for significant advancement that existed in the metal trades. Distinction of status and function among workers in the mines was based more on experience than on formal training."[15] A sympathetic observer of one of the early miners' strikes in Asturias made an almost identical observation. "There, in the great foundry of La Felguera . . . the workers have aspirations and realize them. They start work at 10 or 11 earning two or three *reales* but with the prospect of later earning 12, 16, or 20, even during the industry's bad times. It is even possible to become a foreman and earn 28 or 32 *reales* . . . but the miner enters and leaves, or perishes, and it is always the same. He enters the mine at the same age they enter the foundry and the most he can hope for is to become an interior watchman and make 10 or 12 *reales*." [16]

Age and length of time spent in a particular mine were two crucial factors in determining a worker's job classification. [17] An analysis of workers at three mines in Mieres between 1916 and 1934 reveals the importance of age in various job categories. Certain categories were highly age-specific, especially hewers and assistants. The curve for assistants peaked the earlier of the two, at sixteen to twenty, as many youngsters who started out in this category moved on after a few years. After a precipitous drop between twenty-one and thirty-five, the curve rose again, reflecting the fall back into this category of older men no longer able to do other jobs.

For the hewers the peak came slightly later, between twenty-one and twenty-five, for skills had to be learned. The major fall came after the age of thirty, although the number working at the age of forty was still a third of the maximum. The haulers, a category that put a priority on physical strength, had a similar curve that peaked at twenty-one to twenty-five, but that dropped much more sharply than that of the hewers afterward. Hewers could draw on a wealth of experience to keep up their production whereas haulers had nothing with which to compensate their loss of physical strength.

Timberers and blasters had very different, much flatter age curves. They peaked later, at thirty-one to thirty-five for the blasters and twenty-six to thirty for the timberers, and fell very little thereafter. This was clearly because these two categories required skill and experience more than strength, and offered much longer working lives.

The relative lack of job mobility might have been the basis for a sense of identity among miners, a "solidarity that suggested itself naturally," as E. J. Hobsbawm has written. [18] However, not all miners in Asturias could look forward to similar experiences, and the major line of division was the differing prospects of native Asturian and immigrant miners.

Despite the great emphasis put on the attraction of workers from outside the province for the growth of the industry, it was assumed that they would take a long time to acquire the skills needed to become good miners. By 1914 the percentage of immigrant miners was still quite small, and it appears that they were congregated at the lower levels of the job hierarchy. In Langreo at the beginning of the twentieth century, the immigrants did work "that the natives do not want because they earn more on the inside." [19] The study done by the Dirección General de Minas in 1909 found them to be "less adept at moving the wagons and the inclined planes" than the Asturians and noted that they rarely worked inside the mine. That immigrant workers moved around "too frequently" or only worked during the seasons when their farm work at home allowed did not help them move up into the higher job categories. [20] Their inexperience was often blamed for the sharp drop in productivity during World War I. According to Ramón González Peña, "The majority of the workers from the Castilian steppe and the hills of Galicia knew absolutely nothing about the difficult job of mining and for this reason . . . they could not produce as much as the skilled workers." [21]

This black-and-white distinction drawn before and during the war, of Asturians taking the skilled, highly paid jobs inside the mine and the immigrants being left with the rest, began to change somewhat afterward. In the years from 1919 to 1934 the possibilities for Asturians and immigrants began to converge, although some very real differences did remain. Looking at the presence of immigrants in various job categories at the same three Mieres mines, we see that they were not condemned to the unskilled, poorly paid parts of mine work. The most important observation is that we find immigrants in all five major categories. True, they are overrepresented in the two lowest categories, assistants and haulers, with 28.4 and 24.5 percent, respectively, compared to 23.9 percent of the total sample, but they were even more highly represented among the blasters, a skilled and well-paid category. Here they accounted for 46.3 percent. On the other hand, few (17.5 percent) became timberers, and fewer still (11.2 percent) became hewers.

How can we explain these patterns? Did immigrants enter the mines later in life, thus reducing their chances of entering categories where age was important? Were they less stable than Asturians, staying with companies for shorter periods and losing out on promotions based on apprenticeship within the mine?

An analysis of the age at which 4,007 miners joined four companies in the Caudal valley between 1916 and 1934 indicates a slight difference between the two groups. Three-quarters of the immigrants and 73.2 percent of the Asturians had started work by the age of thirty. The only significant difference was before age twenty, when only 29.8 percent of the immigrants had started compared with 36.3 percent of the Asturians. Forty-five percent of the immigrants began in their twenties but only 36.9 percent of the natives did so. Their having had this slightly later start cannot account for the extremely small number of immigrant hewers, although it would have restricted to some degree their chances of reaching this category.

It is when we turn to the stability of the two groups in employment that we find a significant difference. The immigrants were much more transient. Almost 45 percent of the sample stayed with the company for less than one year, and another 15 percent stayed between one year and two. Only 17.4 percent stayed longer than five years. The natives were considerably more stable. Only 27.7 percent left during the first year and only 12 percent during the second. Almost one-third, 31.8 percent, stayed with the same company for more than five years. Both groups show a marked increase in the number of workers with more than nine years continuous service, but the Asturians out-numbered the immigrants here, too: 14.2 percent to 9.7 percent. When we recall the importance the companies attributed to developing a *stable* work force, the lack of stability among the immigrants must explain a great deal of their inability to reach the grade of hewer.

Geographic origin was one point of division among miners; the varying prestige of job categories, and particularly the distinction between interior and exterior workers, was another. Although this is difficult to document, one gets the distinct impression that these almost constituted two separate castes, an impression reinforced by the opposition of the SMA to identical across-the-board wage increases for all grades. In April 1916 the union executive rejected this on the grounds that it would unduly favor the outside workers, "as the amount of work they do is brutally unequal . . . we would be sacrific-ing the interior worker to the exterior worker." [22]

The interior workers were considered "professional miners," the exterior workers were not. There are also indications that among the interior workers the hewers saw themselves as a group apart. In January 1922 the hewers at Hulleras del Turón met to organize "an exclusive organization, apart from the rest of the workers." This was a response to the attack on piecework rates in the early 1920s, which affected the hewers more than other categories. [23] This incipient sense of superiority is well illustrated by the hostility among miners during a strike at Minas de Teverga in April 1922. A group of eight hewers worked one seam collectively and earned the highest wages at the mine. When they wanted to go on strike, they were opposed by many of the other workers, who refused to stop work "so that eight hewers can earn twice as much as the rest." The meeting called to decide the question nearly ended in violence. [24]

Established labor practices in the Asturian mines came under attack only in the 1920s, as part of the owners' response to the postwar crisis in the industry. Their initial strategy was, as always, to cut wages to cut costs, but as the crisis dragged on and the workers reacted strongly in defense of their incomes, the owners changed tack and tried to intensify production. This had two basic as-pects: the alteration of job roles and the reduction in the number of oncost workers, on the one hand, and the introduction of labor-saving technology, on the other. Both were intended to increase the productivity of the work force.

The first step was to reduce the proportion of oncost workers. Between 1920 and 1923 the percentage of workers involved in extraction rose from 35.8 to 41.9 percent. The only groups of workers beside the hewers to in-crease were the sorters and those in the workshops. Wartime experience had shown that the sorters were unable to "wash, sort, and finish all the coal sent from inside." The percentage of supervisory staff decreased, as falling piece-work rates could be relied upon to encourage workers to maintain productivity levels. Oncost workers were cut again in 1934 with the result that "the number of extraction workers increased dramatically." [25]

The second facet of this intensification of production was the increased mechanization of the mines. When he toured the Langreo coalfield in the 1840s, S. E. Widdrington had difficulty in believing he was in the middle of a famous mining area: "We had been travelling for some time over the rich coalfields of Asturias, but no notice was given of such a district; not a particle of smoke, no carriage road, much less railways. . . . Groves of chestnuts and the most luxuriant vegetation cover the seams which come to the surface in the precipitous hills that bound the deep valley of the Nalón. Amid these groves were seen a few men, who pierced a short distance into a seam with perpendicular walls on each side, working as long as it served their purpose and then seeking another vein. No machinery of any kind is used or required." [26] Nor did the technical level of the industry improve with any rapidity. Company representatives who testified before the 1867 parliamentary tariff commission all but boasted of their refusal to modernize production. According to the Sociedad Santa Ana, the deficiencies of the region's infrastructure dissuaded it from putting production on the same lines used in Britain and Belgium, even though it could do so "easily." [27]

Coal mining was not a high technology industry, and the technical advances made during its "industrial revolution"—from 1850 to 1910 in Britain—were not numerous. The key improvements were in mechanical cutting and underground haulage techniques. Compressed air was first used as a source of power in 1853, and ten years later the first effective cutting device, the disc cutter, was invented. In 1893 electrically operated picks were introduced. The adoption of the new techniques was uneven, but "by the closing years of the nineteenth century coalmining had entered the modern era of mechanical cutting at the face." [28] In Britain, where mechanization lagged behind Belgium, Germany, and even France, there were 483 mechanical cutters, 149 of them powered by electricity, in 1903. Mechanical conveyers at the face were introduced in the 1850s, but in Britain, which trailed here, too, little advance was made on the primitive Endless Rope system before World War I. [29]

The explosion of world coal production in the interwar years, which was the backdrop to the crisis in Asturias, was due to "the higher unit output obtained per unit of capital and labor as a result of mechanization." By 1929, 90 percent of the coal mined in Belgium and the Ruhr and 70 percent of that mined in France were mechanically cut. In Britain, whose coal competed directly with that from Asturias in the Spanish domestic market, the figure was only 30 percent. Britain also trailed in the modernization of underground haulage techniques. In short, "as mechanization developed so too did labor productivity and hence, the greater the effect on the major cost item in coalmining, wages. In general, the greater the advance of mechanization, the greater the rise in output per man-shift."[30]

In Asturias the calls for mechanization intensified in the 1890s, as increasing demand brought colliery operators up against an acute labor shortage. The *Revista Minera* seized on the Spanish-American War as a propitious moment for modernization:

> We recognize that a working population that accepts underground work can only be created slowly; but what we protest against is the small result we get from the work force on which we rely. While our mine owners in general, *and of coal mines in particular*, do not accept that a man should not do work that can be done by a machine we will never surpass this unacceptable increase of 10 percent. . . . While we see interior transport powered by men's backs when it could be done by electric locomotive, while we do not try new coal cutters where they can be used, we will not blame the difficulty in increasing production on the shortage of workers but on the shortage of machines. . . . It is our firm belief that there are machines for every case; the question is to know of them.[31]

Such blandishments had little effect. Between 1904 and 1908 the number of machines in use rose from 107 to 129, and it was not until 1908 that Duro-Felguera introduced compressed air picks into its important María Luisa mine.[32] In 1911 the use of mechanical cutting devices was still very limited. "They have been little used up to now; only in the Lieres mines, where since 1905 they have used one compressed air cutter in the tunnels . . . and three rotation drills in the galleries."[33]

World War I presented a major occasion for a debate on mechanization. As domestic production was called upon to compensate for the termination of British exports, there was concern that the Asturian mines would not be up to the task. Perceptive observers knew that finding more mine workers was not the real issue. Cost had to be cut and productivity increased, and the only way to manage this was to substitute machine power for manual labor wherever possible.[34]

Some investment and improvements were made. Between 1913 and 1918 Duro-Felguera invested 5.3 million *pesetas* on interior electric traction, offices, a power plant, workers' housing, and sinking pits. It was also able to unify its overall operation, "having the mines grouped rationally and in condition to work as a complex instead of having each mine on its own, isolated."[35] The company claimed to have invested over 20 million *pesetas* between 1914 and 1920.[36] Fábrica de Mieres spent 17 million on improvements to its Mariana mine and on other facilities, and the Industrial Asturiana spent 8.5 million on a spur line, buildings, washers, and other installations.[37]

The most significant innovation in Asturian mining was the introduction of pit mining. Pits were first sunk in 1916–17 as the most easily available coal began to run out. In 1918 inclined pits were being put in at Saus, Sociedad Cantabro-Asturiana, Hulleras del Pontico, and Minas del Escobio. Fully vertical pits were under way at Felgueroso Hermanos' Barredos mine and at the Nalona and Sotón mine belonging to Duro-Felguera. By 1933 there were also pits at Hulleras del Turón, Carbones de la Nueva, and the Pumurabule and Mosquitera mines.[38]

Although not negligible, the investments made during the war represented only a small proportion of the vast wartime profits made by the mining companies. The failure to attend seriously to the industry's basic deficiencies, and especially to its lack of mechanization, was felt in the 1920s, and demands for improved methods came from all quarters. SMA president Manuel Llaneza called for the nationalization and rationalization of the mines on the grounds that the owners had proven their incompetence, while *El Socialista* dismissed claims that geology had condemned the Asturian mines to inefficiency.[39] Another SMA official, Cándido Parrado, complained that the owners had not learned the lessons that their Belgian counterparts had. A rumor that Fábrica de Mieres was going to be taken over by the Krupps was greeted as good news: "Far from being surprised by this piece of news we must confess that we are anxious for such a change. . . . We understand that it may be the lever which will lift the town of Mieres from its rachitic state and at same time free the working class from the whip of the incompetence of its owners. . . . We prefer that foreign capital give life to this industry than that the workers emigrate in droves to other countries."[40] Looking to the Krupps as the liberators of the working class! A telling critique of the incompetence of the company's management.

Such views were also shared by the regional branch of the Association of Mining Engineers, which also included supervisory personnel. The industry was suffering a crisis of production that required that production costs be cut, but these cuts could not be borne exclusively by the workers. Technology suitable for Asturian conditions was available, but with rare exceptions the owners had not adopted it.[41] The report of the Aldecoa Commission pointed out that mechanization was under way and that the use of mechanical drills and picks was showing good results, but that there was still a long way to go.[42]

The most knowledgeable critique came from Rafael de Riego, the chief engineer at Hulleras del Turón. He was a harsh critic of the other major companies, chastising them for blaming the failure to change on the workers and charging that it was greed that stopped them from making badly needed investments. What was needed in his view was a comprehensive modernization of the industry: cutting, interior transport, sorting, and washing to lower costs to a competitive level. "The market has to be our own creation; it must be conquered with good products at reasonable prices. We must widen it if it already exists or create it if it does not, and for this we can count on one method only; changing the system of work . . . using machines to help, to complement and to substitute where possible the muscular energy of the physical labor of men." [43]

Riego's opinion carried some weight, as he had overseen the only complete mechanization carried out by a major mining company in the region. Even before the war Hulleras del Turón had studied ways of solving its pressing labor shortage and had decided to make use of "electric energy and compressed air." [44] In 1917 work on the pits had to be held up as the company could not find enough workers for the mines already in operation. The introduction of the seven-hour day for interior workers in 1919 and the onset of the postwar crisis forced the pace, as management realized that wages could not be cut indefinitely. An engineer and a foreman were sent abroad to study the newest techniques and brought back up-to-date machinery, including the latest mechanical drills. [45]

The results were positive and immediate. By 1921 the company had achieved "real savings in the number of workers and the price," and these savings would have been even greater had it not chosen to amortize the costs so quickly. [46] Hulleras del Turón did not have a single losing year in the 1920s and only one between 1919 and 1934. So successful was its modernization program that it was able to absorb the increased costs posed by the reintroduction of the seven-hour day in 1931 and the wage increases that followed. [47]

The major component of this program was the total conversion to mechanized extraction. Before 1920 all the company's coal was cut by hand. By 1923, 23 percent was being cut mechanically, by 1924, 45 percent, by 1925, 54 percent, and by 1927, 86 percent. In 1928 the management declared the changeover complete as over 90 percent of the coal was being mechanically cut. But this extensive use of mechanical cutting was not the only change. Interior transport was improved, and a new Dorr automatic washer and sorter was introduced in 1926. It reduced the amount of dust produced by one-fifth, and earned the company a bonus from its principal customer, Altos Hornos de Vizcaya. [48] By thus mechanizing its entire operation the company had avoided the bottleneck created when mechanized cutting increased production to an extent with which old-fashioned haulage and sorting methods were unable to cope. Increasing the productivity of the hewers accomplished little if that of the haulers and sorters remained unchanged. [49]

Of course, these changes in technique forced changes in the work force. First, the number of workers was reduced. By 1922 it had been reduced by 20 percent while output rose by 150 kilograms per worker per shift and costs fell by 40 percent. [50] Then worker resistance to the new methods had to be overcome. This was particularly strong at the outset, when the new system was not totally reliable. Later on, the ease of advance with the mechanical picks led hewers to ignore timbering the stalls. The company responded by increasing the height of the stalls and "imposing on the worker the obligation of making a uniform daily advance" in order to cut down earnings.[51] All these changes had one effect that management could not have foreseen and certainly did not welcome—the Turón coalfield, scene of the most sweeping changes in work routine in the province, became the only place in which Communism would have a mass following among the miners: "Red Turón."[52]

Other companies stepped up their mechanization programs in the 1920s, but none matched Hulleras del Turón in thoroughness. Duro-Felguera deepened the main pit at Mosquitera, built a new mechanical extraction complex at Barredos, and electrified the spur line between Mosquitera and Brana. It also increased the use of mechanical picks. Hullera Española began to use mechanical drills for digging tunnels, employing both compressed air and electricity, and also mechanized its interior haulage. Production rose by 10 percent between 1928 and 1932, while the work force increased by only 7.5 percent. The mechanization of four of its mines—Mariana, Dos Amigos, Conveniencia, and Turca—allowed new seams to be brought into production and more workers hired. Elsewhere, benzine and even electrically powered locomotives were being used for interior haulage, although animal traction was still much more common.[53]

Can we get a general idea, then, of the degree of mechanization of the Asturian mines by 1934? All the major improvements were being used: mechanical ventilation, mechanical picks and drills, mechanized—and even electrified—interior transport, and modern, self-acting washers and sorters that used the flotation process to cut down on lost coal. By 1930, 1.5 million tons, one-third of the region's production, was mechanically cut. This was a much smaller percentage than in the Ruhr, Belgium, or the Pas de Calais in France, with 91, 89, and 72 percent, respectively, but certainly comparable to Britain, where the figure was 28 percent in 1929 and 38 percent in 1932. Extraction was more highly mechanized in Asturias than in some British fields, including ones in South Wales.[54]

This mechanization achieved its main objectives: to increase labor productivity and cut production costs. Output per worker had fallen drastically during the war, from 135 tons per worker per year in 1913 and 1914 to 102.2 in 1918, 85.6 in 1919, and 92.1 in 1922, due mostly to the opening of new, marginal mines and helped by the tremendous labor strife of 1921–22. At Duro-Felguera, output fell from 904 kilos per worker per day in 1915 to 596 in 1919. However, productivity began to take off after 1922. The index of productivity jumped from 102 to 193 in 1929 (with 1914 as the base). At the same time, wages were pushed down, from a peak of 298 in 1920 to 223 in 1923–24 and 219 in 1929.[55] This progress continued, with only slight setbacks, through 1933.

There was another aspect of the modernization of the mines, which had little to do with compressed air or electricity: the supervision and disciplining of the work force. As we have seen, before World War I discipline was not thoroughly enforced. In part this problem arose from the difficulty of supervising any mine work effectively. The natural conditions of mining provide "an almost unprecedented degree of independence from managerial supervision. . . . The extent of job control exercised by the hewers is unequalled in capitalist enterprise." [56]

As Alvarez Buylla had foreseen in 1860, discipline and supervision were particular problems for the large companies. The growing demands for improved labor discipline and attempts to achieve it corresponded to the beginning of the dominance of the large-scale producer around 1885.

All mines had to confront the scarcity of labor but the new demands made by the large companies put them at a disadvantage. All mines competed for the same workers, who were almost exclusively Asturian mixed workers. As a result, the smaller operations with their greater flexibility proved more attractive. With less rigid rules and timetables and greater contact between mine worker and mine owner, the small mines were able to compete successfully for the available workers. Mine work was much more attractive when it did not require the worker to sacrifice his "liberty." [57]

Faced with the difficulties of direct supervision mine owners used indirect means of supervision. One was subcontracting. Sydney Pollard has described this as a means "to allow entrepreneurs to escape the most urgent, immediate problems of large-scale management." Subcontracting freed owners from the need to supervise operations constantly, but had the major drawback of leaving coal deposits open to damage by subcontractors concerned only with their own short-term profit. The system was generally eliminated "as soon as employers could be certain of being fully in control of discipline," [58] but in Asturias the impossibility of imposing a secure labor discipline meant that subcontracting would be a persistent feature throughout virtually the entire history of the industry.

The earliest form of subcontracting was subleasing. An individual or company would claim a concession that would then be leased to groups of workers who mined it and received a set price for the coal. The workers usually supplied tools, explosives, and lighting oil; the concessionaire, wood, maintenance, and sorting facilities. One common form of lease was the *arriendo a la cuarta*, in which the workers paid a royalty of 25 percent. [59] At the Mosquitera mine in Langreo everything except repairs and some operations requiring special care was done on contracts. Tunnels were paid by linear meter of advance and extraction "for each full wagon extracted and so much for each ton of good coal produced, which depended on the seams." The contracts were made between the company and the leader (*cabecera*) of the team "for two or three months, sometimes more, but always expiring on December 31." The leader was a miner, usually an experienced timberer. The company provided wood and tools and deducted costs for any that were lost or intentionally destroyed. The miners provided their own explosives and lighting oil. At other mines the company demanded a deposit from the contractor, which could be as much as 1,000 *pesetas*.[60]

Not only did subcontracting continue to be used in many Asturian mines, including in some major companies, through the 1930s, but it became stronger as time went on. Felgueroso Hermanos contracted interior haulage when galleries and tunnels were long, a common practice during the war. Carbones de la Nueva contracted the digging of tunnels as well as haulage in areas where direct supervision was difficult. At Hulleras del Turón haulage and construction were on contract in the mid-1920s and at Industrial Asturiana subcontracting was reintroduced in the 1920s, after having been stopped earlier due to worker opposition. Hullera Española still contracted interior transport in 1931, finding this the easiest way of increasing productivity.[61]

Subcontracting was not without its critics. As early as 1863 the *Estadística Minera* blamed "the ease with which concessions are obtained and mines leased out" for hurting the industry.[62] Francisco Gascue was a harsh critic, especially as the system often failed to achieve the intended degree of control over the work force. Contractors were continually demanding revisions in prices due to the irregularity of the seams and threatening to leave if their demands were not met. This constant upward adjustment of the rates eliminated the need to drive the workers to increase output, which was from management's point of view one of the main reasons for using the system. "Any intelligent worker who considers the subject will see that far from being an incentive to work hard this contract will not persuade him to tire himself since at the end he winds up earning exactly the same."[63]

The workers were the strongest and most consistent critics of subcontracting, and the attack on the system was one of the first concerns of the mine labor movement. In his early pamphlet, *Los mineros asturianos*, Socialist organizer Manuel Vigil described the "barefaced robbery" practiced by contractors, especially their cheating of the *picadores*. "Just think, miners, that a rogue in the form of a contractor robs you at the end of the month, paying for centimeters instead of meters. What happens? Of course he does not go to jail and unfortunately we know of many who rob and no one dares stand up to them."[64] A related complaint was the harshness of contractors as employers. This was especially resented because many contractors had themselves been miners. One worker wrote to the Socialist paper *Aurora Social* that "it would not be so bad that men became contractors if the majority of miners who took on this role did not turn into infamous exploiters who flatter the mine owners."[65] In some places the contractor's authority went well beyond the workplace. Miners in Riosa complained that the contractor was also the mayor and the tavernkeeper and "did not permit them to get drunk outside his place and threatened to take care of them if they demanded their earnings." [66]

The return to subcontracting in the 1920s, at a moment when the union movement was in crisis, created discontent. The reappearance of contractors at Industrial Asturiana was denounced as "something the unionized workers did not permit as they considered it contrary to their economic aspirations." [67] One worker from Aller recalled the time "when this local was strong and we called a strike to eliminate the contractors; today we work for them." [68]

Some miners preferred collective contracts whereby they took over the running of the mine without any intermediary. The first such contracts were at Industrial Asturiana, one of the largest companies in the region and the one that had the most problems during the crisis of the 1920s and 1930s. The management sought some way to staunch the losses and turned to the collective contract. By 1922 there were three such contracts at the company, and by 1931 the practice had been extended as a means of avoiding the closure of the mines. [69] The workers took on another contract in 1933, also to prevent a closure. "Faced with the bosses' refusal to continue operations the workers did not hesitate . . . concluding a leonine contract with the company even though they knew it tied them hands and feet because it was forced on them by difficult circumstances." [70] The company had learned from experience that it was incapable of running the mines without incurring huge losses, but that with these collective agreements it could turn a profit with no effort. By 1933 this approach was being used at the Socieded Santa Barbara and Carbones de la Nueva as well as in three mines belonging to Duro-Felguera. It had also been requested by some workers at Hullera Española. [71]

Where neither subcontractors or collective agreements were used, piecework (*destajo*) was intended to force workers to discipline themselves. One mining engineer commented that "we tend to give the miner piecework since given the conditions of the mine any other system would cost too much in supervision." [72] Workers were paid an established rate per linear meter of advance for digging tunnels and per tonnage of coal for hewing and hauling. The prices for hewing varied according to the condition of the seams: those with harder rock or more irregularities were given a higher rate. Often the company provided explosives and then deducted the cost from the workers' monthly earnings. [73]

The earliest reference to the piecework system comes from the Polish traveler Holynski in 1843. By the 1850s it had become a common method of payment, both in the central coalfield and in more peripheral areas such as Riosa. The popularity of this method undoubtedly lay in the positive effect it was seen to have on productivity. In the 1880s Fábrica de Mieres was able to cut its labor costs by 14 percent by putting its employees on piecework, and in 1890 the *Revista Minera* reported that those mines that used this method had the best rates of productivity.[74] A straight daily wage was said to have the opposite effect: "It puts the bad worker on the same level as the good and requires a great deal of supervision, which is difficult to achieve in a mine."[75]

Piecework became the general means of paying hewers for digging tunnels and cutting coal. It was a method of paying the individual worker, and there was very little teamwork. It was also used to pay timberers and haulers, but its frequency varied from mine to mine. At Felgueroso Hermanos all interior workers except assistants were paid on piecework. At the Mariana mine all 1,050 workers except the blasters were on a straight wage. In 1933 it was estimated that some 40 percent of all Asturian mine workers were on piecework.[76]

The setting of the rates was largely a matter of custom. "There are rates which have been adopted through custom, without complaint by the workers, according to the rocks through which they must advance or how the seam looks. Another factor which affects the rate is the amount of explosives that must be used." Thus, the rates were the product of an agreement between employer and worker, and after the beginning of the collective agreements between the SMA and the Patronal they were attuned to the negotiated minimum wage.[77]

However, as we have already noted, wages came under strong attack, especially between 1921 and 1924, as mine owners unilaterally took to lowering piecework rates in their continuing attempts to lower costs. The length of the work day received similar treatment, although the owners had to wait until 1927 to achieve their goal of adding an extra hour.

The length of the work day had always varied from mine to mine, having been as long as twelve or thirteen hours. However, not all of this time was spent laboring. The work day had always been measured from the moment of entry into the mine to the moment of departure. This meant that a significant amount of time, up to an hour and a half, was spent in getting to and from the work site, and the actual working time was reduced to ten or ten and a half hours.[78]

The work day of the inside workers was always shorter, usually by an hour, than that of the outside workers. General José Marvá's 1909 study of conditions in the mines showed that inside workers had a work day that varied from eight and a half to ten and a half hours, while that of the outside workers varied from ten to ten and a half hours. The work day was first regulated by law in 1910, when it was limited to nine hours on the inside and nine and a half on the outside. It was reduced to seven and eight hours, respectively, by the decree of October 10, 1919, giving the Asturian miners the shortest work day in Europe. Mine owners campaigned strongly against this and finally were successful in September 1927, when the eight-hour day was restored for interior workers. In 1931 Socialist Labor Minister Francisco Largo Caballero restored the seven-hour day.[79]

Solidarity did not suggest itself naturally, inevitably, in the working life of the Asturian coal miner. The work itself was essentially individual, and team-work was rare. In very few cases did one miner's wage depend on the work of another. The differing prospects for mobility between native and immigrant miners reinforced differences based on regional origin, while the distinction between interior and exterior workers—and within the former between hewers and the rest—was another point of cleavage.

However, after World War I major changes were introduced into the work routine as owners frantically sought to cut costs and increase productivity: tighter discipline, lower piecework rates, longer hours, increased use of sub-contracting, and the intensification of production through mechanization. The hewers, the heart of the mining operation, bore the brunt of these changes, but no category of mine worker remained untouched by them. The period 1919–34 saw the most sweeping changes in the history of coal mining in Asturias, all of which were detrimental to the interests of the worker, forcing him to work longer and produce more while earning less. And the miners were well aware of what was happening: "All the methods of multiplying the strength of the individual worker, all the means of exploiting the producer, are placed before him by the scientific forces of production, which replace attractive work by forced labor, harshen the conditions of work, and subject the proletariat to a rough and intense despotism."[80] In this way the work place became the classroom for class conflict, providing the miners with the opportunity for overcoming the divisions inherent in the work in the mines, to create a solidarity that otherwise would not have existed.

NOTES

1. *Mercurio de España*, 1821, III, 176. See also J. V. Pereda, *Memoria sobre el carbón fosil* (Oviedo, 1814), 8–9.

2. *Lecciones de laboreo de minas* (Oviedo, 1866), 115.

3. H. Louis, "Coal Mining in Asturias, Spain," in Newcastle Institution of Mining Engineers, *Transactions*, 1904, 421–22; T. Saus, "Prácticas de residencia en la mina Maríana" (Thesis, Escuela Superior de Ingenieros de Minas, 1924), 12.

4. Alvarez Buylla, *Observaciones*, 9; M. Pastor, "Memoria del Grupo Sama" (Thesis, Escuela Superior de Ingenieros de Minas, Madrid, 1926), 11.

5. Pastor, "Memoria," 21; Saus, "Prácticas," 16–21.

6. Saus, "Prácticas," 16–17. See also Louis, "Coal Mining," 422.

7. Pastor, "Memoria," 16; Nicou, "L'industrie," 216; Pérez González, "Cuenca Central," 431.

8. R. Oriol y Vidal, *Carbones minerales de España* (Madrid, 1873), 20; Alvarez Buylla, *Observaciones*, 36; *RM*, 1885, 320; Pastor, "Memoria," 19.

9. Pastor, "Memoria," 19; Saus, "Prácticas," 42; Louis, "Coal Mining," 423; Oriol, *Carbones*, 20.

10. *RM*, 1883, 155–58; 1885, 320; Oriol, *Carbones*, 21.

11. *EMME*, 1884, 133.

12. Louis, "Coal Mining," 430.

13. *EMME*, 1884, 63–66; AHE 45/9.

14. "Memoria de un viaje a las minas de carbón de Asturias en 1884" (Manuscript, Escuela Superior de Ingenieros de Minas); *RM*, 1883, 158.

15. D. Crew, *A Town in the Ruhr* (New York, 1980), 83.

16. Cited in M. Vigil, "Memorias de un octogenerio" (Manuscript, Fundación Pablo Iglesias), 88–89.

17. Pérez González, "Cuenca Central," 311.

18. E. J. Hobsbawm, "The Machine Breakers," in *Labouring Men* (London, 1964), 9.

19. *AS*, 5.XII.1902.

20. DGM, *Informe*, 19.

21. *ES*, 27.VII.1925.

22. *MH*, Apr. 1916, 10. See also *ES*, 9.I.1922, and *Revista Nacional de Economía*, Oct. 1917, 580.

23. *ES*, 25.I.1922; Saus, "Memoria," 44–46.

24. S. Suárez, *Mineros de España* (Oviedo, 1958), 22.

25. *RIMA*, 1.V.1921, 172; 1.XII.1924, 354; *Revista Nacional de Economía*, Jan. 1918, 138; Olariaga, *La crisis*, 27. At the Saus mine the ratio of assistants to hewers fell from the usual 1:1 to 1:3.3.

26. Widdrington, *Sketches*, 83.

27. *Información sobre el derecho diferencial de bandera. Tomo 3: Carbones* (Madrid, 1866), 20–29. See also A. Grand, *Étude sur le bassin houilliére des Asturies* (Paris, 1874), 33.

28. A. R. Griffin, *The British Coal Mining Industry* (Hartington, 1977), 111.

29. N. K. Buxton, *The Economic Development of the British Coal Industry* (London, 1978), 105–12, 178.

30. Ibid., 178–85.

31. *RM*, 1900, 96. Emphasis is added.

32. Comisión de Estudio sobre la Riqueza Hullera Nacional, *Información*, 27; *EMME*, 1908, 585.

33. DGM, *Informe*, 21. In 1904 H. Louis wrote that in Laviana "machines seem to be unknown."

34. *Riqueza Hullera Nacional*, 59.

35. *RM*, 1918, 217–18.

36. *RIMA*, 16.VIII.1927, 241.

37. Ibid.

38. *Revista Nacional de Economía*, 1918, 47; *Boletín Oficial de Minería y Metalurgia*, Mar. 1918, 2–17.

39. M. Llaneza, *Estudio de la industria hullera española y la necesidad de su nacionalización* (Oviedo, 1921), 9–13; *ES*, 28.VIII.1925.

40. *ES*, 31.X.1923, 26.XII.1924.

41. *RIMA*, 16.I.1925, 22–23, 30.I.1925, 376.

42. Aldecoa, *Dictamen*, 45–48.

43. R. de Riego, *La mecanización de los servicios en las minas* (Oviedo, 1929), 17–35.

44. Hulleras del Turón, *Memoria* (Bilbao, 1914), 8.

45. Hulleras del Turón, *Memoria* (Bilbao, 1918), 8; 1920, 6; 1921, 7.

46. Hulleras del Turón, *Memoria* (Bilbao, 1923), 6.

47. Hulleras del Turón, *Memoria* (Bilbao, 1932), 6–7.

48. Hulleras del Turón, *Memoria* (Bilbao, 1922), 8; 1926, 10–11; 1927, 7. See also *NO*, 29.IX.1926.

49. The use of mechanical picks and drills was no advantage in mines with little incline where coal had to be moved by assistants, unless interior haulage was also improved. See the *Memoria* for 1921, 6–7.

50. Hulleras del Turón, *Memoria* (Bilbao, 1922), 6–7.

51. A. Aldecoa y González, "Memoria de prácticas de estancia en la Sociedad Hulleras del Turón" (Thesis, Escuela Superior de Ingeniero de Minas, Madrid, 1925), 103–9.

52. See ch. 7 herein. The expression comes from Grossi, *La insurrección*, 30.

53. S. M. Duro-Felguera, *Memoria* (Madrid, 1926), 5; Ampliación de la resena sobre las minas de hulla de Aller, 1929, AHE 4/2; Rubiera to Barbey y Prats, 5.XII.1932, AHE 12; *RIMA*, 16.VIII.1927, 244.

54. Muniz, *Industria*, 173; *RM*, 1932, 160; 1931, 322; Buxton, *Economic Development*, 179–83. In 1925 there were 58 compressors, 359 mechanical drills, and 381 mechanical picks—270 of which were at Hulleras del Turón—in the province. By 1934 the figures were 120, 818, and 2,236. *EMME*, 1925, 565; 1934, 478.

55. *RIMA*, 16.IX.1920, 291; 30.I.1925, 375; Duro-Felguera, *Memoria* (Madrid, 1920); *RM*, 1918, 218; Ministerio de Trabajo, *Estadística de salarios*, LXII.

56. K. Burgess, *Origins of British Industrial Relations* (London, 1975), 65. For Asturias see Nicou, "L'industrie," 217.

57. Alvarez Buylla, *Observaciones*, 28.

58. Pollard, *Genesis*, 38–47. The management of Hulleras del Turón was explicit about the advantages: "As a way of economizing on supervision we give monthly contracts to old workers in whom we have complete confidence. They take responsibility for their team." DGM, *Informe*, 15.

59. Grand, *Etude*, 35; *EMME*, 1863, 34.

60. "Memoria de un viaje . . . 1884." A report done for the Hullera Española in 1890 found that subcontracting was generally used for interior work in Mieres and Aller and for both interior and exterior work in Langreo. Another report noted that the mixed worker was more prominent in Langreo than elsewhere, but did not connect this to the more widespread use of subcontracting, although such a connection seems likely.

61. J. Fernández Hernández, "Memoria de prácticas en las minas de la Sociedad

Felgueroso Hermanos" (Thesis, Escuela Superior de Ingenieros de Minas, 1915), 63–64; *ES*, 20.V.1928; *AS*, 4.V.1928, 5.IV.1929; Grupo de Legalidad, Nov. 1931, AHE 12.

62. *EMME*, 1863, 37.

63. *RM*, 1883, 399.

64. M. Vigil, *Los mineros asturianos* (Oviedo, 1900), 11. See also *AS*, 7.II.1908.

65. *AS*, 4.IX.1908.

66. *ES*, 2.I.1922; *AS*, 19.I.1901.

67. *ES*, 18.X.1922.

68. *AS*, 4.V.1928.

69. *ES*, 18.X.1922; *EMME*, 1932, II, 328; 1933, II, 561.

70. *AV*, 4.VIII.1933.

71. *RIMA*, 16.VIII.1934.

72. L. Angoloti, "Memoria de Prácticas" (Thesis, Escuela Superior de Ingenieros de Minas, n.d.), 61.

73. DGM, *Informe*, 14; A. Marvá, *El trabajo en las minas* (Madrid, 1975), 70.

74. Holynski, *Coup d'oeil*, 74–75; *RM*, 1855, 315; 1858, 704; F. Gascue, *La industria carbonera asturiana* (Gijón, 1888), 87.

75. *RM*, 1890, 46.

76. Marvá, *El trabajo*, 69–70; Fernández Hernández, "Memoria," 62–65; Saus, "Prácticas," 75–76; *AV*, 30.I.1933.

77. Fernández Hernández, *Memoria*, 62–65.

78. Castaño, *El estado*, 22; *RM*, 1882, 65.

79. Marvá, *El trabajo*, 72; Aldecoa, *Dictamen*, 61–62; *RM*, 1931, 317.

80. *AS*, 8.III.1929.

3

The Conditions of Social Life

Both the miners' origins and their work put obstacles in the way of the development of any group consciousness. Did the same hold true for social life? Or did the patterns of residence and social intercourse help weld them into a unified group? Was there any link between occupation and neighborhood? Was there a spatial or social segregation that meant that "miners and their wives and children were unlikely to come into frequent contact with anyone who was not also a miner or a member of a miner's family?"[1] In short, once he left the colliery did the Asturian miner return to an environment that was likely to reinforce or detract from his identification with his workmates?

The population of the province had always been widely distributed among numerous small groups. In 1858 the total population of 529,529 was spread among 3,787 centers, of which 2,108 were *caseríos*—clusters of farmhouses with fewer than fifty inhabitants. Only sixteen centers had more than 1,000 people and only two, Oviedo and Gijón, over 10,000. What were to become the major mining and metallurgical centers of Mieres, Sama de Langreo, and La Felguera had an appearance that was more rural than urban.[2] One journalist described Mieres as "seven clusters strung out along the highway."[3] In 1858 the municipal district of Langreo had 7,823 people in 118 centers, Mieres had 10,647 in 212, San Martín del Rey Aurelio 3,985 in 191, and Aller 10,426 in 163. By 1930 the pattern had not changed. The population of Mieres had risen to 42,787, but the number of population centers had jumped to 424. In Langreo 39,777 people were divided among 226 centers, in Aller 24,658 among 174, and in San Martín del Rey Aurelio 16,442 among 234.[4]

The major urban centers that did develop came to have an increasing weight. For example, Sama and La Felguera increased their share of the population of the municipal district from 24 to 47.5 percent between 1857 and 1900.[5] However, the pattern of urbanization, which was determined both by the narrowness of the valleys and the rapidity and uncontrolled nature of urban growth, particularly in the second decade of the twentieth century, did not produce a few large centers of concentrated population, but rather spread it out "in a ribbon along the main road." [6] In the town of San Martín del Rey Aurelio only "a few stretches of patched stone sidewalks and the uniform of the municipal police permit it to be called urban." [7]

Despite growth and some urbanization, the population of the coalfields continued to live primarily in numerous small villages and hamlets (table 9). Only 18.7 percent of the total of 131,171 people lived in the seven towns with over 1,000 people, and only 31.8 percent in the thirty with more than 500. Forty-three percent lived in 736 centers with between 100 and 500 people, while fully a quarter of the population lived in the 1,016 villages and hamlets with fewer than 100 people. This pattern of a highly dispersed population was less true for the metalworkers than for the miners, as a historian of Langreo has written: "The metallurgical installations of La Felguera are very important in the urbanization process because they constitute a large center of labor in the plain, compared to the dispersion of mining in small centers dotted on the hillsides, which has favored the native population, which is able to combine mine work with agricultural activities." [8]

One major consequence of this residential pattern was that many miners lived, not clustered around and constantly in sight of their place of work, but instead a considerable distance from the mine. When the Escuela de Capataces (Foremen's School) was established in the 1850s, the organizers recognized

Table 9. Population Distribution in 1930

Municipality	0/100	100/500	500/1000	1/2000	2/5000	5000
Aller	12.6	24.4	33.2	—	29.8	—
Langreo	17.7	43.9	5.6	—	32.8	—
Laviana	38.6	26.5	—	—	34.9	—
Mieres	25.0	46.7	10.4	2.6	—	15.2
Ríosa	51.4	48.6	0	—	—	—
San Martín del Rey Aurelio	46.8	38.0	15.2	—	—	—
Siero	9.2	67.7	23.1	—	—	—
Total	25.2	43.0	13.1	.9	12.1	5.7

Source: *Nomenclator de la provincia de Oviedo en 1930* (Oviedo, 1931).

Note: All data are given in percentages. For Mieres, Ríosa, and San Martín del Rey Aurelio all parishes were analyzed. For the rest only those that included mining zones—Boo, Moreda, and Cabanaquinta (Aller), Ciaño, Lada, Sama, and Tuilla (Langreo), Pola de Laviana, Tolivia, and Villoria (Laviana), and Arenas, Feleches, and Valdesoto (Siero)—were examined.

that the schedule had to be adapted to the special conditions of the region. Classes could only be given on days when there was no work "because the workers live in small villages and must travel half a league to get to work." [9] All subsequent testimony bears this out. In 1882 the *Revista Minera* noted that miners had to spend between forty-five minutes and one hour getting to work. Many lived as much as six kilometers away. Workers at Hullera Española had to come large distances, many of them four or five kilometers on bad roads, to vote in a strike referendum in 1917. [10]

In 1925 the *Revista Industrial Minera Asturiana* lamented "the frequent occurrence" that workers were having to walk up to seven kilometers to get to work, and called on the mining companies to build housing close to the mines. [11] One of the doctors employed by the Hullera Española has left us an interesting description of the situation:

> With few workers in my district I have to go to Villallana and from there to the villages in the parish which are in the mountains . . . and in the winter after visiting Villallana I have to go back to Sovilla in order to return along the right bank of the river. . . . All these places have workers of ours and they are dispersed on opposite sides of the river. . . . Although there are not that many *caseríos* in Ujo there is Villar on one bank and Ubriendes, Casones, and Conforcos on the other. . . . Santa Cruz has Granedo and Grillero and others it would be monotonous to name. . . . *The problem is not in the numbers but in the distance.* [12]

A second important consequence stemmed from this dispersal of the mining population. Asturian coal miners were not ghettoized in homogeneous settlements where they had little opportunity to mix with other types of people. Ramón Pérez is correct in saying that the coal companies built housing near the mines and that this led to a buildup in the valleys. However, these company residences never housed a significant proportion of the mine work force, and his contention that miners were concentrated into a "strongly monolithic" group is, I believe, untrue. [13]

The available literary evidence, which is slight, suggests that at least until World War I miners were not isolated from other Asturians. Dr. Muniz Prada, an instructor at the Foremen's School and an authority on worker hygiene, felt that this mixture of population, with miners spread among farmers, was useful in preserving levels of "morality." He warned against the massive introduction of outside workers, especially if they were to be bunched together in separate districts: "Now they are mixed in with the sober and docile peasants of these valleys among whom the healthiest traditional and religious practices prevail. . . . This must make us ponder how unknown workers from outside shall be admitted and how the working population of tomorrow is to be formed; for if the idea of barracks predominates we believe the system of dispersed housing to be much healthier." [14] One historian of Mieres writes that until 1914 it still looked more like a group of farming villages than a city and that "artisans, miners, factory workers, and some white-collar workers and professionals lived there in neighborly harmony." [15]

The only municipal censuses available for our period, for Mieres in 1910 and Laviana in 1930, indicate that the mining population was widely dispersed and did not dominate, although this began to change over time. As we see in table 10, in only three districts of Mieres (Rozadas de Bazuelo, Murias, and Vegadotos) did miners represent over 20 percent of the population, and in only two others (Santa Rosa and Villarejo), 15 percent.

When we turn to Laviana in 1930 (table 11), we find a greater predominance of mine workers and their families. In two parishes, Carrio and Entralgo, over 60 percent of the households had a miner as member and in two others, Tirana and Villoria, over 50 percent did. Miners represented a significant part of the population in each of the eight parishes except Condado and Lorio. In all, there were miners in 37.9 percent of the households of the municipality, and 42.6 percent if we discount the parish of Condado.

In the absence of other censuses we can turn to the electoral registers to get some idea of the situation. In addition to their notorious unreliability, the electoral registers have another shortcoming for the analysis of professional structure: the vagueness and inconsistency of the job definitions. This is particularly the case with *obreros, peones*, and *jornaleros*, vague terms for workers that give no indication of the type of work done. Still, the registers can offer at least an indication. Table 12 shows the evolution of the professional structure of Mieres, Langreo, and Aller between 1893 and 1922.

What conclusions can we draw? First, the miners came to have an increasing weight in the population of Mieres and Langreo over these thirty years, but in Aller the percentage remained almost stable. Second, industrial workers of all types dominated the population by 1922, with 72 percent in Mieres, 73.3 percent in Langreo, and 46.4 percent in Aller. The coalfield municipalities, with the mines and foundries, were very much a workers' world, but not a miners' ghetto. Third, only one other category—the farmers—accounted for more than 10 percent of the population. Their presence did diminish, absolutely as well as relatively, but they retained a surprisingly high profile in the coalfield municipalities: 9.9 percent in Mieres, 7 percent in Langreo, and 41.8 percent in Aller in 1922. In Laviana they represented 37 percent, and in San Martín del Rey Aurelio 13.4 percent, also in 1922. [16]

It is clear, then, that although miners were never entirely ghettoized in Asturias, they comprised an increasingly larger part of the population and, inevitably, came to have more contact with each other outside work. However, we should now recall the division of the mine work force into two distinct groups, Asturians and immigrants, to see whether increasing contact necessarily turned into sociability.

Table 10. Number and Percentage of Miners in the Population of Mieres, 1910

District	Cédulas	Total Population	Miners	Percentage
Consistorales	470	2,389	262	11.0
La Pasera	455	2,432	125	5.1
La Peña	311	1,497	94	6.3
Rozadas de Bazuelo	128	628	136	21.3
Murias	363	1,785	357	20.0
Sta. Rosa	147	743	127	17.1
Vegadotos	142	704	163	23.0
San Tirso	124	625	30	4.8
Rebollada	349	1,745	1	0.05
Baiña	124	620	0	0.0
Loredo	349	1,814	0	0.0
Seana	292	1,454	122	7.7
Figaredo	273	1,348	31	2.3
Villarejo	240	1,199	181	15.1
Cuna	162	807	113	14.0
Gallegos	188	943	116	12.3
Ujo	317	1,602	8	0.5
Sta. Cruz	290	1,312	42	3.2
Villabazal	329	1,753	213	12.9
Villandio	172	863	107	12.4
Urbies	172	833	5	0.6

Source: Padrón, 1910, Archivo Municipal de Mieres.

Note: *Cédulas* were the documents issued by municipal governments to each head of household.

Table 11. Miners' Households in Laviana, 1930

Parish	Households	Miners' Households	Percentage
Carrio	85	51	60.0
Condado	260	2	0.8
Entralgo	120	75	62.5
Lorio	323	56	17.3
Pola	559	191	34.2
Tirana	438	243	55.5
Tolivia	155	61	39.4
Villoria	406	213	52.5

Source: Padrón, 1930, Archivo Municipal de Pola de Laviana.

Table 12. Professional Structure of Mieres, Langreo, and Aller, 1893–1922

Category	Mieres			Langreo			Aller		
	1893	1915	1922	1893	1915	1922	1893	1915	1922
Miner	1.9	22.7	34.9	9.6	24.2	33.8	28.2	25.5	28.6
Worker[a]	48.1	36.4	28.4	44.9	45.2	26.9	4.0	14.5	12.8
Employee	2.1	4.3	6.9	1.2	3.3	6.7	0.6	0.7	2.0
Foreman	1.2	1.3	9.8	1.1	1.0	1.5	0.6	0.3	0.6
Skilled Worker[b]	2.3	9.0	8.7	4.5	8.8	12.6	3.2	2.9	5.0
Shopkeeper[c]	1.0	2.1	2.9	1.7	2.7	3.3	0.9	1.4	2.7
Industrialist	1.3	2.1	1.9	1.6	2.1	2.8	1.8	0.6	2.0
Notable[d]	2.3	2.4	3.1	2.6	1.8	2.5	1.8	2.1	2.0
Farmer	39.2	15.6	9.9	30.8	10.0	7.0	58.0	50.0	41.8
Other	0.5	4.1	1.9	1.1	1.7	2.8	0.4	1.1	2.6
Total	3,174	5,397	6,369	2,463	5,965	4,780	1,355	3,501	3,623

Source: *Censos Electorales de la Provincia de Oviedo*, 1893, 1915, 1922.

Note: All data are given in percentages.

[a] Includes *obrero, jornalero, peon, trabajador,* all of which mean wage workers.
[b] Includes carpenters, masons, machinists, puddlers, plumbers.
[c] Includes tailors, shoemakers, barbers, millers, pharmacists, printers, grocers.
[d] Includes solicitors, lawyers, priests, officers, notaries, judges.

All mining in Spain brought together workers from various parts of the country, and Spanish miners earned a reputation as rabid regionalists after their own fashion. In her memoirs Communist leader Dolores Ibarruri, whose husband had been a miner, mentions the practice of managers in the Basque iron mines of pitting one regional group against another.[17] Anarchosyndicalist leader Angel Pestaña, who spent his childhood in the mining communities of Leon and Santander, was deeply impressed by the "race hatred" he saw among the miners and of which the Galicians were everybody's favorite target:

> The Aragonese and Navarrese, for example, did not mix with the Basques or Asturians, and if they fought among themselves they also formed a group apart from other regions. When they were attacked by others they came to an agreement and defended themselves. . . . Those from the Rioja also worked by themselves. But where this race hatred was most notable was between the Galicians and the rest. Everyone united against the Galicians. They were the butt of all the jokes of that disparate and heterogeneous world. They were insulted in every way possible, even in songs. They sang songs like these:
>
> > They say that a *gallego* has died.
> > If only twenty would die—
> > The more *gallegos* who die,
> > The more hides for oil.
> >
> > When the *gallegos* in Galicia
> > Go in procession
> > They carry a cat for a saint
> > And an old woman for a banner.[18]

This type of antagonism was certainly present in the Asturian mines. Its earliest form was a general dislike of outsiders. As Francisco Gascue observed in 1883, "Here there is a . . . certain narrow, local spirit which opposes anything which is not from the province, and believes that it is impossible for people from elsewhere to become miners."[19] In a letter to Alejandro Pidal y Mon, a leading national political figure in the Conservative party, the mayor of Moreda complained about the problems caused by the immigrants working for Minas de Aller: "The disorderly conduct of the outsiders who work there has often created problems for which the residents have had to go to the courts . . . and this is expensive. . . . They also have to close up their houses every day after dusk and dare not use the roads for fear of being surprised and exposed to trouble."[20] Such hostility continued into the twentieth century: in 1901 and 1902 *Aurora Social* reported hostility to outsiders—they were blamed for unemployment—and attempts were even made to remove them physically from the mines.[21]

The regional rivalries described by Ibarruri and Pestaña were also present, and the hatred of Galicians was, as elsewhere, particularly intense. In February 1919 a fight between Catholic and Socialist miners in Boo was followed by one in Moreda between Catholics and Galicians. An injured Galician was taken to the Hullera Española company doctor in the town for treatment when "a socialist worker, revolver in hand, said to the doctor that the Galicians should die in the street. . . . There were twelve Catholics and Socialists there when the Galicians arrived shouting "Long live Galicia." *As the others understood that it had nothing to do with ideology but only regionalism* they started to fight with the Galicians, and if it had not been for the intervention of Vicente Madera, Catholic miners' union leader, there would have been much to lament." [22] Any sentiment that could unite Socialists and Catholics must have been amazingly strong.

The origins of this hostility to the Galicians is unclear, but one of the miners' songs from the October revolution provides one possible explanation: the Galicians were identified with the hated Guardia Civil.

> Inside the bullring
> The Galicians in three-cornered hats
> Used us to play bullfighter.
> Some used sabres
> And others whips,
> And the policemen from Galicia
> Kicked us as well. [23]

Likewise, Alfonso Comín dedicated his account of the Asturian revolution, *El Valle Negro*, "To Jose Garci-Crespo, who loves Asturias free of moors, of the Legion, and of Galician troops." [24]

Immigrants undoubtedly had their own networks of communication and contacts. Some were formal, such as the Centro Gallego started in Aller in 1919, which quickly had 200 members, or the Colonia Vallisoletana in Turón, which in September 1920 "decided to throw out the large number of members who are slow in paying [their dues] and whose names will appear in the press of Valladolid." [25] The Castilians did not have such formal organizations but did consider themselves enough of a community to hold meetings about questions of common interest. [26]

Of course there were also more informal grapevines that served to attract men from a province, a region, or even a village to a particular mine. In his study of the industrial working class of late nineteenth-century Moscow, Robert Johnson stresses the idea of *zemliachestvo*, the close relationship among men of a particular region that led them to the same urban neighborhoods, to the same companies, and to the same social activities. [27] Something similar was undoubtedly at work among the immigrants to the Asturian coalfields. The personnel registers of the mining companies indicate that in some mines hiring patterns were likely to have been influenced by just such relationships. At the Tres Amigos mine, 111 of 1,184 men hired after 1916 came from the province of Lugo, with 16 coming from the village of Palas del Rey. Orense sent 81 men to the mine, 23 came from La Mezquita and 12 from Gudiño. Of the 57 from Pontevedra, 33 came from Campo Lameiro. At the Coto Sama mine, of the men hired between 1916 and 1930, 30 came from Jaén, and of these 21 came from Linares. Thirteen of the 55 from Zamora were from Moraleja, 12 of 92 from Orense were from Celle, 11 of 72 *vallisotelanos* from Villalón, 8 of the *leoneses* came from Valencia de Don Juan, and 9 of those from Lugo were from Sarria. The Saus mine hired 2,316 men between 1914 and 1919: twenty-nine came from Villalón in Valladolid, and 39 from Peñaranda in Salamanca.[28]

If immigrants were drawn together into provincial or even village groups at work, were they also drawn together in their residences? Before World War I immigrant workers were most common in Mieres and Langreo, the only places with available rental housing. This was of extremely poor quality but very expensive, and as a result most immigrants to Mieres headed for the old core of the town, La Villa. Of 309 registered immigrants to Mieres in 1908–10, 35.9 percent (111) lived in La Villa, including 44.7 percent of those who came from other provinces.[29] According to Ramón Pérez this indicates "a clearly selective integration of the resident miners" and "the social depression of La Villa, due to which the immigrants ended up there."[30]

The 1910 Mieres census shows that immigrant miners were not so tightly concentrated. Only 24 percent lived in the district of Consistorales, which included La Villa, and they represented only 14.8 percent of all miners living there. Fifteen percent of the immigrants lived in Murias but accounted for only 7 percent of the miners in the district, while 13.3 percent lived in Villabazal where they accounted for less than 10 percent of the mining population.[31] Thus if there were a tendency, usually the result of economic necessity, for immigrant miners to reside in the same areas, this did not remove them from contact with native Asturians. Nor is there any evidence that immigrants from individual provinces clustered together.

The practice of lodging served to lessen the potential isolation of the newcomers. A report on the *huelgona* of 1906, done by the Instituto de Reformas Sociales, stated that in Mieres, "in contrast to the situation in Vizcaya," there were no lodging houses.[32] Single workers who needed such accommodation found it in "the six or eight residences that Fábrica de Mieres has built, or in private lodgings, generally offered by the established miners."[33] In Aller many of the Industrial Asturiana's workers lodged with employees of Hullera Española, often in company housing.[34]

Whether or not they lived in the same house or neighborhood, all miners shared one thing in common, the low quality of housing in the coalfields. This had always been the case. The farmhouses of the mixed workers had the advantage of being away from the crowded and dirty towns, but were themselves small, dark, and badly ventilated. Conditions in the coal towns were, if anything, even worse. "In general they are hygienically inadequate in every way: small, dirty, dark, badly ventilated, and this is a significant factor in the exaggerated disease levels there." [35] Conditions had not improved and may even have deteriorated further by the eve of war. One of the doctors employed by the Hullera Española described the housing provided by the company in the following way: "The housing of the workers . . . is truly intolerable. I was attending one person with typhoid in whose bedroom three other people slept, two during the day and one at night." [36]

The vast increase in the population due to the wartime immigration only exacerbated the problem. In an interview with *El Comercio*, Manuel Llaneza said, "In the coalfields even stables are used as houses, and as proof of their lack of hygiene there is the smallpox epidemic which swept the entire area last year and ravaged the families of the working class. They sleep on straw mattresses in horrible promiscuity. I could cite cases of a married couple, a twenty-year-old girl and a thirteen-year-old boy sleeping in the same bed. Young siblings of the opposite sex sleep together, and three lodgers sleep in the same bed, one having to get up so the other can lie down." [37] In Ciaño and Sama de Langreo the ratio of residents to dwellings rose from 8:1 to 8.5:1 between 1910 and 1920. In 1919 the municipal administration requested that a commission be set up to study the housing question, "keeping in mind that working class families are living in filthy holes, terribly overcrowded, without separating the sexes, with detriment to virtue and exposure to contagious diseases." [38] Some new housing had been built after 1915, but not nearly enough to relieve a situation, which remained appalling.

Conditions in Laviana were little different. In Pola de Laviana, the capital, there was some newer housing, but it was not much better than the old—and neither was hygienic. According to *El Socialista*, "Complaints about the scarcity and cost of rental housing are daily events . . . and the dwellings in which the workers live could not be worse." [39] In 1930 there were 4.84 people per household in the municipality as a whole, but the average for miners' households was 6.15. In Turón, which had the highest rents in the region, the situation was so bad that tenants formed a Liga de Inquilinos with a miner, Baldomero Alvarez Díaz, as president to assure that housing met the minimum prescribed standards. [40]

In Mieres the mayor, Manuel Llaneza, tried to interest the mining companies and others in providing low-cost housing and offered to put up 10 percent of one million *pesetas* and to amortize the entire sum over twenty years. The Constructora de casas baratas para obreros, Sociedad Cooperativa was a failure, as was another attempt, the Cooperativa de casas baratas para empleados y obreros municipales. The Mieres local of the SMA did manage to build a dozen units, and Fábrica de Mieres had its own cooperative, which built one housing complex. On the whole these attempts were "rachitic" and did not even begin to solve the problem.[41]

The housing crisis was only part of the general deterioration of social conditions in the coalfields after 1914. They had not been an attractive place to live before the war, and a chaotic, completely unregulated urban growth made things much worse. Complaints about the lack of social services abounded. Everything was missing: roads, electricity, schools, washing facilities. In February 1927, the Turón Socialist organization wrote to the Mieres town hall that "from April to October there is no water, good or bad, and the immense majority of houses do not have toilets because there is no sewage system. . . . Nor are there laundry facilities for the women. . . . It is the same with education . . . and of the state of the roads it is better not to talk because as soon as a dozen drops of rain have fallen you cannot leave the house. . . . The river is used as a slag heap."[42]

Shortage of water for washing, cooking, and drinking was a constant and pressing problem. Residents of the valleys had always drawn their water from the rivers and creeks, but the growth of coal mining caused these to be either polluted or blocked up. As early as 1863 the Mieres town hall began to receive complaints that "we cannot wash our clothes or cook or even let the cattle drink."[43] The "rivers" files in the municipal archive contain numerous such complaints directed against the mining companies.

In Sama complaints that the mines were fouling the rivers and that women were having to get up at 5:00 in the morning to collect water began in 1900. The water shortage was chronic, and a study commissioned by the town in 1918 concluded that the natural problems of the area were being exacerbated by rapid growth. Pollution had made the Nalón and its offshoots completely useless, the sewage system was inadequate, and the streets were filthy. The study recommended that nothing should be done at the moment as the cost was far too high, but that plans should be drawn up to take advantage of the least costly of the available alternatives so that work could be completed as quickly as possible when the proper moment arrived.[44] The problem continued through the 1920s. "The companies have repeatedly been asked to supply water for public use and until now we have gotten only a little, and that of poor quality. At the moment the capital of the district has water at certain hours only . . . and the situation is the same in other municipalities."[45]

Not surprisingly, with poor housing and insufficient and polluted water, disease was a problem. In 1885 cholera hit Aller for the first time, although Mieres and Pola de Lena had suffered from earlier outbreaks. Infectious diseases were a continuous cause for concern. There were typhus epidemics in 1911, 1914, 1916, and 1927, which doctors blamed on poor sanitation and sewage systems. "As well as to the infraction of the most basic rules of hygiene in most miners' homes this can be attributed to two factors: the toilets which drain into the receiving tank and the tank itself; the first as a vector for the germs and the second as a receptacle from which they draw water for washing and other domestic uses. In this way there is a vicious circle against which medical efforts are useless." [46]

Tuberculosis was another prominent disease, and one whose presence was often blamed on the mining industry. Naturally enough miners suffered from various respiratory problems. The district doctor for Moreda saw 3,113 workers between 1919 and 1922, of whom 947 had respiratory problems, 363 had skin diseases, 107 had eye problems, and 24 suffered from anemia. During the same period, 5,072 men applied for jobs. Four hundred fourteen were rejected on medical grounds, 106 passed, and the rest had some sort of job-related illness or injury. [47]

It was common for middle-class commentators to claim that mining had improved the standard of living in the region, in terms of both clothing and diet. Dr. Muniz Prada wrote in 1885 that the development of the mining industry, in addition to the cultivation of the potato, had led to the improvement of the Asturian workers' diet. In his view miners ate better than the residents of the "isolated parishes." [48] Jové y Canella shared this opinion. The meager and monotonous diet of the past, which had led to a high incidence of pelagra, improved as industry grew. In San Martín del Rey Aurelio meat, eggs, coffee, and chocolate had become part of the daily diet, while the widespread access to land meant that many workers were able to grow "a large part of the products required for subsistence." [49]

Such optimism is highly questionable. The Asturian agricultural system had provided a relatively balanced diet, which included meat and dairy products, even if it could not guarantee enough food to meet the needs of the population that depended upon it. With the growth of the coal industry came other problems: the adulteration of food and, most serious, the high cost of living. "Because of the high cost of basic necessities and the high birth rate the workers' income does not provide the necessary sustenance." [50]

This had prevented the mine owners from attracting immigrants before 1914, but the wartime inflation made the situation much worse in spite of significant wage increases. Food prices rose 159 percent between 1914 and 1920, while rents rose between two and four times. [51] Figures offered by the SMA in April 1920 showed that a family's daily needs had increased in price from 4.59 *pesetas* in 1914 to 10.94 *pesetas* in 1920. The *Revista Nacional de Economia* called these figures "very sober . . . irrefutable." [52]

The drastic cut in mine wages after 1922 was not accompanied by an equivalent fall in the cost of living. The estimated daily family budget offered by the SMA had risen from 10.94 *pesetas* in 1920 to 12.15 in 1922, although this did include 50 *centimos* for entertainment. The miners' standard of living fell in absolute terms during the 1920s, but they also became poorer than other sectors of the Asturian working class. The real wages of inside workers fell from base 100 in 1914 to 98 in 1930, after having risen to 120 in 1920. At the same time, the index of all wages in the province rose from base 100 in 1914 to 190 in 1920 and 218 in 1930, while the index of prices for basic necessities rose to only 172. In fact, it fell during the 1920s from 203 in 1920 and 195 in 1925. Thus it appears that living standards improved slightly in the province as a whole, while in the coalfields, where wages were falling rapidly and the cost of living was higher than elsewhere, the mine workers were experiencing both a relative and an absolute impoverishment.[53]

Taken together the poor and deteriorating social conditions in the coalfields had a debilitating effect on the working class. As one company doctor wrote very eloquently in 1922, "Allowing boys of 11, 12, and 13 to work in the mines, the double shifts that wear the workers out, the falling wages and the rising cost of living, the high rents, produced by excessive demand, and the consequent overcrowding . . . the poor sanitary conditions, inappropriate for human beings, even in purpose built housing . . . the lack of drinking water in many of them, and the faulty drainage systems all contribute to the evolution of *a new, truly degenerate race of beings.*"[54]

Two other much-commented-upon aspects of social conditions in the coalfields were alcoholism and crime. These were said to be interrelated, and both caused by the spread of industry. Socialists like Manuel Vigil joined middle-class commentators in denouncing alcohol as a vice harmful to the working class.[55] The director of Hullera Española claimed that the company's workers preferred to go drinking than to attend church on Sunday, and its police vigorously enforced the law on Sunday closing of taverns because "instead of attending church most go to the tavern."[56] The state mining engineers felt that this was the most common vice among the miners: "On holidays and paydays there are too many examples of disorderliness, primarily in the Mieres and Langreo valleys."[57]

In turn, alcohol was held responsible for the increase in crime in the region. A study published in 1900 showed that crime was increasing in those areas that had both population growth and industry, leaving the rural districts untouched. The judicial districts that had the highest crime rates were those with the greatest alcohol consumption. In sum, workers, and especially miners, were much more likely to find themselves in court than were farmers.[58]

The crimes committed by workers were of a limited type. They were "crimes of passion," not crimes against property, and they increasingly came to feature new types of weapons, pistols and razors instead of "the classic and picturesque club which the peasants handled with so much skill."[59] The Hullera Española police force regularly checked workers for weapons and frequently found them. Fights were such a regular part of life that in 1900 Manuel Vigil could promote unionization by claiming that it would reduce the violence among miners: "The friendly relations among miners of one mine and another, and one valley and another, will grow. . . . The disputes which arise with lamentable frequency because of trivialities will disappear as you will think only of using your force against those who exploit and mistreat you. You will not be beaten by the Guardia Civil for having fought among yourselves, and you will not go to jail for having wounded a workmate." [60] This quotation further indicates that there were subgroups or subidentities among the miners that served as a basis for division, even to the level of fighting.

A major reason for the popularity of the tavern was the absence of other recreational and cultural facilities. Taverns were the locale for live music-hall style entertainment. In 1909 one Moreda bar offered the "Turn of the Century Operetta," which included such characters as "the anarchist" and "the village priest." [61] As the union movement grew in wealth and size, the absence of public facilities was partially offset by the creation of workers' *ateneos* (cultural centers) and the Casas del Pueblo of the Socialists, "to such an extent that it can be said that there is no center of relative importance in the coalfields that does not have a cultural center where the workers can go to talk, read, or listen after work or on the holidays." [62] Both the *ateneos* and Casas del Pueblo offered lectures, theater performances, choral groups, and libraries. [63] The SMA Casa del Pueblo in Mieres had a library of 17,000 volumes at the outbreak of the Civil War.

These institutions did not succeed in drawing the miners out of the tavern, away from less "useful" pursuits such as drinking and gambling. In the 1920s trade union activists complained bitterly that many miners were more concerned with having a good time than anything else and that as a result they were uninterested in union affairs. These charges had a definite generational basis, with the men who had fought to establish the union before the war attacking the younger men who had entered during the wartime boom.

During the May 1922 congress of the SMA, Llaneza spoke of a new generation of mine workers, which did not have the same values as his own generation. This new generation "does not know or want to know our history, does not understand that they have lived in an extremely unusual time, and that instead of dedicating themselves to the conquest of knowledge to raise themselves from their condition of inferiority, they let themselves be seduced by the glitter of a flame . . . which will do away with the virtues that have always been identified with the miner." [64] He returned to this theme in a speech in December 1926, saying that the young were uninterested in the union and that "with few exceptions they are given over to things inappropriate to the class to which they belong." [65] Echoes came up from the base. Lucio García from Barros wrote that young miners were not concerned with social issues, and L. Leon called on them to give up their current life-style, "delivered over to vice, proper only for men for whom vice and corruption are daily fare." [66] The leadership of the Sama local despaired of its youth who were, they said, interested in nothing but the tavern and "the damned vice of football." [67]

Poor—and deteriorating—social conditions and a declining standard of living were the common lot of all Asturian miners, particularly after World War I. Inadequate housing, water shortages, poor roads, inadequate sewage disposal, and exposure to infectious diseases, as well as endemic work-related illnesses, were things they all experienced together and more or less equally.

However, in their social life as in their working life the miners of Asturias had much to overcome before they could have any sort of group identity or consciousness. Miners were never ghettoized in large homogeneous settlements that restricted the range of their social contacts, but rather were widely dispersed, usually in centers of less than 500 people, always in close contact with other social groups, and often at some distance from the mine. Within the mining population there were a number of internal divisions, of which geographic origin was the strongest. Regional rivalries were rampant in the coalfields, and the hatred for Galicians was especially intense, on occasion transcending the bitter ideological differences between Socialists and Catholics. There also undoubtedly existed informal but effective networks among immigrants from a region, province, or even village that further solidified this division. In addition, there was at least a potential rivalry based on the workplace, as well as a generational split that made the men who entered the mines during the wartime expansion the object of the criticism of the older men, and particularly the union activists, during the crisis of the 1920s.

NOTES

1. D. Crew, *Town in the Ruhr*, 191–94.

2. F. González Valdés, *Topografía médica del concejo de Oviedo* (Oviedo, 1911), 14; F. de Luxán, "Viaje Científico a Asturias," in Real Academia de Ciencias, *Memorias* (Madrid, 1861), 106; *Nomenclator de la provincia de Oviedo* (Madrid, 1860), 640–700; Criado Hernández, *Población*, 21.

3. P. G. Solís, *Memorias asturianas* (Madrid, 1890).

4. *Nomenclator*, 640–700; *Nuevo nomenclator de España* (Madrid, 1876); *Nomenclator de la provincia de Oviedo en 1930* (Madrid, 1931).

5. Pérez González, "Cuenca Central," 218.

6. Jové y Canella, *Topografía . . . San Martín del Rey Aurelio*, 50.

7. La Felguera to the Mayor, 26.II.1913, Fuentes (Turón-Urbies), AMM.

8. Fernández García, *Langreo*, 15.

9. 30.XI.1853, Legajo 6069, Archivo de la Administración, Alcalá de Henares.

10. *RM*, 1882, 65–66; M. Arboleya, *El caso de Asturias* (Barcelona, 1918), 190.

11. *RIMA*, 30.I.1925, 397.

12. Memorandum, 25.IV.1901, AHE.

13. Pérez González, "Cuenca Central," 19, 217–18. For a complete discussion of company housing, see ch. 4 herein.

14. N. Muniz Prada, *Apuntes para la topografía médica del concejo de Mieres* (Oviedo, 1885), 60–61. See also R. Fuerte Arias, *Asturias industrial* (Gijón, 1902), 139.

15. L. Fernández Cabeza, *Proceso de la Economía Mierense en los Tres Cuartos del Siglo Ultimo* (Mieres, 1977), 13.

16. Censo electoral de la provincia de Oviedo de 1922, Archivo Historíco Provincial, Oviedo.

17. D. Ibarruri, *They Shall Not Pass* (London, 1970), 19–20.

18. A. Pestaña, *Lo que aprendí en la vida,* in *Trayectoria Sindicalista* (Madrid, 1975), 142–43.

19. *RM*, 1883, 372.

20. Pando Arguelles to Pidal y Mon, Jan. 1891, AHE 2/5.

21. *AS*, 5.IV.1901, 5.XII.1902, 21.V.1909.

22. Jiménez to Montaves, 18.II.1919, AHE 55 /4. A week later the Centro Gallego asked to join the local Socialist organization and was turned down.

23. Songs of the October Revolution, Archive of the SMA, FLC.

24. A. Comín, *El Valle Negro* (Mexico City, 1938).

25. *NO,* 1.IX.1920. These miners retained close ties to their home province.

26. *NO,* 8.XI.1919.

27. R. E. Johnson, *Peasant and Proletarian: The Working Class of Moscow in the Late Nineteenth Century* (New Brunswick, 1979), 67–79.

28. Registro de Personal, Mina Tres Amigos, Archivo Pasivo de HUNOSA, Mieres; Registro de Personal, Grupo Sama, Archivo Pasivo de HUNOSA, Ciaño. Of the twenty-eight registered heads of household who went from Leon to Mieres in 1908, thirteen were from the same village.

29. DGM, *Informe*, 19–36; Inmigrantes, AMM.

30. Pérez González, "Cuenca Central," 679–80.

31. Padrón de 1910, AMM.

32. IRS, *Informe sobre Fábrica de Mieres*, 25.

33. *RIMA*, 16.V.1928.

34. Jové y Canella, *Topografía . . . Laviana*, 70.

35. 1899, AHE 57/4.

36. ? to Montaves, 9.VII.1913, AHE 57/6.

37. *MH*, Mar. 1917, 4. For a novelistic description, see I. Acevedo, *Los topos* (Madrid, 1930), 111–12.

38. Fernández García, *Langreo*, 212. By contrast, the ratio in the metal workers' district of La Felguera fell from 12.1:1 to 10.9:1.

39. *ES*, 8.VII.1923.

40. Jové y Canella, *Topografía . . . Laviana*, 74; Padrón de 1930, AMPL; Comas to Montaves, 13.III.1917, AHE 57/6; *ES*, 22.VII.1927; Liga de Inquilinos to Mayor, 21.III.1932, Sanidad, Higiene, y Vivienda, AMM.

41. Junta Local de Fomento de Habitaciones Baratas to Instituto de Reformas Sociales, 27.VIII.1922, AMM. See also Pérez González, "Cuenca Central," 767.

42. *AS*, 11.II.1927. See also 26.XII.1926, 8.VIII.1930, 10.VII.1931; *NO*, 13.IX.1924; *ES*, 1.XII.1926, 15.XI.1927.

43. Mieres, Requejo, Cuestivil, and Río Turbio to Mayor, 27.VI.1863, Ríos, AMM; Pérez González, "Cuenca Central," 857–58.

44. *AS*, 8.III.1900; F. Casariego, *Saneamiento de Sama y Langreo* (Madrid, 1918), 5–16, 112–18.

45. *ES*, 11.X.1923. For the effects on outlying villages, see *ES*, 6.III.1922, 17.VII.1927, and *AV*, 9.VIII.1933.

46. Pando Arguelles to Parent, 19.X.1885, AHE 17/2; Comas to Montaves, 13.I.1911, AHE, 57/6; Cervino, nd, AHE 57/7.

47. Jové y Canella, *Topografía . . . Laviana*, 129–30; AHE 53/4.

48. Muniz Prada, *Apuntes*, 43.

49. Jové y Canella, *Topografía . . . San Martín del Rey Aurelio*, 85, and *Topografía . . . Laviana*, 99.

50. Pérez González, "Cuenca Central," 720; Madera to Montaves, 29.V, 27.XI.1917; Martínez to Rubiera, 13.II.1918, AHE 3/12; 1899, AHE 57/4.

51. Pérez González, "Cuenca Central," 720.

52. *Revista Nacional de Economía*, 1920, 328.

53. Ministerio de Trabajo, *Estadística de Salarios*, CLVIII, CLIV–V; *ES*, 27.V.1922; *NO*, 12.III.1924.

54. Report, Moreda District Physician, 26.IX.1922, AHE, 53/4.

55. *RM*, 1883, 388.

56. Montaves to Parent, 16.IX.1887, AHE 56/1; 1899, AHE 57/4.

57. DGM, *Informe*, 27.

58. M. Gimeno y Azcárate, *La criminalidad en Asturias* (Oviedo, 1900), 30–33, 39–46.

59. Ibid., 69.

60. Vigil, *Los mineros*, 23. For a literary portrayal of the violence of the miners, see the story "La Prueba" by R. Pérez de Ayala in his *Obras Completas* (Madrid, 1964), 1:997.

61. Costa to Montaves, 19.VI.1909, AHE 55/2.

62. Vigil, *Los mineros*, 27; D. Benavides, *El Fracaso Social del Catolicismo Español* (Madrid, 1970), 550.

63. Castaño, *El estado*, 29.

64. *ES*, 15.V.1922.

65. *AS*, 24.XII.1926.

66. *AS*, 15.X.1926.

67. *AS*, 11.II.1927.

4

Morality, Discipline, and Social Control
The Social Practices of the Mining Companies

No sooner had the first large-scale capitalist mining enterprises been created in Asturias than their owners and managers as well as observers concerned with the rational exploitation of the coalfields began to complain about the inadequacy of the available work force. It was at once undisciplined and in short supply. Two remedies were frequently proposed: the mechanization of the mines to reduce the number of workers needed, a process that did not get under way until after World War I; and the provision of social services by the companies to attract new workers into the coalfields and turn them into productive miners.

Owners and managers began to act quickly on this second front. By 1862 the Real Compañía Asturiana de Minas had "a complete staff of loyal, intelligent, and submissive workers" as a product of its housing program.[1] A year earlier Alvarez Buylla reported that Fábrica de Mieres had created a savings bank for workers "to assure their well-being and preserve their subordination."[2] The connection between social provision and efficiency was drawn by Francisco Gascue. Likening the worker to a machine, he emphasized the importance of keeping him well maintained: "We must worry about the worker's diet, which is his fuel, his cleanliness, and his housing. . . . We must determine what is the effort he can make each day in his benefit and in ours. . . . As he must know the longevity of the machine he uses in order to replace it, so must we know his. . . . Philanthropy goes hand in hand with self interest. If a worker is well-educated he will be more productive than the totally neglected miner of today."[3]

However, the provision of social services was given an intellectual justification that camouflaged the underlying intent of control and exploitation. This was generally phrased in terms of the need to improve the morality of the miner, to shape him both as a worker and a citizen. As one commentator wrote in 1910, "Like all workers, and perhaps more than others because of his isolation, the miner must be educated so that he will become a useful member of society. He must be instructed so that his labor will yield the maximum, so that he begins to plan for his future."[4]

The corollary to the importance of properly molding the worker was the danger of failing to do so. The theorists of paternalism saw the worker as an infinitely malleable material, who when left to his own devices was easy prey for the unscrupulous agitators who would manipulate him for their own purposes: "If the worker is well led and well instructed and his virtue stimulated, it is possible to make him into a valuable element for the regeneration of society. He is excellent raw material. But if he is allowed to leave the limited sphere in which his meager intelligence can cope, he will inevitably fall into the clutches of those who will exploit him without compassion."[5]

Naturally, it was the middle class that determined the form this instruction was to take, and it included what Sydney Pollard has called "the attack on working-class morals."[6] The point is well illustrated in the essay on workers' housing, *Hogar y Patria*, published in 1906. The mere provision of housing was in itself insufficient. The dwellings had to be carefully designed to help the worker overcome his bad habits. Even worse than putting the worker in badly designed housing was isolating him in a proletarian ghetto where there were no healthy, middle-class models to emulate.

> If the worker is isolated from the rest of the population he will be isolated from the ideology of social peace, since the division of society into classes will be given physical form. A purely workers' district, lacking any close contact with educated people, would be a terrible place, a forge of hatred against those above. The worker who lives in the attic of a gentleman's house unconsciously acquires a certain amount of education which he would never get in an isolated district. . . . Will this worker, his wife and children, be capable of committing any unjust act against the ruling classes? No![7]

In practice, however, it was found that land prices dictated the location of workers' housing some distance from the center of population. In these circumstances the separation of the worker was inevitable, but steps could be taken to prevent the impression of having created ghettoes. The designers of the housing blocks built by the Fábrica de Mieres cooperative in 1921 were concerned that these dwellings not look like the usual *cuarteles*: "The four-story building with its facade full of windows and balconies will eliminate the image of the barracks and with it 'that sentiment of social inferiority that workers' houses usually project. Instead it will give the sensation of well-being, comfort, and hygiene which every honorable, hard-working household desires.' Therefore the facade was designed to offer the image of the strength, austerity, and modesty which characterize working-class life."[8]

83

We have seen that alcoholism and the crime that followed were perceived as a growing problem in the coalfields, and the aspect of working-class life that came under strongest attack was the miners' notorious fondness for the tavern. The problem was not so much the effect of alcohol on the miners but on the working of the mines. According to Gascue, alcohol was responsible for turning the miner from his normal "quiet, honest, tranquil, and good-natured" self into a brawling ruffian, "useless for work." In the end, the mine owners were the ones who paid for the miners' vice.[9] Nor was drinking a problem limited to the early stages of the development of mining. In 1911 the government mining engineers condemned drinking as a widespread vice, especially on holidays and paydays.[10] According to Jové y Canella it was on the increase after World War I. "Since the Great War more money has been spent in Langreo on alcohol than on bread," and in San Martín del Rey Aurelio "the tavern is a moneymaker without equal. It never fails."[11]

The problems arising from the miners' fondness for the taverns was a principal reason for the provision of housing by the mining companies. They reasoned that if the miner had a comfortable home to which to return, he would be less likely to be drawn into the tavern. Muniz Prada criticized the barrack-style housing offered by many companies, recommending instead individual homes with gardens "where the worker can pass time far from the bar, cultivate an intimate family life, and, as a result, develop a love of work, frugality, and good habits."[12]

Alcoholism, drunkenness, and inefficiency were not the only problems that the mine owners and their representatives saw arising out of the tavern. They also drew a direct connection between the tavern and "socialism." *The Boletín Oficial de Minería y Metalurgia* urged the companies to provide bath houses, schools, and recreational facilities for their workers. "In this way the worker will become clean, and taken away from the taverns and so-called workers' circles where they do nothing but plan strikes."[13]

Company social provision was intended to have two other major effects. The first, as we have mentioned, was to attract immigrants into the valleys. In the early days of the industry this was particularly important. Potential immigrants were frightened off by the poor conditions, the scarcity of housing, and the unusually high cost of living in the coalfields. In the 1880s Fábrica de Mieres built housing and started a cooperative, as well as improving conditions within the mines, to assure itself a stable work force.[14] Hulleras del Turón, another of the largest companies, recognized the importance of attracting workers immediately. The *Memoria* for its first year of operation noted that "workers' housing is one of the most pressing needs in the Turón valley," and undertook to add fifty new residences to the fourteen it had already built.[15] This was far from sufficient, and two years later the *Memoria* noted that the shortage of housing was having an effect on production.[16]

The housing problem reappeared, and with greater urgency, during World War I. A commission of inquiry into the ability of the industry to respond to wartime circumstances warned that "either we find 20,000 new mine workers or we find a way of doing without them." Social services had a key role to play in this recruitment, "drawing workers from other regions and easing their difficult apprenticeship. If they are encouraged by clean houses, schools, hospitals, saving banks, and, above all, a pension based on consecutive years of service," the problem would be more rapidly resolved.[17]

As it was, there proved to be little difficulty in finding the required workers, as the high wages of the war years drew countless poor farmers from Castile, Galicia, and elsewhere into the mines. The number of workers needed dropped substantially with the crisis that followed the end of the war, but some observers feared that the outflow would be so great as to create a new labor shortage. As early as June 1917 the *Boletín Oficial de Minería y Metalurgia* addressed itself to this problem. Recognizing that the boom would end when normal conditions were restored and that wages would have to be cut, it suggested that the blow could be softened and massive emigration avoided by "trying to improve the social conditions of the working population in order to endear the coalfields to them."[18]

The experience of Hulleras del Turón illustrates the potential effectiveness of this approach. From 1912 on it increased its production more than any other company in Asturias, and by 1917 it had become the second largest producer in the region. According to Rafael de Riego, this success was due to a combination of an ambitious program of mechanization begun during the war and the use of social provision to develop a numerous and obedient labor force. "The difficult problem of manpower could only be overcome by a social policy which made Turón more attractive than the other valleys: abundant, cheap, and sanitary housing, well-stocked stores where savings would be noticeable, schools to educate the children, and, complementing all this, a transformation of the methods of production."[19]

The second major function of social provision was to serve as a prophylactic against social unrest. In 1871 Pedro Duro, founder of Duro-Felguera, told the parliamentary commission looking into the condition of the working class that his policy of offering steady work and social services kept his workers happy; twelve years later Gascue seconded Duro's opinion on the virtues of paternalistic management, citing various examples from other countries.[20] José Suarez, the government mining engineer for the province, agreed: "Everything that contributes to organizing the worker's life . . . will be another motivation for his retaining good relations with his employer."[21] The mining engineers who reported on social conditions in 1911 were convinced that there were fewer labor problems in those companies that cared for their workers and that "strikes are more violent where workers are poorly housed or where they pay high rents." [22] However, despite the oft repeated importance of such measures, the services that were actually offered varied greatly from one company to another.

The most urgently needed service, and the one most commonly supplied, was housing. We have already seen the attention paid to this problem by Hulleras del Turón. In 1892 it had fourteen buildings under construction and had tendered contracts for fifty more. By 1899 it had four buildings in Cabajal, six in San José, and twelve under construction at Prado Longo to serve the San José and San Francisco mines. Before 1914 housing was virtually the only service the company provided, except for the barracks for the Guardia Civil, but even so these dwellings housed only ninety families at a time when the company employed almost 1,500 workers. [23]

The wartime expansion of the work force made further building essential. Between 1918 and 1922 four blocks containing 227 residences were built, but even with the reduction in the number of workers after 1920 housing remained "a real problem whose solution we will continue to study when circumstances permit." [24] Circumstances were not so kind, and the housing problem in Turón became so acute that residents formed a Liga de Inquilinos (Tenants' Association) to denounce violation of housing and hygiene regulations to the municipal authorities. [25]

In contrast to Hulleras del Turón, Fábrica de Mieres did not pay much attention to housing its workers until the war. In 1911 it had only twenty-four residences for a work force of 2,405, and the state mining engineers judged its overall performance as poor. "Considering that it is located in one of the largest towns in Asturias it is disgraceful that a company so important does not have more and better housing for its workers, and the fact that the majority are local farmers is no excuse. Many workers live in very poor conditions." [26] The company did respond to the attempts of the city's mayor to initiate cooperatives to build low-cost housing for workers. In April 1921 it started its own cooperative and developed a plan for sixty-eight residences. [27]

Duro-Felguera, whose growth had led to the creation of the populous proletarian town of La Felguera, faced problems similar to those of Fábrica de Mieres, and began to deal with them only at the end of the war. In 1918 it spent one million *pesetas* to acquire land "where the first block of houses, each with four units surrounded by a garden, so that all the houses will be independent, will be built." Called the Pueblo Obrero Pilar, this project was expected to house 2,200 people and contain churches, schools, bath houses, a theater, a co-op, and a workers' club. [28] A second project, the Barrio Obrero Marqués de Urquijo, was also being planned. [29]

The influx of workers from outside the province between 1914 and 1920 prompted the major companies to increase the pace of construction of workers' housing, although the problem was never resolved. At the same time the nature of this housing underwent a significant change. The single-family dwelling with garden gave way to terraced housing and large apartment blocks (*cuarteles*).

Ramón Pérez suggests that the initial choice of the single-family dwelling resulted from the concern of the companies not to "overly upset the new workers" by exposing them to an environment totally different from that which they had known before entering the mines.[30] This would seem unlikely: it was precisely at this time of movement from one environment to another that the new miner was most vulnerable and therefore a more malleable object for those who wanted to turn him into a disciplined industrial worker. We might suggest instead that in the years preceding the war, in which immigration was slight, the available company housing was directed at Asturians who wanted to establish their own homes but would consider only single-family dwellings with land attached.[31]

After housing, the most common service offered was the mutual aid society, *caja de socorros*.[32] These were established and run by the companies, and although there was often some worker participation, it was ineffective where not totally symbolic. As membership was almost always obligatory and the societies were financed by deductions, usually of 2 to 3 percent from the workers' wages, these institutions very quickly became the target of complaints by the miners and of attacks by the unions. During a number of strikes in 1902 miners included in their demands decreases in the amounts deducted, independence of the societies from the company, and public accounting for the use of the funds.[33] The mutual aid societies were responsible for providing a number of benefits for their members, of which medical care was the most important. In return for their contributions workers and their families received free medical attention and free or cheap medicines, sick pay, disability pensions, and funeral expenses. Retirement pensions were occasionally provided as well.

At Carbones de la Nueva the society was founded with a donation of 1,500 *pesetas* from the company and deductions of 2 percent from the workers' wages. It provided a school, sick pay of 50 percent of regular wages, and retained a doctor. The *caja* at Minas de Figaredo, La Unión Verdad, was not obligatory. Members paid monthly dues of 1.50 *pesetas* if they earned more than 2.25 *pesetas* per day, and half that amount if they earned less. In return they received one *peseta* per day sick pay and free medical care for up to six months.[34]

Education was a less frequent provision, and only a few companies—Duro-Felguera, Fábrica de Mieres, Carbones de la Nueva, and Unión Hullera—supported their own schools. Duro-Felguera spent most in this regard. In 1904 it paid seven Hermanos de la Doctrina Cristiana to teach 1,050 children, 450 between six and fourteen years old during the day and 600 between fourteen and sixteen in the evening, presumably after finishing work. According to the mining engineers, this was the "perfect model for an educational establishment."[35] The company's *Memoria* for 1920 showed it supporting the following schools: for children of both sexes in Santa Ana and Sotón, for boys and girls separately in Mosquitera and Peña Rubia, for adults in Santa Ana, Sotón, and Peña Rubia, one unspecified school in La Felguera, and an arts and crafts school. Between 1915 and 1919 the enrollment increased from 842 to 942.[36]

The Unión Hullera had a school at La Justa, "old, rundown, and very small," where forty children were taught. In addition it paid two or three *pesetas* per day so that its workers' children could attend the municipal schools at Villar, Las Cubas, and San Andrés free of charge.[37] Fábrica de Mieres founded a school in 1900, which was run by Dominican nuns who taught the miners' daughters. The boys' school had a summertime attendance of 130, which dropped sharply during the winter due to the large distances the students had to travel from their "isolated villages and homes." In addition, the company gave financial support to two municipal schools.[38]

The schools run by Duro-Felguera and Fábrica de Mieres were entrusted to nuns and priests. This exclusively religious education was very much consistent with the desire of the companies to have a moral work force. However, it could also backfire and lead to protests from those workers who wanted a secular education for their children. In February 1930, 200 workers at Duro-Felguera presented a petition to the management protesting the lack of education at Ciaño-Santa Ana: "We asked the company to provide two male and one female teacher. That is what they promised when they built the school at Santa Ana. The Dominicans are now using all three buildings as they wish and have even turned one into a chapel to help them win friends and money. . . . Many children have to leave school because they do not attend mass when the priests say so and this does not include those whose parents want other people entrusted with this important mission."[39] During a strike at this same company in 1932 workers demanded that the schools be taken out of the hands of priests and given over to lay teachers.[40]

Control of the schools was not the only presence the Catholic church had in the social provision of the mining companies. Minas de Saus maintained a chapel, and Solvay spent 500 *pesetas* per year for a chaplain to say mass.[41] The religious presence was especially strong at Fábrica de Mieres, particularly after the *huelgona* of 1906 in which the company had been able to destroy the existing union. The most important facet was the Agremaición Católica, which was founded to prevent the spread of socialism. The company built "a beautiful chapel decorated with elegant paintings, altar pieces, and sculptures of much merit" and was active in charitable work.[42]

Another important aspect of the social practice of the companies was the provision of stores. Initially the company opened, or allowed an employee to open, a shop that was run as a moneymaking enterprise. In the 1880s Gascue criticized these *abastos*, even when well run, as troublesome, and recommended that they be replaced by either *economatos*—nonprofit stores run directly by the company—or by cooperatives. And considering the "intellectual and moral condition" of the Asturian miners he gave preference to the former.[43]

Hulleras del Turón opened its *economato* in 1894 "so that the food is good and nutritious and to avoid the exploitation that always takes place in these circumstances."[44] Minas de Saus, owned by the Felgueroso brothers, had "a shop since the nearest town was 10 kilometers away. The workers take whatever they need, often in excess of the value of their wages. This exceptional practice is only possible in a company like this, with its paternalistic management and a stable work force drawn entirely from the local population."[45] This practice of allowing workers credit in excess of their wages immediately calls to mind debt-servitude practices used elsewhere to keep the labor force tied to the employer, but it is unlikely that this was the case here. If the work force was "stable and local" and therefore presumably mixed workers, there would have been no need to keep them bound to the company through debt. In addition, the Felguerosos were generally well liked by their workers, a product of their willingness to deal with them personally.[46]

Given the workers' inevitable suspicion that "a store set up by the company would only be interested in getting back the wages paid out," these *economatos* were less common than cooperatives. Some co-ops were independent of the companies and run entirely by workers, but it was more common for the company to organize and manage it with the participation of a workers' committee. Fábrica de Mieres opened its co-op in 1875. Members paid an entry fee of 25 *pesetas*, which entitled them to spend up to two-thirds of their wages in the shop. Wine and alcohol were not sold. Only a small percentage of the workers were members, but at Minas de Teverga 231 of 400 miners belonged, and at Unión Hullera there were 1,450 members.[47]

This of necessity haphazard survey of the social provisions of the mining companies leads us to two observations. First, despite the rhetoric devoted to the question of social provision and the theoretical importance attached to it, the mining companies approached the problem in a piecemeal manner. Each firm dealt with its own work force as it felt best, or necessary, but none achieved a comprehensive set of services. Second, the services we have mentioned date almost entirely from before World War I. In part this is a question of sources. The only thorough analysis of company social provisions is the much cited *Informe* of the engineers of the Dirección General de Minas. However, this in itself is only a reflection of the reality. The massive influx of non-Asturians into the mines between 1915 and 1920 removed one of the major reasons for providing social services, the attraction of workers into the coalfields. And the virtual monopoly of the national market enjoyed by the Asturian industry, which freed mine owners from the need to produce cheaply and inefficiently and thus allowed them to function in a way which under normal conditions would not have been possible, removed the other, the inculcation of labor discipline.

There was, however, one company that did attempt to provide a comprehensive set of social services for its workers and that approached the whole question in a much more serious manner than the others, Hullera Española. Given the ownership of the company, this is hardly surprising. The company had been acquired in 1881, when it was known as Minas de Aller, by the first Marqués de Comillas. In 1891 his son, the second Marqués, reorganized the firm under the name of Sociedad Hullera Española. The Marqués, whose base was in Barcelona, was one of Spain's leading landowners and industrialists, and he owned the important shipping company, the Transatlántica, among many other enterprises. He was also the most important lay proponent of social Catholicism in Spain, and his religious and moral principles were imparted to his businesses. One sympathetic biographer has called the ships of the Transatlántica "floating parishes." [48] (The Marqués has subsequently been proposed for canonization.)

As did the other mining companies, Hullera Española always claimed that its social practice was directed at improving the moral well-being of its workers, but behind these claims lay the two more important motives we have seen at work in the general Asturian context. The first was to attract and retain workers. To this end the company paid bonuses for long and continuous service, "an increase in salary differing with each case but never less than 25 *céntimos* per day periodically to workers after a certain length of continuous service, so that for any particular job the worker with the most seniority is the best paid." There were also more unusual means of keeping workers with the company: "In order to facilitate the recruitment of miners to make up a capable work force, the retirement fund gives young workers with five years' continuous service prior to their being called up, amounts which permit them to purchase exemption from military service." [49]

Much more important, however, was the second aim—to have a work force that was stable as well as docile and not attracted to "socialism." This aversion to the labor movement was stronger at Hullera Española than at any of the other large companies, and it was the only important firm not to join the Patronal Minera, precisely because this organization dealt with the SMA. The desire to prevent the spread of the labor movement among its workers was the driving force behind the company's social provision, a result of the general strike of May 1, 1890.

The company reacted harshly to the strike, firing anyone involved or even suspected of sympathy with it. [50] Even after such exemplary measures the company president, Santiago López, remained uneasy, and in January 1891 he expressed his concerns about the next May 1 strike to the head of operations, Felix Parent. In this letter he proposed the use of social provision as a solution. The workers must see that the company is attending to their needs, but this attention must not appear to be a response to the threat of a strike.

> The retirement fund has been in operation since January 1 and the workers have been informed of our new project: houses for outstanding workers, land, prizes for seniority, etc. But do not forget that in general workers do not appreciate such efforts unless they benefit directly from them, and therefore all our efforts on their behalf will have little or no effect on the upcoming strike. Therefore it will be useful to immediately build the three or four houses for this year. Construction will be simple. It will not take long and should not require many workers. The houses will not be awarded before May as this would make it seem as though we were reacting to the threat of the strike and in fear of it; but the fact that the workers see that they are being built and know that they will be given to those who have behaved themselves best, will give us a better result.[51]

Such bluntness was not meant for public consumption, and it was usually disguised behind the rhetoric of morality. As we have seen, the tavern was a prime target of criticism, especially as it was considered the breeding ground of the dreaded socialist virus: "There are taverns which stand out as havens for the propagandists of strikes and even murder, such as the Confitería in Moreda. . . . They make propaganda in these places because they understand that they have no place in our good order and therefore they patronize all vices and bad habits."[52] Religion was presented as the most effective treatment: "The best way to moralize the workers and protect them from the socialist plague is, without doubt, the opening of a workers' club in the Catholic Center where the bond between workers and employers will be strengthened. That alone will shut the door on propaganda, on the exploitation of the ignorance and docility of the workers of Aller."[53]

This manicheistic perspective—taverns=Socialism and religion= morality—was well illustrated in the speech given by Manuel Montaves, the chief engineer, to open the Círculo Obrero in Bustiello: "Where can the worker best dedicate Sunday to God? In the Catholic Workers' Circle, where he receives instruction for his body and his soul, or in those dens of vice called taverns, where he learns the most abominable ideas about everything worthy of respect and where God is blasphemed? In the tavern he is taught the most absurd and crazy notions about the social order, he wastes his money and his health, for in many back rooms other vices such as gambling reign."[54]

Such rhetoric was little different from that used by other companies and by observers of the industry. What distinguished Hullera Española was its willingness to act according to the logic of its rhetoric. Not only did it provide housing, schools, religious and recreational facilities, and medical care, but also it attempted to use them to make its property a separate world, to seal it off as much as was possible from its surroundings, and to exercise complete control over the lives of its workers and their families. The company's police force, its managers in Asturias, and even the president in Barcelona concerned themselves with the most insignificant details of the workers' lives, all in the name of morality.[55]

The town of Bustiello was a model of what the company hoped to achieve. It was completely distinct from the typical village of the valleys, built from the beginning "according to a precise plan. Everthing is set out so that the visitor's first impression is of geometric precision." The square, usually the heart of social life, "is away from the center, away from the residential area, and therefore not part of the daily round of activity." The town was administered directly by the company and did not depend on the town hall of Mieres, as did the surrounding towns.[56]

Bustiello was conceived as a "miners' village composed of model miners," and the initial residents were very carefully chosen. They either rented their homes or owned them as a result of having won the lottery run by the company. This status was passed on to their children. The residences were all identical: duplexes comprising two floors and an attic surrounded by 200 square meters of garden. Any modification of the appearance of the house had to be approved by the company, so that the "aesthetic aspects" would not be disturbed.[57]

The depth of control exercised by the company over the residents of the town, and initially over all its workers, is astounding. Two documents from the archive, "Matters dealt with in Ujo, October 14–19, 1892," and "Various matters to be resolved by the Honorable Marqués de Comillas during his stay, September 29 to October 10, 1893," illustrate the degree to which Hullera Española intervened in the lives of its employees. The second document reveals how the Marqués dispensed favors more in the style of a feudal lord than of a nineteenth-century capitalist. Of the 107 matters to be discussed, 51 were requests from individuals—workers, ex-workers, or widows—for favors such as loans, jobs for children, or pensions. The following examples are illustrative.

The widow of one of the mayor of Moreda's tenant farmers requested that an extra room be added to her house. This was refused.

> She is vice ridden by nature. Even when her husband was alive her behavior was the cause of much gossip, and since he died she has led a very licentious life. Her last lover was one of our workers, whom we had to fire because of the scandal they caused. She has a 14-year-old son who works in the Legalidad mine, and who so far has been a good boy, hard working and obedient. He became aware of his mother's behavior while very young and has suffered because of it. . . . She is

so insistent in her request because she wants greater privacy in which to carry on. She does not deserve help, and the best thing would be to prohibit any of our workers from visiting her house.[58]

A foreman who asked for a loan of 4,000 *pesetas* to pay the dowry for his daughter who wanted to enter the convent of the Dominicans in Valladolid was told that "he should try and raise the money and then report back, when a decision will be made." [59] The widow of a worker killed in one of the company's mines had better luck. As she was "of good conduct and each month sends part of her wage to her parents and therefore has little left for herself . . . all the reports on her are good," she was given a job as a crossing guard, which paid more than the sorting station where she had been working.[60]

Housing was one of the first aspects of social provision considered by the company. In 1891 it had three blocks containing sixty dwellings. These were preferred to single-family dwellings, as they lent themselves better to the disciplining of the residents. "We prefer blocks to individual houses because we want to discipline personnel whose habits are somewhat primitive, and to inculcate the habits of cleanliness and respect for property, which they do not have in the least." Each block of twenty residents was well supervised "by an employee of higher rank than the others—foreman, etc.—who reports abuses and oversees a general cleaning every week." [61]

Ironically, it appears that this type of housing had exactly the opposite effect. The doctor for the Moreda district sharply criticized the blocks and recommended they be replaced by single-family dwellings. However, such houses were seen as rewards for levels of morality already attained, not as a means of developing it. The houses in Bustiello went precisely to "model workers," and the conditions for eligibility for the raffle of houses—ten years' continuous service without any unfavorable reports from superiors and no criminal convictions or even charges—demanded total acceptance of the code of conduct laid down by the company. Loans were available to workers deemed deserving to allow them to build their own homes, and land was available to those who wanted to cultivate a vegetable garden in their spare time.[62]

In whatever form, blocks or individual houses, the housing provided by Hullera Española was far from sufficient to meet the needs of its work force. In 1924 *El Noroeste* estimated that only 10 percent of its workers lived in company housing, a figure given credence by the company's own statistics. In 1935 it owned 88 buildings containing 471 dwellings. In 1933 it employed 3,627 workers. Most of the rest lived in extremely poor conditions described by the Gijón daily as "unhealthy attics and cellars." [63]

Another of the early services offered was the *caja de socorros*, which was started in 1885 as a "professional mutual aid society." It had three classes of members: white-collar workers paying 1.5 percent of their monthly salary, blue-collar workers paying 3 percent, and retirees paying 1 percent of their pensions. Blue-collar workers were entitled to all the services offered by the society: medical care for themselves and their families, free schooling for their children, pensions for widows, orphans, and disability, 1,000 *pesetas* for burial, and 30 *pesetas* per month maintenance for twins. White-collar workers and retirees received only free medical care.[64]

This was the most important of the *caja*'s services. The company's property was divided into four zones—increased to five in 1921 and six in 1934—each with a doctor and an assistant. The company also retained specialists and paid consultation fees to an X-ray service, as well as maintaining a hospital that in 1911 was described as the best in the province.[65] Medical care was seen as a major weapon in the war against socialism in the region. In 1918 Santiago Romero, one of the company's physicians, emphasized the need to extend the service to keep up with the wartime expansion of the work force: "as well as serving the many members who live in the town it will help attract people away from the troublesome Socialist mutual aid society."[66]

Of course religion had a prominent place in the social practice of the Hullera. The firm spent 848,000 *pesetas* on building and restoring the churches of Bustiello, Ujo, Moreda, Santa Cruz de Mieres, Boo, and Villallana and paid the salaries of four chaplains. The management issued a document, the "Instrucción sobre el servicio religioso," which outlined the duties of these special employees. The head of the service was the *capellán mayor* who lived in Bustiello, where he presided over the community of the Brothers of the Christian Doctrine, the hospital, the schools, and all aspects of religious life, "overseeing the scheduling of services, especially Sunday and holiday mass, arranging with the parish priests not to schedule services all at the same time, to facilitate the attendance of workers and their families so that no one need miss them." There were two chaplains in Caborana, one each for the boys' and girls' schools, and one in Ujo, for the school there.[67]

The chaplains, who were appointed by the company, had a wide variety of duties: to say daily mass and preach a sermon on Sundays, to offer services for the young on Sunday afternoons and holidays, to preach one sermon each month in the school, to provide a half hour of religious instruction daily, to hear confession on Sunday afternoons and in the evening before holidays, to organize a monthly confession for schoolchildren, to arrange annual spiritual exercises for the older children, and to provide spiritual direction for the religious brotherhoods, *cofradías*.[68]

The company also arranged for special religious functions, in particular the celebration of the festival of Santa Bárbara, the patron saint of miners. In the early years of the Hullera this was a major event: in 1895 eighteen priests presided at mass, and between 450 and 500 employees took communion. This was followed by a procession: "Everyone had his designated place. . . . Fifty contractors served as marshals, and miners holding candles blocked the way of anyone who tried to cross the route." The day ended with a *romería*, the traditional Asturian outdoor celebration. "There was singing and dancing, good spirits and good order. Over 7,000 people came, many from Mieres, Turón, and Lena. Many of the workers from Turón behaved as they do at other celebrations, but they were immediately taken care of and no one, neither inside nor out, raised their voice." [69] The company continued to spend sizeable amounts on these celebrations—between 1,000 and 1,200 *pesetas* per year from 1912 to 1915—but this could not prevent the decline in popularity of the Santa Bárbara of Aller. [70]

In the week before Easter the company arranged for a mission, usually performed by the Jesuits, "to make the workers fulfill their Easter duties." Santiago López ordered the manager to make arrangements with the supervisory staff "so that all our workers are given every opportunity to attend all the acts, especially the general communion at the end." [71]

The company's interest in religion was, however, conditional upon its ability to maintain control over it and to use religious personnel for its own ends. The issue of control arose almost immediately. In September 1887 the coadjutor of Ujo published an article in *El Siglo Futuro* and *La Cruz de la Victoria*, which charged that Hullera Española failed to respect Sundays and holidays, prohibited its workers from hearing mass, and was responsible for the undermining of good habits. The company denied all charges. Of more interest are the attacks on the clergy made by the company's managers, which make it clear that the priests were tolerated only so long as they did what they were told:

> Sr. Parent, I hate to say it but with very few exceptions the priests here are more likely than we to do away with *good habits and faith*. . . . God save me from having to fight them again. . . . I suspect that they want to dominate, and if this were to happen it would be very bad. Every day they would ask for more. . . . All this causes a great deal of harm, and the priests are the main conspirators against good order and the interests of the Marqués. What I would give in order to be able to operate freely! I assure you that it will be best not giving in to them at all. . . . I can also assure you that they have given me no end of trouble, and probably an ulcer as well. [72]

Not only did the company expect the clergy to be docile, but also it used them to inform on the workers. Among the chaplains' duties listed in the "Instrucción sobre el servicio religioso" was the following: "The chaplains will learn the religious and moral behavior of the workers and inform the Chaplain of the mines and the parish priests." [73] The parish priests then informed the management. "We have the practice of asking some of the parish priests for information about our workers. . . . When we inquire they respond by mail." [74]

The first efforts in education were directed at women, the wives and daughters of the miners. In 1891 a seamstress was brought in from Barcelona to teach the women of the working class to make clothes, "in order to develop a taste for work among the wives and daughters of our workers, and to permit them to contribute to the family income." The company even considered opening a clothing department in the *economato* to sell their work.[75]

The main thrust of the educational provision was directed at the children. The Hullera had schools in Caborana (one for boys and one for girls), Ujo, and Bustiello as well as a Sunday school in Caborana. In 1934 these had an enrollment of 2,053 and a teaching staff of fifty-eight. The weight of religion in this education was readily apparent. Students were required to attend mass on Sundays and holidays at the hour designated by the chaplains. Of the fifty-eight teachers, thirty-two were nuns and fifteen were Brothers of the Christian Doctrine. There were eleven lay teachers. The religious orders received some two-thirds of the entire budget of 156,340 *pesetas*, while the lay teachers received only about 8 percent.[76]

Within the mining communities the schools could play a role that went well beyond education. The following account describes the place of the Hermanos de la Doctrina Cristiana and their school in the social life of Bustiello:

> In order not to lose contact the graduates had the Marian Academy, also run by the Brothers, in which there were all kinds of games: domino, chess, football and basketball, courses of study, and talks. It had its own magazine, *El Cris*. . . . It had an arts group which put on plays (but only males took part; when there was a woman's role it was played by a man).
>
> The school had a "Children's Battalion" with uniforms, guns, military hierarchy, training days, and expeditions to surrounding villages. It had 100 members. . . . There was no bar in the village. All recreation was controlled by the Brothers. There was a choir and a library. . . . Around 1920 they formed a football team coached by the Brothers. It played on a field donated by the company, and even reached the regional first division. The company supplied the equipment.[77]

There were also recreational facilities outside the orbit of the schools but not of the church. The Hullera spent 41,000 *pesetas* to build the Catholic Circle in Bustiello, which had a priest as one of the directors, and 16,000 on the building for the Sindicato Católico in Valdefarrucos, as well as contributing to the Recreational Club in Caborana. In addition, it spent large sums on sports, music, cinema, and theater and provided free train service to the Catholic Circle on Sundays.[78]

Hullera Española produced a weekly illustrated magazine, the *Semana Popular Ilustrada*. This was published in Barcelona between July 1890 and May 1892 and sold for 10 *céntimos*. The contents were varied: travel, science, poetry, literature, and the lives of famous people. The purpose of the magazine was explained in its first issue:

We propose that the popular classes enjoy, at least once a week, the advantage of having an entertaining magazine. . . . We are moved by the sincere wish to free the public from abject publications which corrupt without providing recreation and are only interested in scandal. We want the worker with even the most meager resources to have, like the comfortable classes, a magazine which brightens his home during the week and contributes indirectly to the education of his family.

The poor man is assured the freedom to become rich through labor, virtue, and thrift; the rich man to become poor through vice and sloth.[79]

The magazine itself offered no indication of who was responsible for this "publication specially dedicated to the working class," as its subtitle proclaimed. There was certainly nothing to suggest that it was the Hullera Española or the Marqués de Comillas. However, in a letter to David Sampil, in which he commented on this journalist's offer to the Fábrica de Mieres to start a newspaper "to increase the morality of the workers," Felix Parent explained the principle behind the Hullera's putting out its own magazine: "As a business proposition it would be a disaster, but as its purpose is to distract the worker from vice through reading, the business aspect disappears. . . . The price should be as low as possible. This is the system we have used in our mines with *La Semana Popular Ilustrada*."[80]

Strict control was maintained over all publications allowed on company property. The management drew a sharp division between the "good press"— *El Carbayón*, *El Debate*, and *ABC* (all Catholic)—and the "bad press," which included all Socialist and anarchosyndicalist publications. One of the topics discussed during the visit of the Marqués to Ujo in 1893 was Tomas Zapico, "distributor from Mieres who continues to bring papers which it is not convenient for our employees to read (*Liberal, Imparcial, Globo*)."[81] One of the primary tasks of the company police force was the surveillance of the press distributed among the miners. "The persecution of the bad press on the company's land is not only one of the things I most urge on my staff . . . but I also dedicate as much of my own time as possible to it."[82]

All recreational activities were kept under equally strict surveillance, even by the president of Barcelona. When a carpenter employed by the Hullera opened a cinema in Caborana, Santiago López wrote demanding that "from now on all films to be shown be subject to prior censorship."[83] Nor was the management averse to using threats. "I have warned him that he will be fired if he shows morally questionable films or allows immoral behavior there." Censorship of films fell to Santiago Romero, one of the company's doctors, and a guard was stationed in the cinema at all times "to preserve morality and order during the performances. A couple of Civil Guards generally attend as well."[84]

Similarly, the content of music hall performances was scrutinized. When the parish priest of Moreda complained about the show being put on in a local

97

café, the head of the company police force attended, in order to check that "there was nothing immoral about it." As a result he ordered that the owner of the cafe have the social content of the skits removed: "In the 'Turn of the Century Operetta' an individual played a number of roles including the 'Anarchist' and the 'Village Priest.' I had to tell the owner that these two roles could not be repeated, and he obeyed, promising that they would not." [85]

Even apparently harmless activities such as childrens' games and dances were supervised by the head office. In 1908 López ordered Montaves to take measures against boys who swam nude in the rivers, "as this offended public decency." [86] Mixed dances were considered particularly dangerous, and López repeatedly expressed his concern about possible abuses and demanded that they be stopped:

> Our company is not against those forms of entertainment which offer honest and legitimate diversion, but it cannot remain indifferent before the existence of others which constitute a danger to the good habits and conduct of its employees. Thus you will inform our workers living in and around Ujo that this office views their attendance or that of their families at the dance in question with great displeasure, and trusts that in the future they will refrain from attending. By so doing they will avoid our having to take measures which we will deeply regret but which we will indeed take. [87]

Taverns were considered great danger spots. In 1904 the head of the police force organized a special patrol to note and denounce those taverns that violated the Sunday closure law. [88] Nor was alcohol to be tolerated under other circumstances. When the widow of a miner requested permission to open a stall to sell beer and lemonade behind one of the blocks of company housing, she was told that "it is not permitted to have any kind of stall on company land which sells drinks that might lead to rowdiness." [89] There were strict sanctions against drunkenness, a 5-*peseta* fine for the first offense, loss of five days' pay for the second, and dismissal for the third. Blasphemy, "whether drunk or not," was punished by immediate dismissal. [90]

However, despite all the time and money it spent on social services, Hullera Española was only marginally more successful than other companies in achieving the desired result, a moral and disciplined labor force. In October 1933, at a heavily attended meeting, workers agreed to withdraw their children from the company's schools to protest the continuing religious content of the teaching. [91] The management expressed its concern over occasional indications that its efforts were not proving effective. When some miners went on a riotous binge in Moreda, Santiago López complained that these "excesses reveal a state of savagery inappropriate for any moderately civilized place" and that they represented the breakdown of order and discipline. "Even more saddening, if possible, is the evidence of the breakdown in the discipline of a good part of our personnel . . . and that the previously peaceful towns of Moreda and Carabanzo have become centers of riot and scandal where the regulations and orders we have so often repeated are shamelessly ignored." [92]

These were, however, only momentary indications of the sentiments of a few workers, or rather, of the sentiments attributed to them by the management of the Hullera. But how did the mass of its workers feel about the company? On May 9, 1925, a committee was formed to plan the erection of a statue to the Marqués de Comillas, and it proposed that the statue be partially financed by the donation of one day's wage by all of the employees. It requested that each mine canvas its workers and report back. The committee cannot have been pleased with the result. Barely half the workers whose reply is recorded, 1,204 of 2,283, were prepared to make the suggested donation and only another 50 were willing to offer a lesser amount. The number of outright rejections—1,038 or 45 percent—was very high, considering that the company's readiness to discipline those who contradicted it was well known and that the survey was taken at a time of acute economic crisis and high unemployment, when few workers would have been prepared to risk their jobs. This danger was not imaginary: on the lists sent in by managers there appears beside the names of those who refused to make a donation, in red ink, their marital status and number of children.[93] We do not know if the company actually imposed any sanction, but this notation is an unmistakeable sign that it considered doing so. In any case, if we take this as a kind of referendum—in which all the circumstances favored the company—on the effectiveness of the social practice of the Hullera Española, it is abundantly clear that it had failed in its attempt to create a moral and disciplined work force loyal to the company.

The ineffectiveness of the social provision of the mining companies is not surprising. Its fundamental weakness was the false premise on which it was based: that the workers were an infinitely malleable material without any independent ability of mind and easily seduced by the bosses' generosity. Even so, with the exception of Hullera Española, the companies did not approach the problem in a comprehensive manner, nor act according to the logic of their own rhetoric. When World War I freed them from the conditions of labor shortage that had originally led them to provide social services, they ceased to do so. As one concerned observer wrote in the 1920s: "Since 1914 the mine owners have intensified extraction to the maximum without bothering themselves with anything other than the greatest production for the greatest profit. The only thing they have given the mining industry is more machines and installations, which are more gains for themselves. They have totally ignored social questions and shown that they take no interest at all in their workers. Apparently it does not suit them to recognize the problems of housing, sanitation, culture, and education." [94] This critiqiue of the situation in San Martín del Rey Aurelio, which is nothing more than a statement of the guiding principle of industrial capitalism, can be extended to the entire Asturian coalfield and serves as an epitaph for so many grave concerns and good intentions.

NOTES

1. *Boletín Oficial de Fomento*, 1862, 71.

2. Alvarez Buylla, *Observaciones*, 25.

3. *RM*, 1883, 372. See also *Revista Nacional de Economía*, Jan. 1919, 162.

4. A. Vasconi, *Sobre el régimen de trabajo en las minas españolas* (Madrid, 1910), 29–30.

5. Fuerte Arias, *Asturias industrial*, 139.

6. Pollard, *Genesis*, ch. 4.

7. A. de Llano, *Hogar y Patria: Estudio de casas para obreros* (Oviedo, 1906), 12. See also N. Muniz Prada, *Nociones del higiene* (Oviedo, 1886), 80.

8. Pérez González, "Cuenca Central," 779.

9. *RM*, 1883, 388.

10. DGM, *Informe*, 22.

11. Jové y Canella, *Topografía . . . San Martín del Rey Aurelio*, 59.

12. Muniz Prada, *Nociones*, 79.

13. *Boletín Oficial de Minería y Metalurgia*, Mar. 1918, 33.

14. *RM*, 1885, 320.

15. Hulleras del Turón, *Memoria* (Bilbao, 1892), 16.

16. Hulleras del Turón, *Memoria* (Bilbao, 1895), 11.

17. Comisión de Estudio sobre la Riqueza Hullera Nacional, *Información*, 58.

18. *Boletín Oficial de Minería y Metalurgia*, June 1917, 47; Mar. 1918, 33.

19. *NO*, 6.VII.1934.

20. P. Duro, *Contestación* (Madrid, 1871), 21; *RM*, 1883, 402.

21. *EMME*, 1892, 244.

22. DGM, *Informe*, 23, 47.

23. Hulleras del Turón, *Memoria* (Bilbao, 1893), 15–16; 1899, 5–6; DGM, *Informe*, 41.

24. Hulleras del Turón, *Memoria* (Bilbao, 1919), 9.

25. Liga de Inquilinos de Turón to mayor, 21.III.1932, Higiene y Viviendas, AMM. For another description of conditions in Turón, see Suarez, *Mineros de España*, 66.

26. DGM, *Informe*, 41.

27. Junta Local de Fomenta y Mejora de Habitaciones Baratas, AMM; Pérez González, "Cuenca Central," 770.

28. *Boletín Oficial de Minería y Metalurgia*, Mar. 1918, 29.

29. *RM*, 1918, 407.

30. Pérez González, "Cuenca Central," 761.

31. DGM, *Informe*, 36–37.

32. In 1932 there were fourteen mutual aid societies in the province, with 21,879 members. *EMME*, 1932, II, 325.

33. DGM, *Informe*, 27; Vigil, *Los mineros*, 12; *AS*, 8.XII.1900; *ES*, 16.XII.1898, 31.VIII.1900, 11.VII.1902; Huelga de Obreros del Coto del Musel, 1902, AMPL.

34. DGM, *Informe*, 27–29.

35. Ibid., 31–34, 49–50; J. Pla, *El carbón en España* (Madrid, 1904), 58–59.

36. Duro-Felguera, *Memoria* (Madrid, 1921), n.p.

37. DGM, *Informe*, 49.

38. Ibid., 52–53. See also Fuerte Arias, *Asturias*, 146–47.

39. *AS*, 7.II.1930.

40. *ES*, 29.IV.1932.

41. DGM, *Informe*, 53–54.

42. Benavides, *Fracaso*, 43; Fuerte Arias, *Asturias*, 147–48.

43. *RM*, 1883, 401–2.

44. Hulleras del Turón, *Memoria* (Bilbao, 1895), 11. In October 1898 some of the company's workers tried to set up their own co-op "to free themselves from exploitation, not only in the local stores but even in the company's own cooperative." *ES*, 7.X.1898.

45. DGM, *Informe*, 47.

46. *AS*, 10.XI.1900. "Mr. Victor Felgueroso does not allow injustices and is not above dealing with the workers. . . . He discusses their demands with them and until now has been able to avoid strikes."

47. *RM*, 1883, 401; DGM, *Informe*, 43–49. For a critique of the *economatos*, see *AS*, 18.IV.1930. Nor were the cooperatives free from abuse, most especially the ability of the company to restrict sales or even close the stores entirely during strikes. See *NO*, 3.X.1919, 4.IV.1920, 25.X.1925.

48. S. Nevares, S.J., *El patrono ejemplar* (Madrid, 1936), 39.

49. "Institutions en faveur de personnel ouvrier," Oct. 22, 1891, AHE 4/2. Wage increases could serve the same purpose if limited to workers with five or more years continuous service. "This was intended to make the workers more stable. Before, they left the mine easily, but with the incentive of extra money plus schools, etc., many of them settled permanently, and it was possible to have a regular work force, educate the families and make them moral." Nevares, *Patrono*, 138.

50. "Asuntos tratados en Barcelona," June 1890, AHE 4.

51. López to Parent, 29.I.1891, AHE 2/5.

52. Montaves to Parent, 28.III.1891, AHE 2/5.

53. Penanes to Parent, 5.IX.1897, AHE 56/4.

54. Montaves, 5.V.1895, AHE 56/4.

55. The Socialists certainly saw it this way: morality was a pretext "to persecute workers for whom they could find no other reasons to persecute." *AS*, 30.IX.1927.

56. J. L. García, *Antropología del Territorio* (Madrid, 1976), 197, 205–9.

57. "Institutions en faveur," AHE 4/2; García, *Antropología*, 208–12.

58. "Asuntos varios tratados durante el viaje del Sr. Marqués de Comillas a Ujo en 1893," AHE 2, folio 6–7.

59. Ibid., folio 5.

60. Ibid., folio 1.

61. "Institutions en faveur," AHE 4/2.

62. 26.IX.1922, AHE 53/4; "Institutions en faveur," AHE 4/2; Sorteo de casas, 7.VI.1902; Correspondencia Constantino Bayle, S.J., AHE 4/2; DGM, *Informe*, 38–39.

63. *NO*, 23.I.1924; Bulloso to Satrústegui, 16.V.1935, AHE 4/2.

64. DGM, *Informe*, 28–29, 36.

65. Rubiera to López, 30.IX.1921, AHE 57/3; Datos estadísticos de la Caja de Socorros, June 1935, AHE 4/2; DGM, *Informe*, 30–31.

66. Romero to Rubiera, 29.XII.1918, AHE 57/3.

67. "Instrucción sobre el servicio religioso," AHE 56/12.

68. Ibid.

69. Montaves to Parent, 5.XII.1895, AHE 56/4.

70. Miranda to Rubiera, 29.XI.1917, AHE 56/4.

71. López to Montaves, 5.III.1910, AHE 12/3; Cuadrado, S.J., to Montaves, 26.II.1909, AHE 56/9.

72. Montaves to Parent, 16, 18, 19.XI.1887, AHE 56/1.

73. "Instrucción sobre el servicio religioso," AHE 56/12.

74. López to Rubiera, 22.XI.1916, AHE 12/4.

75. AHE 4/2. For a description of the homemakers' school, see Nevares, *Patrono*, 62.

76. AHE 32/1, 32/2, 32/7; Notas, 4/2.

77. Cited in García, *Antropología*, 204–5.

78. According to Nevares, the sum was 46,500 *pesetas* per year. *Patrono*, 64. *ES*, 11.XI.1898.

79. *Semana Popular Ilustrada*, 31.VII.1890.

80. Parent to Sampil, 15.V.1891, AHE 2/5.

81. "Asuntos varios . . . 1893," AHE 2. In 1902 López objected to a new Catholic publication, *El Zurriago Social*, "not because of its form but for the violence of its language. The good press should not use insults as its weapons because in this way it imitates the bad press, and instead of convincing the enemy it angers him and alienates him even more. . . . Since reason and truth are, of course, on the side of the Catholic press, it should respond clearly and calmly to the errors of our enemies." López to Montaves, 9.VI.1902, AHE 12/2. On Catholic attempts to promote the "good press," see I. Sánchez, "La Iglesia española y el desarrollo de la Buena Prensa," in *Les Élites Espagnoles à l'Epoque Contemporaine* (Pau, 1984).

82. Bonnin to Rubiera, 19.IX.1915. In November 1910 the parish priest of Moreda informed the police of the arrival of a package of photographs of Francisco Ferror, the radical educator executed following the Tragic Week in Barcelona in July 1909, wrapped in a copy of *La Escuela Moderna*. Costa to Montaves, 9.XI.1910, AHE 55/2; Costa to Montaves, 2.XI.1910, AHE 55/2; Bonnin to Montaves, 19.V.1912, AHE 55/3; López to Rubiera, 29.VIII.1927, AHE 12/7.

83. López to Rubiera, 22.II.1915, AHE 12/3.

84. Jiménez to Rubiera, 1.VIII.1922, AHE 12/5.

85. Costa to Montaves, 19.VI.1909, AHE 55/2.

86. López to Montaves, 9.VIII.1908, AHE 12/3.

87. Bonnin to Rubiera, 12.II.1915, AHE 55/3; López to Montaves, 28.VII.1910, AHE 53/3; López to Montaves, 14.VI.1910, AHE 12/3.

88. Costa to Montaves, 22.II.1904, AHE 58/3; Costa to Montaves, 12, 21, 29.X, 18.XI, 9.XII.1904.

89. López to Montaves, 8.I.1908, AHE 58/4.

90. Bonnin to Montaves, 14.XII.1912, AHE 55/3. The company even organized a series of anti-blasphemy rallies in Aller. López to Montaves, 31.VIII.1912.

91. *AV*, 9.X.1933.

92. López to Montaves, 23.III.1909, AHE 54/3; 14.V.1912, AHE 12/3.

93. Estatua, Marqués de Comillas, AHE 4/12.

94. Jové y Canella, *Topografía . . . San Martín del Rey Aurelio*, 79–80.

5

From the First Strike to the Seven-Hour Day, 1873–1919

In the years following the introduction of large-scale capitalist mining in Asturias, mine owners and managers had to contend with one fundamental problem, a chronic shortage of labor. Before World War I they were unable to resolve it either by seducing large numbers of new workers into the coalfields with the provision of social services or by mechanizing the mines to reduce the number of workers required. The workers they did have were overwhelmingly from the coalfields or the immediate surroundings and were neither sufficiently numerous nor appropriately disciplined for the requirements of large corporations such as Fábrica de Mieres and Duro-Felguera.

This lack of the desired industrial discipline was seen by owners and managers as an indication of the failure of the workers to adapt to what was a new and—in their opinion—undoubtedly better world. Their unthinking confidence in the value of progress was well expressed by Rafael de Riego, director of Hulleras del Turón, when he described the effect of his company's growth on the way of life in the Turón valley: "There were only a few dozen houses dispersed throughout the valley, connected by a few treacherous roads, and life was dictated by a meager agriculture. With the arrival of Hulleras del Turón a new life, which has blossomed as the company has grown, has flourished, and the workers have adapted to the mines we have cut into the rich flesh of the mountains." [1]

But the inhabitants of the coalfields did not inevitably share this enthusiasm for the new life, which cut into their old way of life as much as into the "rich flesh of the mountains." One of the first casualties was what Alvarez Buylla had called "their old independence and natural liberty." Thus, their lack of discipline did not signify a failure on their part, but rather was a rejection of the new order, a means of self-assertion. Even after mining had become well established and a major part of Asturian life, the idea that something better had existed shortly before lingered on, even among the most advanced sectors of the working class.

> The healthy and robust farmers lived in their own houses in the valleys or on the hillsides. They made their own clothes, and on their feet they wore the comfortable *madreñas* [wooden shoes] which they made during the enforced leisure of winter. They consumed the produce of their own fertile fields watered by the plentiful and as yet unpolluted rivers, and the milk, cheese, butter, and meat which came from their animals. In the heat of the summer they restored their energies in natural springs fed by the crystal clear waters of the Lena, Aller, Caudal, Turón, and other rivers.
>
> Then came Fábrica de Mieres and its collaborators, in the task of finding among these peaceful and honest farmers a cheap, abundant, and subservient labor force.[2]

It was here, in the collision between two antagonistic worlds, that the roots of labor protest in Asturias are to be found. In holding out against the pretensions of the mine owners, the workers learned where their interests came into conflict with those of the incipient industrial order. This shared experience provided the raw material from which labor organizers could fashion the trade unions and political parties that would eventually form the Asturian labor movement. However, this was in itself no guarantee that a strong and effective labor movement would develop. That depended on circumstances and the ability of the organizers. In fact, it was only in 1910, with the creation of the Sindicato de Obreros Mineros Asturianos (SMA), that the mine workers of Asturias had such a union organization. The delay was not due to the docility of a labor force composed predominantly of mixed workers, as some have claimed.[3] Discontent, strikes, and even occasional violence long antedated the labor movement, and there were no significant changes in the composition of the work force, the organization of work in the mines, or in social relations that could have made 1910 a watershed. There would be such changes, but only after 1914 when the union was already well established.

The first miners' strike in Asturias took place in Langreo in 1873, but little is known about it. This was followed by others, in February 1879 and February 1884 in Mieres, and in April 1881 and April 1887 in Langreo. All but the last of these were defensive, to protest against wage reductions, and were spontaneous. They took place without any permanent organization, although committees did emerge to deal with the immediate situation. The strike of April 1887, which affected all of Langreo and parts of Siero, was the first one in which miners demanded increases in pay. As the local correspondent for *El Liberal* described it, the strike was both massive and entirely peaceful.

It seems that the strike began in the mines nearest to Carbayín. Five hundred men took the initiative, and they were joined by the rest of the workers from the coalfields whose help they had requested. All of this took place peacefully.

They all went to Sama and in the afternoon returned by way of the houses of La Felguera, asking the women who were on the balconies for bread. Those of us on the sidewalk decided to distribute 20 four-pound loaves of bread. . . . Such was the hunger of these poor people that they did not let us divide the bread but went away thanking the people of La Felguera and envious that they all had bread to eat while the [miners] got only a little corn and a few sardines.[4]

Strikes were part of a labor protest that included absenteeism, the refusal to work overtime, and a general resistance to the imposition of labor discipline. Most of this early protest was directed against the immediate, visible agents of authority. The early issues of *Aurora Social* are full of letters from miners complaining about the "despotism" of foremen and contractors, such as indiscriminate fines and suspensions and cheating workers out of their full earnings on piecework jobs. For example, in August 1901 "one of the exploited" complained about the behavior of a foreman in the Tudela-Veguín mines: "He wants to get in with the bosses at the expense of the workers. He takes centimeters away from their advance and does everything possible to ensure that they earn as little as possible. . . . Miners who have worked there since they were children are replaced by newcomers who are neighbors of his."[5]

Most often the miners' response to such situations was to appeal to the mine owners against the foremen and contractors, blaming them for the lack of harmony between owners and workers. In March 1909, *Aurora Social* responded to the decision of foremen to cut piece rates by urging workers to let the owners and authorities know about it through a manifesto. On the other hand, mine owners who dealt with their workers face to face, like the Felgueroso brothers, were picked out for praise. "Don Victor Felgueroso is not afraid of dealing with the workers, from whose ranks he comes. He discusses their claims with them, and so far has been able to reach agreements and avoid strikes which would have cost him more than the concessions he has made, and has not lost any of his authority as an employer."[6]

Such attitudes suggest that mine workers' protest was as yet uninformed by the ideology of the labor movement, and workers continued to view the mine owners as the ultimate—and essentially benevolent—arbiters in labor questions, not as part of them. The weakness of the ideological and organizational penetration of the labor movement in the nineteenth century is well illustrated by the series of food riots that took place in Oviedo, Gijón, Trubia, and Mieres in 1897 and 1898, especially the last one, which because it took place on June 22, 1897, the festival of San Juan, the patron saint of Mieres, came to be known as the *Sanjuanada*.[7]

The authorities blamed the disturbances on the Socialists and arrested Eduardo Varela and another member of the party, but these men denied having any part in it and claimed that the riot contradicted all Socialist practice. Descriptions of the events read more like an eighteenth-century food riot than a modern, organized labor protest. The miners were the protagonists. For a number of days before the 22nd there had been rumors of discontent among the miners over the recent increase in the *consumos*, the municipal tax on food items. On the morning of the 22nd miners from the Mariana and Peña mines marched into town, collecting workers as they went. They were led by a man on horseback carrying a black banner with the slogan "Down with the *consumos*! Death to the mayor!" Another account had the banner bearing no slogan at all. A number of workers from Hulleras del Turón also came. "Ours left work very peacefully at midday and went to demonstrate. Three were wounded in the leg, one seriously, and they returned at nightfall quite beaten up. About a third of our workers, especially the young lads, went to Mieres [on the 23rd] and there are many absences today because of the rumors that the workers of Mieres were going to demonstrate because of the Corpus [Christi]." [8]

A crowd of some seven to eight thousand people, dominated by some 2,900 striking workers, the vast majority miners, gathered in the square in front of the town hall shouting "Down with the rogues and idlers! Down with the *consumos*!" The mayor, accompanied by the local judge and the commander of the Civil Guard, met a five-member delegation that demanded "energetic measures" to lower the tax on basic necessities and to assure that bakers indicate the weight of their loaves and that merchants give full weight to their products, make periodic checks of their weights and measures, and inspect meats. [9]

The mayor agreed to some of the demands and promised to look into the others, but then trouble broke out. According to his report, the crowd tried to break into the town hall, and pistols were fired at the Civil Guard, who returned the fire, killing two and wounding seventeen; but according to *El Carbayón*, Francisco Martínez, who had farmed the *consumos* in Mieres for a number of years, threw a bottle into the crowd from the balcony of the town hall and injured a demonstrator, and this triggered the violence. In either case, when Martínez left the town hall, the crowd "followed him to his house with whistles and other unpleasant signs." There further trouble broke out when one of the women of the house allegedly flung boiling water on the crowd in the street. Martínez was taken off to jail, as the crowd had demanded, but more as a protective measure than anything else. By 7:00 in the evening, when a train arrived from Oviedo carrying more Civil Guards and two companies of soldiers, the show was over. [10]

Despite the existence of labor protest in the coalfields, however, the miners proved strangely resistant to the organized labor movement. In general terms, both socialism and anarchism spread inland from the coast, starting with the dockers and metalworkers of Gijón. The first unions in the coalfield municipalities were created by metalworkers in the foundries located there. Between October and December 1871 they organized and affiliated with the Federación de la Región Española, the Spanish branch of the First International (IWMA), but this, like the FRE as a whole, which was prohibited in January 1874, was short-lived.[11] A census of working-class organizations in Asturias in 1887 listed only two whose aim was "the defense of the workers' economic position," and neither was in the coalfields. The other twenty-six organizations were either mutual-aid societies or educational and recreational groups.[12]

Socialist propagandists reached the coalfields in late 1892, and five years later branches of the Socialist party were set up in Mieres and Sama de Langreo. But the real strength of Asturian socialism lay not with the party but with the unions affiliated to the Unión General de Trabajadores. The first period of growth for socialist unionism came with the Spanish-American War. In 1899 there were only two unions and 200 organized workers in the coalfields; by 1902 there were seventy unions with 4,000 members, of whom 2,600 were Socialists and 1,400 anarchists. In May 1900 miners at Arenas (Siero) joined the UGT, and two months later the 600-member Agrupación General de los Obreros del Valle de Langreo, most of whose members were miners, also joined. By 1901 the UGT had 4,224 members in Asturias. Oviedo, with 1,749, was the fourth most important center in the country, and Mieres, with 1,061, the sixth, figures that reflect the general weakness of early Socialist unionism rather than the strength of Asturian socialism. In 1902 Mieres had 1,080 members and was the seventh Socialist stronghold.[13]

This growth of the mine labor movement and a subsequent upsurge in strike activity during the Spanish-American War, which authorities attributed to "American gold running through the mines to paralyze production and leave the fleet without coal,"[14] led the civil governor to send an alarmist report to Madrid: "Socialist and anarchist associations are numerous in this province and there are frequent strikes in the mining region of Mieres, Sama, and Langreo, with the danger that the disturbance of order might become grave."[15] The precariousness of public order in Spain and the authorities' irrational fear of the labor movement explain his alarm. A description of that same period offered in 1917 is much more accurate. The unions had grown under the favorable circumstances created by the war with the United States, but these were all local unions, without any central organization, which succumbed easily once the war had ended, leaving "only a few nuclei here and there, impotent and incapable of doing more than keeping the sacred fire of rebellion burning in a few."[16]

In fact, the early mine unions were destroyed in two major strikes, one at Duro-Felguera in 1903, the other the so-called *huelgona*, or "great strike," at

Fábrica de Mieres in 1906. In March 1903, 1,500 workers at Duro-Felguera went on strike to protest a 10 percent wage cut, and in May they were joined by workers at Unión Hullera and a number of other mines, bringing the total number of strikers to 12,000. The strike lasted until mid-June before collapsing, and the company then took its revenge. A wage cut was imposed, and a number of workers fired.[17] As the firm's annual report stated, "At the end, and happily without the authorities having to use force, the sensible majority of the workers returned to their jobs, and our Director was able to make the necessary selection in the personnel and eliminate the rowdy elements who caused the indiscipline."[18]

The *huelgona* was an even more catastrophic defeat. The roots of the strike were in a 10 percent wage cut ordered by the Fábrica de Mieres for January 1, 1905. This triggered a six-day strike, which ended when the company agreed to delay the cut for six months. Subsequent increases in coal prices led to demands that wages be restored to their previous level, and on February 7, 1906, a strike started in the Baltasara mine. The next day it had spread to all the company's other mines. This strike, like the one in 1905, was opposed by the Socialist miners, who were forced to take part "against their will." According to Vigil, the strike was the work of the younger miners who, "without the agreement of those most experienced in these struggles and without counting on the metalworkers' and miners' unions, imposed a strike on the foundry and the mines. This lasted a few days and was a disaster. They did not get what they asked for and even lost some of the gains won earlier."[19]

Taking advantage of the strike having been called during a crisis of overproduction, the company fired the entire work force and evicted those who lived in company housing. It planned to reduce costs by hiring fewer workers—570 fewer in the mines and 300 fewer in the foundry—and to destroy the miners' union by carefully screening the workers who were rehired. This was left to two employees in whom the director had absolute trust; they came to be known as the *gabinete negro* (black cabinet).

> The worker who wanted a job got a form in the office which he had to complete, indicating his personal circumstances, the type of work he wanted, and the installation in which he wanted to work. He was then called for a medical checkup, and if he passed he had to present himself to the relevant department head, who in turn sent him to the director to request work. The director checked with the two employees . . . and accepted or rejected the request. In the first case the worker's name was written on a board that was hung each day in the foundry. From the first day it was apparent that any worker who had belonged to the Unión Socialista or who had in any way stood out during the strike—and the management had a complete list of the names—did not appear on the board. . . . The list of names was compiled during the strike by the foreman of each group.[20]

As the *Revista Minera* so succinctly put it, "With the separation of the rebels and leaders and a new order among its personnel, it is likely that the company will work peacefully from now on." [21]

This policy was supremely successful. According to the president of the Unión Socialista, 95 percent of those workers who were not rehired were Socialists and the organization was reduced from 800 members to 100, of whom only fifty paid dues, "and it should be noted that there are not any among them who work in the foundry. In the mines there are eight who still pay dues, but they do so secretly." [22] Sales of the Socialist press also fell: *El Socialista* from 300 copies before the strike to sixty in 1907, and *Aurora Social* from 500 to 125. Those workers who continued to subscribe to one or another of these papers did not do so openly. "Juan González, the president of the Unión Socialista, receives the packets and distributes the papers himself, taking all kinds of precautions." Likewise, company guards watched the *centro obrero* so thoroughly that workers were afraid of being seen there, and the lectures of the University Extension had to be cancelled for lack of audience. [23]

The effect on the labor movement was dramatic. In 1907 the UGT had only 927 members in thirteen locals in Asturias, and this according to Socialist party sources. The following year Maximiliano Arboleya credited it with 2,318 members, barely half the 1901 figure, and most of these were farmers. The Mieres organization, which had been one of the strongest in the entire country, was completely smashed, and many of its leading militants, including Manuel Llaneza, were forced to leave Asturias to find work. Many others left later as wage cuts and layoffs continued. [24] There were a notable number of strikes in the province as a whole between the *huelgona* and the creation of the SMA in 1910, but the center of gravity had returned to Gijón and the anarchists. There were few miners' strikes, and those for which we have information were defensive reactions to intolerable conditions—the extension of the working day for outside workers at Carbones Asturianos to twelve hours, the nonpayment of wages for three months at Hulleras de Riosa, and a 40 percent cut in piece rates for hewers at Duro-Felguera. [25]

The definitive organization of the mine workers only began in 1910, with the creation of the Sindicato de Obreros Mineros Asturianos (SMA) under the leadership of Manuel Llaneza. While in France, where he had spent three years following the *huelgona*, Llaneza had carried on a debate with another Asturian, Juan González, over the best form of union organization, "whether it was better to organize locally and then federate, or, as Llaneza claimed, to create the organization from the center outward, with a single leadership and a single treasury." [26] When he returned to Asturias in 1910, Llaneza was determined to avoid the decentralized format of the first miners' unions, which had been destroyed so easily, and to build a union modeled on the unions of northern France. "The locals were not autonomous, and they could only make demands or call strikes through the executive committee. Dues went to the union treasury, and the locals retained only the minimum to pay essential expenses, after getting permission from the executive in Mieres." [27]

In 1911 and 1912 the union adopted an aggressive policy that allowed it to establish itself quickly (table 13). This aggressiveness was essential, for with the exception of Duro-Felguera, which "looked on impotently as its workers organized, without daring to forbid it," the major companies resisted the union vigorously.[28]

The first test came in May 1911 at Fábrica de Mieres. Following the *huelgona* the company had financed a Catholic Workers' Circle "with the three classic aims of the Catholic Círculos: religion, education, and recreation." By 1908 it had 1,300 members, but its strength was an illusion, for "it had never fought for the workers' interests and appeared only as a tool of the owners." [29] When the SMA made its appearance, the Agremiación Católica was unable to resist it. In May 1911 the company fired twenty-seven of 300 workers who had not worked on May 1. The SMA called a strike, and after fruitless interventions by the mayor of Mieres and the civil governor, the company was forced to give in and reinstate the men.[30]

The next challenge came from Hulleras del Turón, which fired the most active SMA organizers in August 1911. A union delegation was received by company officials "with gross gestures and insulting words for our organization, saying that they would deal with their workers only." [31] As the company continued to be totally inflexible, the union prepared for a strike, which it saw as a matter of life and death. On September 11 it called a general strike that was supported by the entire mine work force. The strike ended four days later with a solution proposed by the mayor of Mieres, that the one worker who had not yet been rehired be readmitted.[32]

Despite these victories, which were followed by a massive three-day strike in solidarity with Basque workers, the SMA still had to face its most determined opponent, Hullera Española. As we have seen, this company tried to use the provision of social services as a means of establishing control over the lives of its employees. When this did not work, it adopted more direct means. In 1890 it created a police force of six men armed with revolvers and Winchester repeating rifles, which—besides the usual functions of guarding company property and installations—was charged with "the maintenance of order and discipline." In practice this meant preventing the spread of unacceptable ideas among the workers, liberal reformism as well as socialism and anarchism. When the SMA began to organize in Aller in 1912, the force was expanded to twenty men.[33]

The company police prevented the circulation of the "bad press," and kept Socialist organizers off company property. Both Eduardo Varela and Manuel Vigil had been prevented from doing their job of "delivering magazines and

Table 13. Membership of the SMA, 1911–20

Year	Membership	As Percentage of Work Force
1911	1,800	11.7
1912	10,000	62.2
1913	8,653	48.6
1914	10,000	54.8
1915	12,867	64.5
1916	11,907	49.8
1917	13,593	47.5
1918	19,583	59.3
1919	28,883	84.5
1920	24,551	62.8

Sources: *Minero de la Hulla; Revista Minera; El Noroeste;* and *El Socialista.*

serialized novels to the homes of subscribers" and were made to hand them over to a guard.[34] The first meetings addressed by Pablo Iglesias in Asturias, in 1892, were attended by the company police, who made lists of the company's workers who attended, "no doubt with the holy purpose of firing them."[35]

When the SMA threatened to undermine the company's ideological control over its work force in 1911 and 1912, the management's response was unambiguous. A special night patrolman prevented the distribution of *Aurora Social* in Sovilla, and the head of the firm's investigation department recommended the careful screening of all prospective workers, which continued at least until 1922.[36] He also had all Socialist meetings in the area watched and even claimed to have infiltrated the Socialist organization. "I had some people in the audience at the Sunday meeting in Turón and *another in the private meeting that took place afterward.*"[37] As the men of his department were not familiar with the work force, he suggested that "someone who knows the workers and has your trust go to Turón to report on who attends."[38] The company forbade anyone going to a Socialist meeting to cross its land and posted guards at the bridges across the river to make the order effective. Eventually all this proved to be a strain on the manpower of the force, and in September 1915 the commander complained that he was short of staff "as we have to keep an eye on the Socialist question, which is getting larger every day."[39]

This war against the SMA had a certain short-term effect, undoing the union's initial attempts to organize the company's men. The first strike called by the SMA at Hullera Española was in May 1912, to protest the dismissal of five workers. It lasted eighteen days and ended when the management promised to rehire the men, a promise that it did not keep. When nine union members were fired in September, the SMA called another strike and forced the company to readmit them. In the wake of its first victory in "the fief of Comillas," the union established locals at Moreda, Boo, Carabanzo, Pinera, and Santa Cruz, but this success was short-lived. The company returned to the offensive, "persecuting the most enthusiastic militants and firing them. In this way it was able to break up our nascent organization. The Moreda, Santa Cruz, and Ujo locals survived the disaster, but remained very weak and drew their members from miners who did not work in the fief of Comillas." [40]

Policemen and dismissals were not the only weapons Hullera Española used against the SMA. It also tried to undermine the appeal of the Socialists by promoting an alternative Catholic union. From its beginning Catholic unionism in the Asturian coalfield had had one overriding objective: to serve as a prophylactic against socialism. In April 1901, when he was asked by the chaplain of Hullera Española for advice on how to prevent the spread of socialism into Aller, Father Maximiliano Arboleya, the outstanding figure of social Catholicism in Asturias, said that only Catholic unions that copied the methods of their rivals would be successful and that the paternalism practiced by Hullera Española would be a failure. Arboleya was unable to put his ideas into practice in Aller, however, because the management would not tolerate a genuine union, Catholic or any other kind. "The otherwise intelligent directors of that company . . . felt that I was much more dangerous than [Socialist party leader] Pablo Iglesias, for he did not need to wear a cassock to preach socialism. . . . A little later a noted religious orator from Oviedo preached three sermons to the miners in Aller, principally designed to show them it was necessary to suffer in this world in order to enjoy the next." [41]

In July 1912 Arboleya returned to Aller at the invitation of the Hullera Española management, which wanted him to draw up the statutes for a Catholic workers' organization, "not the company's thing, but something belonging to the workers, so that they could defend themselves from the company if need be," but once again his approach was rejected. In September he distributed the statutes and began to publish a paper, *La Defensa del Obrero*, but ran into opposition from managers "who found it difficult to control that new power." [42] Arboleya's plan was rejected in favor of one drawn up by Father Gabriel Palau, S.J., which was characterized by "a clear, mutualist, and charitable tendency dictated by the owners." The new Sindicato Católico de Obreros Mineros de Asturias was run by actual mine workers; the white-collar workers who had been prominent in running its predecessor, the Asociación de Obreros Católicos de Aller, were eliminated. [43]

In 1913 the major mining companies formed the Asociación Patronal de Mineros Asturianos and agreed to accept the SMA as the mine workers' bargaining agent. Hullera Española refused to recognize the Socialist union and did not join the Patronal. Instead it dealt with the Sindicato Católico, which it tried to build up as a counter to the SMA. In September 1913 the union and the Patronal agreed on a minimum wage, which went into effect in January 1914. The response of Hullera Española was to grant a "regulatory wage" equivalent to the minimum wage. The company always made sure that its wage levels matched those contained in the SMA-Patronal collective contracts, and in 1917, when the SMA received a payment of 1.25 *pesetas* per ton from the mine owners, Hullera Española gave its workers a 20 percent increase, thereby putting its wages above those set out in the collective agreement.[44]

This strategy was not particularly successful. "While the [SMA] got stronger by *conquering* improvements, the Catholic Association *received* them, and generally 'thanks to the Sindicato Minero,' or at least so it appeared."[45] In June 1916 the SMA called its first strike against Hullera Española since 1912. The occasion was the dismissal of a worker, but the central demand was union recognition, which was eventually accepted. However, when the company refused to accept the 1917 *convenio*, "the workers spontaneously and unanimously went on strike." After the company backed down, the Sindicato Católico also went on strike, "to show that it, and not the Sindicato Minero, was the stronger." In effect the Socialist miners were locked out, and they went "in an orderly fashion and with the banners of their locals to demand that work be resumed."[46] The lockout lasted nineteen days before the Instituto de Reformas Sociales sent General José Marva to find a solution. He arranged a referendum among the company's workers; the SMA won easily. The company refused to open the mines for sixteen more days but was finally forced to do so by the government.[47]

The SMA had managed to establish itself in Aller, but this did not mean an end to the struggle with the Sindicato Católico, which remained bitter and violent. "Here, in the coalfields of Asturias, we need men with *balls*, ready for anything," wrote one Catholic organizer in 1918.[48] There were occasional street fights among Catholic and Socialist miners, but the climax of the violence came in April 1920 with the so-called events of Moreda, in which eleven workers, including Vicente Madera's brother, were killed, and thirty-five wounded in a shoot-out between the two groups. "The tragedy of Moreda is not a sad accident produced by the strike, but the consequence of the state of affairs created by the company," concluded *El Noroeste*.[49] In the end the SMA won the war. Membership in the Sindicato Católico (which in April 1918 became the Asturian section of the Sindicato Católico de Obreros Mineros Españoles) fell from 2,242 in 1919 to 1,020 in 1924, and its sole outpost outside the "fief of Comillas," in Mieres, was wiped out. Even among workers at Hullera Española the SMA was stronger. In 1929 it defeated the Catholics by 1,200 votes in the elections to the arbitration committees (*comités paritarios*) created by the Primo de Rivera dictatorship, and the following year it won the election for members of the directorate of the firm's mutual aid society by 1,554 to 932.[50]

The SMA also had another rival, the anarchists centered in Sama de Langreo, although this struggle was initially much less violent than that against the Catholics. Although anarchism antedated socialism in Asturias and had proven more popular in Gijón, with its dockers and metalworkers, it did not have much appeal among the coal miners. This lack of success is intriguing and difficult to explain. The strongest anarchist presence in the coalfield municipalities was not among the miners but among the metalworkers of La Felguera. But not all metalworkers were anarchists: those at Fábrica de Mieres were Socialists. The strength of anarchism at La Felguera would seem to explode explanations of the popularity of anarchism in Spain based on structural considerations, such as the relative backwardness and the smallness of the units of production in the Catalan textile industry. But why in La Felguera and not in Mieres? As to the miners, the unimportance of Andalusian immigrants among this group of workers, compared to their significant numbers in Barcelona, may be of some relevance.

The one anarchist stronghold among the miners was Sama de Langreo. The only Asturian miners' union to attend the 1919 CNT congress was the Sindicato de Mineros de Langreo, which had 800 members.[51] Sama was a trouble spot for the SMA. An earlier anarchist group, which had published a paper, *El Despertar del Minero*, had joined the SMA, although "some continued to cause us trouble from outside, using calumny and defamation as their weapons."[52] Those who did join soon found themselves chafing at the union's strict centralization, and in July 1915 Sama called a local strike without the authorization of the executive and "did not even let any official of the organization get involved."[53] A special congress was held in October 1915 to deal with this lack of discipline; it resolved "to act with full vigor against those members or locals which do not respect the regulations on calling strikes."[54] But this did not resolve the problem: in 1916 there was opposition to the union's demand for a 20 percent wage increase, with the dissidents calling for an increase of one *peseta* per day for all workers. Finally, in 1917 the original anarchist elements abandoned the union.[55]

As we have already mentioned, all major mining companies except Hullera Española joined the Employers' Association (Patronal), which almost immediately recognized the SMA as the miners' bargaining agent. This opened a period of labor relations that lasted until 1917, during which time the union was able to win a number of important gains. One observer described the process in the following way: "The workers asked what they thought just, what the circumstance permitted. The owners at first said no, but the matter would be taken to the Employers' Association, would be discussed by both parties, and by means of a common give and take an agreement would be reached." [56]

On January 1, 1914, the minimum wage agreement negotiated the previous fall came into effect. The next year the SMA won its main demand, a wage increase of 50 *céntimos* per day and 50 percent extra for overtime. In 1916 the union won a 20 percent wage increase and a moving scale for wages tied to the price of coal. The 1917 agreement included a 15 percent wage increase plus a payment to the union itself of 200,000 *pesetas* and 1.25 *pesetas* per ton of coal produced. [57]

This is not to say that the coalfields were free of strikes in these years, but the Patronal successfully avoided any prolonged massive general strike. Paralysis of production was the last thing it wanted while it enjoyed a captive market and relentlessly rising prices and profits. The Patronal was only too happy to forego confrontation for "the tranquil and serene sphere of reason and discussion." [58]

There was one glaring exception to the relative social peace of the war years, the revolutionary general strike of August 1917. This had nothing to do with the miners' own material interests, but rather was the third and final wave of protest against the Restoration monarchy and its disintegrating political system. The crisis of 1917 was the result of the temporary confluence of a set of diverse and incompatible demands for change by disgruntled army officers, Catalan regionalists led by Francisco Cambó, and the Republican and Socialist parties. Early in 1917 the *Juntas de Defensa*, corporate organizations of middle-ranking army officers, demanded pay increases and improved conditions. They also made vague noises about more general reform, which attracted Cambó, who tried to weld an alliance with Republicans, Radicals, and Socialists to impose political reform from above. When Prime Minister Eduardo Dato closed parliament, Cambó called a meeting of dissenting deputies to serve as a National Assembly and create a new constitution that would include wide regional autonomy. The assembly met briefly in July before it was closed by the police. The fragile and unnatural nature of the alliance became apparent during the August general strike, which had been planned by the Socialists and Reformists. This mass movement frightened both the officers and the essentially conservative Catalan regionalists, who once again fell in behind the monarchy. [59]

In Asturias the strike received massive support, and "even the farmers, until now far removed from this type of struggle, abandoned their work and stopped supplying food to the warehouses." [60] It was also orderly and nonviolent. Llaneza's claim that "there was not a single act of violence against individuals, property, or the army in the entire coalfield" [61] was supported by Arboleya, who wrote that "neither churches nor priests nor storekeepers nor any part of the bourgeoisie was bothered in a significant way by those tranquil revolutionaries." [62] Nevertheless, the authorities reacted with extreme severity. On August 17 the military commander, General Ricardo Burguete, published a notorious decree in which he promised to "hunt the rebels in the mountains like beasts." He even had a train loaded with soldiers go along firing indiscriminately. This "death train" killed at least two people. Through all this Llaneza, public enemy number one of the strike, stayed at large until mid-October, spending a good deal of time in the house of Reformist leader Melquíades Alvarez. [63]

In Asturias the strike continued for two weeks longer than elsewhere in the country, in support of the railwaymen whose own walkout had triggered the movement. However, in the face of the intransigence of the railroad company Ferrocarriles del Norte, the railway strike came to an end and with it the general strike as a whole. As Isidoro Acevedo, one of the Socialist leaders, wrote, "We studied the spirit of the mass of the strikers . . . and we saw that all resistance was useless. Moreover we leaders ran the risk of not being obeyed if we insisted on continuing the struggle." [64]

The general strike was a failure nationwide. In Asturias, and for the SMA in particular, it was a disaster. Llaneza and other leaders and hundreds of miners were imprisoned, and the Patronal took advantage of the situation to impose a 10 percent pay cut and dismiss workers, especially SMA officials. The honeymoon between the union and the Patronal ended abruptly. In the words of Andrés Saborit, the Socialist deputy for Asturias, "Under the cover of a strike which was not directed at them, the mine owners want to undo the union and take away the improvements which had already been achieved." [65] Finally, the inability of the SMA to resist this attack opened a new breach within the membership; a radical wing emerged that would later be attracted to the Russian revolution and the Third International, foreshadowing the divisions that would weaken the union from 1920 through 1922.

There is little parallel between the general strike of August 1917 and the revolution of October 1934. First, the general strike formed part of a national movement aimed strictly at political change, and it emerged out of events at the national level—the "state of national unrest" caused by the crisis of the *Juntas de Defensa* and the Assembly of Parliamentarians. As Juan Lacomba has described it, the strike of August 1917 was "the Jacobin action within the bourgeois revolution that was already under way." [66] In contrast, the revolution of October 1934 did not address itself to a political system in crisis.

Second, the strike of August 1917 was carried out under the direction and control of a political and trade union leadership. The initial revolutionary committee, which included the Reformists of Melquíades Alvarez, the Radicals of Alejandro Lerroux, and the Republicans of Marcelino Domingo, never lost its grip on events. In October 1934 the situation was reversed, and the putative leaders were carried along by the uncontrollable radicalism of their followers. And insofar as there was a political higher command in 1934, it did not include any organization to the right of the Socialists.

Finally, it does not appear that August 1917 resurfaced in the collective memory during October 1934, to be used as a symbol of the glorious struggle or as a past defeat to be avenged. By October 1934 miners had been so radicalized that the political goals of August 1917 appeared irrelevant.

The SMA attempted to recover from the disaster of the general strike and to silence the dissidents by pressing for an increase in wages and an abbreviation of the workday. On October 1, 1919, some 30,000 mine workers struck to demand a seven-hour day for inside workers and eight for outside workers. Officially the strike was called by the Federación Nacional de Mineros, and it spread to some mines outside Asturias. After eight days the government conceded. In winning this strike the SMA had won the shortest mine workday in the world, "seven hours from pithead to pithead," as Llaneza jubilantly told a crowd of 12,000 in Langreo.[67]

El Noroeste exulted in the miners' victory, calling it "the culmination of the union's previous achievements and the full realization of an ideal—the redemption of the mine worker." [68] Indeed it was a monumental achievement and the climax of an eventful decade. Between 1910 and 1919 the SMA had brought the organized labor movement to the Asturian mines and established itself as the single strongest union in Spain. All this had been achieved in favorable circumstances, however, mostly during the wartime boom that was already beginning to wind down. After the boom came a depression, and with it a vigorous attempt by the mine owners to save their profits at the expense of the workers and the workers' wartime victories. The internal dissension that had begun to emerge was amplified as the Llaneza leadership became ever more timid and defensive and the appeal of the Russian Revolution and Communism more alluring. Despite its glorious beginning, the future of the SMA was anything but secure.

NOTES

1. *AV*, 12.V.1932.

2. *ES*, 10.VII.1922; Alvarez Buylla, *Observaciones*, 20.

3. J. M. Fernández Díaz-Faes, *Lo social en la Asturias del siglo XX* (Oviedo, 1966), 22–24; Ruiz, *Movimiento*, 96; S. Canals, *Asturias—su presente estado* (Madrid, 1900), 129.

4. *EMME*, 1873, 74; Santullano, *Historia*, 142–43; Vigil, "Memorias," 67–72.

5. *AS*, 27.X, 10.XI, 8.XII.1900, 19.I, 20.IV, 23.VII, 10.VIII.1901, 18.I, 19.IV.1902, 28.VIII.1903, among many others.

6. *AS*, 31.VIII.1901, 19.IV.1902, 10.XI.1900. See also Vigil, "Memorias," 254–55.

7. *ES*, 13.V.1898; Vigil, "Memorias," 149; *Eco de Mieres*, 27.VI.1897.

8. *Eco de Mieres*, 27.VI.1897. *AS*, 27.VI.1897; *El Carbayón*, 23.VI.1897; Hulleras del Turón to Parent, 24.VI.1897, AHE 2/2.

9. *Eco de Mieres*, 27.VI.1897; Asuntos relativos a los sucesos conocidos con el nombre de SANJUANA, AMM.

10. Asuntos relativos . . . ; *Eco de Mieres*, 27.VI.1897; *El Carbayón*, 23.VI.1897. Instead of going to Mieres, the workers at Hullera Española went to ask Felix Parent to intervene on their behalf. Parent to Gutiérrez, 23.VI.1897, AHE 2/2.

11. Ruiz, *Movimiento*, 46, 93; Santullano, *Historia*, 142–43; Vigil, "Memorias," 67–72.

12. Gobernación, Legajo 575, Fondos Modernos, Archivo Histórico Nacional.

13. Vigil, "Memorias," 80–87, 143–44, 212, 231–32, 328, 386; Ruiz, *Movimiento*, 96; *Revista Socialista*, 1903, 337–39; Vigil, *Los mineros*, 30.

14. Vigil, "Memorias," 164.

15. Civil Governor to Minister of the Interior, Dec. 1903, Legajo 6A, Expediente 24, Fondos Modernos, AHN.

16. *MH*, Oct. 1917, 6.

17. *ES*, 20.III, 22.V.1903; *AS*, 10.IV, 8, 15, 29.V, 5.VI.1903.

18. Duro-Felguera, *Memoria* (Madrid, 1904), 5–6.

19. IRS, *Informe sobre Fábrica*, 11–13; Vigil, "Memorias," 456–57.

20. IRS, *Informe*, 13–14. See also Ruiz, *Movimiento*, 95–96.

21. *RM*, 1906, 228.

22. IRS, *Informe*, 22–25.

23. Ibid., 30.

24. *ES*, 18.X.1907; Benavides, *El Fracaso*, 38–45; *AS*; 26.V.1909; IRS, *Informe*, 10.

25. Ruiz, *Movimiento*, 97; *AS*, 5.II, 26.III, 16.VII.1909. As a result of the strike at Duro-Felguera, the rates were cut by only 20 percent.

26. *ES*, 25.I.1931.

27. Vigil, "Memorias," 483–84; *MH*, Nov. 1914, 12; A. Saborit, *Asturias y sus hombres* (Toulouse, 1964), 156.

28. *MH*, Oct. 1917, 7.

29. Arboleya, *El caso de Asturias*, 70–75.

30. *NO*, 3–7.V.1911; Ruiz, *Movimiento*, 108; *MH*, Oct. 1917, Sept. 1916, 5.

31. *MH*, Sept. 1916, 6–7.

32. *NO*, 11–15.IX.1911.

33. "Asuntos tratados . . . 1890," AHE 2; "Institutions en faveur . . . ," AHE 4/2; Bonnin to Montaves, 31.X.1912, AHE 55/3.

34. Vigil, "Memorias," 330–31.

35. Ibid., 101.

36. Bonnin to Rubiera, 19.IX.1915, AHE 55/3; Costa to Rubiera, 11.IX.1922.

37. Costa to Montaves, 14.II.1912, AHE 15/4. Emphasis is added.

38. Bonnin to Montaves, 24.VII.1912; Costa to Montaves, 25.VII.1912, AHE 55/3. In August 1912 a Socialist was attacked and beaten up by a company guard who then turned him in to the Civil Guard. *NO*, 17.VIII.1912.

39. Bonnin to Rubiera, 15.IX.1915, AHE 55/3.

40. *MH*, June 1916, 1–2.
41. Arboleya, *El caso*, 41, 63.
42. Ibid., 93–96.
43. Benavides, *El Fracaso*, 44; Ruiz, *Movimiento*, 107. The resistance to authentic Catholic unions was shared by the Conde de Mieres, owner of the Fábrica de Mieres, who also a rejected a plan of Arboleya's. According to Benavides, the chief opponents were the Jesuits. *Democracia y Cristianismo en la España de la Restauración* (Madrid, 1970), 279–84.
44. Arboleya, *El caso*, 97–98; *RM*, 1913, 451, 476; 1914, 78–80; Fernández Díaz-Faes, *Lo social*, 33; *RNE*, Oct. 1917, 306. In 1917 the *Revista Minera* commented that the Hullera Española gave its workers whatever they wanted.
45. Arboleya, *El caso*, 99, 161.
46. *MH*, June 1916, 1–6; Aug. 1916, 8–11; Apr. 1917, 1–5.
47. *MH*, Apr. 1917, 4–5.
48. Cited in J. J. Castillo, *El Sindicalismo amarillo en España* (Madrid, 1977), 153n29.
49. *NO*, 10–14.IV.1920. See also Ruiz, *Movimiento*, 136.
50. *El Minero*, 1.V.1918; Castillo, *El sindicalismo*, 206–7; *ES*, 3.X.1929; *AS*, 31.X.1930.
51. Villar, *El anarquismo*, 40–47; R. Alvarez, *Eleuterio Quintanilla* (Mexico, 1973), 257.
52. *MH*, Feb. 1917, 2.
53. *MH*, Aug. 1915, 1–5.
54. *NO*, 12.X.1915.
55. *MH*, Apr. 1916, 10–11; Feb. 1917, 2.
56. E. García de la Fuente, *El problema hullero* (Mieres, 1921), 15.
57. *RM*, 1914, 78–80; 1915, 189, 233, 247–48, 259; 1916, 159, 194, 204.
58. *RIMA*, 16.VII.1916, 517.
59. *NO*, 14–29.VII.1916; Ruiz, *Movimiento*, 115; I. Acevedo, "La huelga de agosto de 1917," in *Nuestra Bandera*, 1947, 507. On the crisis of 1917, see J. A. Lacomba, *La Crisis Española de 1917* (Madrid, 1970).
60. A. Oliveros, *Asturias en el resurgimiento español* (Madrid, 1935), 116; *MH*, Sept. 1917, 6.
61. M. Llaneza, "La huelga de agosto en Asturias," in *España*, 134, 1918, 7.
62. Arboleya, *El caso*, 193.
63. *Historia de Asturias*, VIII (Salinas, 1980), 167–68; Acevedo, "La huelga," 574.
64. Acevedo, "La huelga," 576.
65. Cited in Ruiz, *Movimiento*, 119–20.
66. Lacomba, *La Crisis*, 278.
67. *NO*, 24, 29–30.IX, 1–13.X.1919.
68. *NO*, 9.X.1919.

6

Depression and Dictatorship, 1920–30

The year 1920 was a watershed. The depression that had begun in the mining industry in 1919 now gripped it by the throat, threatening to throttle it to death. As the conditions that had made possible higher wages and a shorter workday disappeared, the SMA dropped the aggressive policy that had established it as a popular, strong, and wealthy industrial union. In the face of unfavorable new conditions and the determination of the mine owners to save themselves at the expense of the workers, the union adopted a timid, defensive strategy based on negotiations with the owners and with the state and avoidance of strikes whenever possible. The division of Spanish socialism over adherence to the Third International and the coup by General Miguel Primo de Rivera in September 1923 produced further problems.

The SMA entered its second decade forced to develop strategies to confront totally new circumstances. Its choice of moderation would drive many miners to frustration and desertion of the union. The 1920s would take a heavy toll; 1930 saw the SMA in decline, under attack from its anarchosyndicalist and Communist rivals in the Sindicato Unico Minero, and still unpopular with much of the rank and file for its inability to cope with the ongoing depression.

The wartime boom had been predicated on the disruption of normal trade patterns, especially British coal exports. Once these resumed, the Asturian coal industry sank back into its chronic state of crisis, now exacerbated. As cheap British coal flooded into Spanish ports, prices plummeted. Many marginal mines that had been opened after 1914 closed down: in 1919 there had been 1,426 mines covering 54,805 hectares in Asturias; by 1921 there were only 1,232 covering 47,199 hectares; by 1923, 1,130 and 45,937.[1]

Some effects were felt as early as 1919, but it was only toward the end of 1920 and the beginning of 1921 that the miners experienced the full impact of the new situation. Mine closures were not the only effects. Owners and managers also sought to make their coal more competitive through the intensification of production—reducing the number of oncost workers, cutting piece rates, and introducing labor saving technology. In short, they tried to make their coal cheaper by producing more using fewer workers who were receiving less pay.[2] The extent to which they were successful is shown in table 14.

Behind these global figures and indices was a situation of great hardship. In 1921 and 1922 layoffs were the order of the day. In March 1921 *El Socialista* reported that "workers were fired daily at all the mines."[3] Hulleras del Turón usually gave six days' notice—when it did not, it gave workers six days' wages and the price of a train ticket to their home village. Clearly it was the immigrants who were being let go first. Unemployed miners were turning up in Langreo from other parts of the coalfield to find that there were absolutely no openings, a situation that one company used to blackmail its hewers: unless they doubled their output, there would be layoffs. Those miners who hung on to their jobs often were on a short week: usually five days, but sometimes four or even three, and sometimes with alternate weekly layoffs.[4]

On May 9, 1921, *El Socialista* reported that "in Langreo workers are losing two and three days per week, and their situation, which was already unbearable because of wage reductions, has become even worse, creating a state of great excitement."[5] According to the regional representative of the Instituto de Reformas Sociales, "On seeing their wages and work week reduced, the workers are beginning to express their unhappiness with the difficult situation in which they have been placed, because the cost of living is the same as before, and even with their former wages they could not meet the absolutely essential needs of their families."[6]

The growing restiveness of its rank and file was a problem for Manuel Llaneza and the other leaders of the SMA, especially as it came in the middle of their struggle to retain control of the union against the challenge of the pro-Communist faction led by longtime Socialist militant Isidoro Acevedo. The Sindicato Minero, like the UGT and PSOE as a whole (and the CNT as well), was divided by the question of allegiance to the Third International.[7] The PSOE debated this at congresses in 1919, 1920, and 1921. At the last of these, in April 1921, it was decided not to adhere to the new International, although only after an extremely bitter and divisive debate. In December dissident former members of the Socialist executive joined with the leaders of the Socialist Youth who had abandoned the movement in April 1920 to found the Partido Comunista Española (PCE). Among their prominent supporters in Asturias were Lázaro García, who had been a delegate to the 1920 PSOE congress, and Acevedo, the editor of the regional Socialist weekly *Aurora Social*. The provincial Socialist federation had shown its sympathy for Communism by voting to join the Third International, but with the rider that it would accept the deci-

Table 14. Workers, Wages, and Productivity, 1914–29

Year	Number of Workers	Wage Index	Productivity Index
1914	18,223	100	100
1917	28,606	154	115
1918	33,020	211	136
1919	34,177	245	93
1920	39,093	298	121
1921	34,031	265	120
1922	29,648	215	102
1923	29,834	223	153
1924	30,759	223	162
1925	31,023	222	160
1926	31,232	217	171
1927	28,244	216	165
1928	25,803	218	175
1929	27,074	219	193

Sources: *EMME*, 1914–29; *Estadística de Salarios*, LXII.

sion of the full party. In his memoirs Manuel Vigil estimated that about one-fifth of the Asturian Socialists were prepared to leave the party.[8]

The stronghold of Communism in the coalfield was the Turón valley, the home of Hulleras del Turón. This was the first company to respond to the crisis and the only one to undertake a thorough program of mechanization. While the company was fairly generous in its provision of social services, which it counted as an important contributor to its economic success, it was also quite ruthless in dismissing workers who were not needed. Also Turón was an area in which the deterioration of social conditions had been particularly acute. In short, it was in Turón that the changes in the miners' working and social lives were most rapid and most marked, and it was there, in November and December 1920, that the first expressions of impatience with the moderation of the SMA leadership emerged.

Llaneza later referred to the Turón general strike as the beginning of the union's internal divisions. The strike evolved out of three separate strikes, each relatively insignificant but displaying the willingness of the miners to defy the authority of the union. It drew 5,000 men out to support the company's office workers, who had been fired for organizing a union of their own. At the Coto del Musel mine three SMA locals, at Tolivia, at Villoria, and at Las Quintanas, had called a protest strike when a company guard fired on a group of workers entering a closed-off gallery, and the miners at Barredos were demanding the dismissal of a foreman at the Duro-Felguera mine there.

The union called a congress to discuss the situation. The Executive had to "use every method at its disposal to prevent the passage of a radical motion" and only with difficulty succeeded in getting a motion to negotiate approved. However, the locals that had called the Barredos strike without the approval of their regional committee continued their rebellion and were joined by the Barredos local. As negotiations stalled the union called and then postponed a general strike for the whole coalfield. Finally, on December 2, the strike began, paralyzing all mining operations, even at the Hullera Española, where the Sindicato Católico had urged the men not to go out. The strike continued until December 31, when the last of the companies, the Hullera Española, accepted the agreement that had been worked out in Madrid, in which the companies recognized the freedom of association of their employees and promised to rehire all those fired during the strike.[9]

The disruptive effects of the Turón strike were evident at the January 1921 union congress, in particular during the debate over whether the authority to call strikes lay with the executive or with the locals. Llaneza argued that it was dangerous to let the locals have such authority and referred to the general strike of the month before: "In this struggle Turón has drawn all the other workers on strike, and this must not happen again. The guarantee of triumph is unity. You have an Executive with which you must consult before taking any decision, not for the advice it might give you, but because it is the axis of the union."[10] Dissatisfaction with the Executive increased a few months later when it refused to fight the pay cut of 3.75 *pesetas* imposed by the Employers' Association. At the congress held on May 29 the Executive came in for some harsh criticism, to which it responded that this was the work of Communist agitators: "It is clear that the propaganda of some comrades from Madrid has had effect. In order to win converts they, like the anarchists and syndicalists, blame Llaneza for the drop in wages."[11]

In June the Executive won a referendum on its management by 5,332 to 851, but in August it was defeated. Llaneza claimed that the Executive had refrained from calling a strike against a pay cut because the workers had shown no enthusiasm for it, but he was contradicted by another member of the Executive, José Vila, who criticized the strategy of relying on negotiations in Madrid and blamed the Executive for the lack of spirit among the miners. The committee was censured in a vote of 4,782 to 2,988, and a motion for its resignation was approved by 4,567 to 3,413.[12] A new Executive was elected, dominated by Communists and headed by Isidoro Acevedo, but it survived only two months and was turned out by yet another congress in October.

The return of Llaneza to the leadership of the SMA did not turn out to be a victory for moderation. Rather, Llaneza inherited a situation of deepening crisis and growing restiveness within the union rank and file that despite his determined efforts he was unable to restrain. In November 1921 the town councils from the coalfield municipalities met in Mieres to demand relief from the government, threatening to resign en masse if nothing were done by the end of the month. The provincial administration did meet with the employers' association and officials of the SMA, but the end result was nothing. The situation only deteriorated further, and on December 9 the first important closures were announced, at Minas de Olloniego. Three days later Duro-Felguera announced that it would shut its mines within a week, and Fábrica de Mieres quickly followed suit.[13]

The union responded by issuing a manifesto calling for a general strike in the coalfields if nothing were done by mid-December. The day before this deadline a temporary arrangement was patched together by the union, the Employers' Association, and the Ministry of the Economy, allowing for two weeks in which the miners would be guaranteed five days work. Word of the arrangement was late in reaching some locals, and the strike went ahead at a number of mines, but it was called off two days later.[14]

This temporary peace was shattered when the Employers' Association announced its proposed changes in the organization of labor in the mines, which would have effectively turned the clock back to 1914. The proposals included lowering piece rates to 1914 levels plus 20 percent, revising rates for galleries and pits and introducing a two-shift system, reducing the number of hewers and assistants to meet the productivity rates of 1914, increasing the number of outside workers, and paying overtime at the regular rate. Any worker who lost his job would be given preference when future openings occurred.[15]

This announcement "upset the miners to an extraordinary degree," and on January 2 strikes broke out spontaneously in Sama and spread rapidly over the entire municipality, exempting only those mines where the new program was not going to be implemented.[16] On January 5 the Sama local of the SMA made the strike official, and at a congress held three days later the union declared a general strike against all the mining companies in the province except the Hullera Española, which was not a member of the Employers' Association and had not implemented the new conditions. By January 11 there were 14,000 to 15,000 men on strike, mostly at Duro-Felguera, Fábrica de Mieres, Hulleras del Turón, Tudela-Veguín, and Industrial Asturiana.[17] The civil governor's proposal of a guaranteed minimum wage and the participation of an arbitration committee in the revision of piecework rates was accepted by the union on the 17th, but when put to a referendum it was approved by a majority of only 500 votes. Support for continuing the strike was strong in Langreo, which had been hardest hit by the crisis, and the strike continued in parts of the municipality for another week as a protest against those companies that did not admit all their workers. At Industrial Asturiana the strike dragged on until February 15, as workers refused to return until one miner who had scabbed during the strike was dismissed. He was eventually transferred to another of the company's mines.[18]

The crisis continued in the next months of 1922. The period from February to May was marked by the response of the miners to pay cuts, changes in working conditions, and dismissals. The reports of the Instituto de Reformas Sociales emphasized the high degree of militancy and solidarity among the miners. "The deep-rooted spirit of solidarity which predominates, sacrificing individual convenience to the collective interest, and the constant resistance to whatever involves a change in the organization of labor or the minimum wage, with unceasing opposition to individual contracts, and refusals to accept wage cuts they consider unjust because they know they are being made to work with greater intensity."[19] On April 11, then, when the Patronal announced that it was again studying wages and ten days later announced a reduction of 20 percent, the reaction was not the least bit surprising: "great agitation, refusal to accept new wage reductions, as they consider that the reduction will make life in the coalfields impossible due to the high cost of basic necessities."[20]

The SMA congress held on May 6–7 voted to hold a referendum on whether to strike, but the Executive's position was made clear when Llaneza's speech recommending an extra hour's work in return for no cut in wages was printed and distributed to the members. Llaneza claimed that "at this moment it is the owners who are most interested in a strike, as the circumstances are favorable for their defeating the working class," and he urged workers to stay on the job until conditions had changed to favor them. Only ten locals accepted this proposal: thirty-nine opposed it, twelve wanted negotiations, and five pushed for an immediate strike. The employers yielded nothing during negotiations, and another congress was held, followed by a referendum. Forty-four locals voted for a strike and only fifteen voted against. The strike was called for May 22 and was to effect all mines except the Hullera Española, which had not ordered a wage cut, and the Campanal mine, which was run by workers under a collective contract. The dissatisfaction with the Executive was evidenced when a motion by the Turón delegation expressing its lack of confidence in the ability of the Executive to lead the strike and calling for the creation of a special strike committee was defeated by only 665 votes, 3,695 to 3,030.[21]

But even before the congress and referendum there was a series of spontaneous strikes in Pola de Lena, Langreo, Mieres, Turón, and Siero. About 4,000 men stayed away from work, 3,000 of them in Turón. On the 18th this spontaneous outburst had paralyzed the entire coalfield except for Aller and parts of Langreo.[22] The official strike began on the 22nd and continued until August 9 and was characterized by the refusal of the rank and file to accept a compromise recommended by the union Executive. On June 7 the Employers'

Association agreed to a proposal of the minister of labor to provide financial support for those mines that remained open and did not cut wages by more than 10 percent. The union announced it would hold a referendum and "abide unfailingly" by its decision. The result was a major defeat for the Executive: 6,470 against and only 60 in favor. Locals in Mieres, Turón, Figaredo, Vegadotos, and Ujo had announced beforehand that they would not even bother to vote.[23]

The miners received substantial support during the strike. The metalworkers' union gave 1,000 *pesetas*, the shopclerks' association 200, the Madrid masons 5,000, and the printers another thousand. The bakers of Turón each donated 160 three-pound loaves per day. By June 20 the Socialists claimed to have collected 81,000 *pesetas*, and the Asturian Communist Federation 77,750. Of particular note was the support given by farmers in nearby municipalities such as Pravia, Salas, and Grado, where SMA official Ramón González Peña reported that "from the offers of help already made by the farmers, the amount of foodstuffs, especially beans, potatoes, and salt pork, which will be available, will be considerable."[24]

The strike wore on, and all proposals that meant a reduction in wages were rejected by the workers. When negotiations broke down at the end of July, the minister of labor decided to intervene personally, and on August 3 he arrived in Oviedo. Llaneza was prepared to accept a cut of 5 percent until productivity rose by 15 percent, and on August 5 the union and the Employers' Association agreed to the minister's proposal of a 5 percent pay cut, which would be revoked when output increased by one-fifth. If by November 1 it had not risen by 10 percent, a joint commission would establish wage rates for the following months. This was put to a referendum and approved by 5,471 to 2,295, with 40 abstentions. Work resumed on the 9th.[25]

The general strike of May to August 1922 was also characterized by a growing antagonism between Socialists and Communists. In June the Communists proposed the creation of a United Front, but this was rejected by the SMA, which claimed that it was the Communists who had disrupted the unity already achieved by the union. The Communists later criticized the SMA for negotiating, claiming that it was betraying the workers who were striking for "not a penny less, not a minute more," and also charged that the negotiations had been set up beforehand in order to freeze them out. As a settlement was drawing near, the Communists sent out handbills urging miners to stay on strike and abstain from voting in the referendum. Miners in Lena and Lieres did stay out an extra six days, a very limited success, although the small number of votes cast in the referendum, fewer than 8,000, indicates that many miners were not pleased with the settlement but were not prepared to prolong a strike that had already lasted nearly three months.[26]

The acute labor conflict in Asturias was only one of the problems, and not the most pressing, that faced Spanish governments in the immediate postwar years. The two dynastic political parties, Liberals and Conservatives, continued to disintegrate into numerous squabbling cliques. The escalating warfare between anarchosyndicalists and government-aided "free" unionists turned Barcelona into a shooting gallery, and made the Catalan bourgeoisie welcome the iron fist of General Severiano Martínez Anido. Between 1918 and 1921 southern Spain was rocked by outbreaks of land seizures and other violence known as the *trienio bolchevique*. Most important, in 1921 the Spanish army in Morocco was decimated by tribesmen at Anual, and this shocking defeat led to a commission of inquiry that threatened both the army and the king. Under these circumstances General Miguel Primo de Rivera carried out a *pronunciamiento* on September 23, 1923. He claimed that his stay in power would be brief, ninety days, after which he would return the country to constitutional rule. In the end he stayed on for almost seven years, until January 1930.[27]

Primo's seizure of power changed the political backdrop against which the labor movement had to act, but it did nothing to alleviate the coal crisis that continued through the decade. During 1923 Minas de Teverga, which employed 500 people, was not open three consecutive months, and many workers left the area entirely. In November 1924 Fábrica de Mieres closed for two days each week and fired 350 workers at its Cobertoria mine; in October 1925 both Fábrica de Mieres and Duro-Felguera shut down for a month, although some of the former's installations stayed closed even longer, leaving several hundred men out of work. The Mieres municipal government tried to relieve the subsequent hardship by distributing vouchers worth 10 *pesetas* per day to 200 families, but this was clearly insufficient. As one miner wrote to *El Noroeste*, "We are reaching the limits of despair. Hungry stomachs cannot wait days until someone gives them the needed bit of bread." [28]

Unemployment was reflected in emigration. This first took on notable proportions during the general strike of May-August 1922, when many immigrant workers and even native Asturians began to leave. But this was due not merely to the strike and the financial aid given by the SMA to those who wanted to leave. In December 1922 *El Socialista* noted that "many of our most enthusiastic comrades" had migrated.[29] When Fábrica de Mieres reopened following the shutdown of October-November 1925, many workers were not present "because they have returned home or gone to other regions to look for work." [30] In May 1926 *Aurora Social* reported that many miners in Onedines had had to return to their place of origin or go to other countries.[31]

The crisis deepened even further in 1927. "In the Mieres valley the small mines began to close or work only a few days per week, and then El Peñon closed, throwing hundreds out of work." Industrial Asturiana laid off 250 in May, and the following month Hulleras del Turón closed two mines and laid off 450. In July Fábrica de Mieres laid off 300, and Ortiz Sobrinos 200.[32] According to the civil governor, the number laid off "exceeds 1,000. In many mines they are working four days, and others have closed completely." [33] From July to September the situation deteriorated further. Fábrica de Mieres had dismissed 1,200 men and put the rest on the three-day week. Llaneza announced that 4,000 men were out of work and that 20,000 were on a short week. On November 26 the Industrial Asturiana closed completely, leaving 1,500 men unemployed.[34] The authorities were getting nervous, and the civil governor warned Madrid that unless something were done for the miners, "disruptive elements could take advantage of the situation." [35]

The year 1928 was no better. According to González Peña there were 4,000 unemployed in May, and in June the Desquite mine at Caborana introduced a four-day week. In August Hulleras del Turón followed suit, while a number of other sizeable companies announced layoffs or closures. *El Noroeste* estimated that there were between 5,000 and 6,000 men laid off in October 1927 who were still without work and reported that in Lena many miners between the ages of twenty-five and forty had been reduced to begging.[36] The number of working miners at Huería de San Tirso had fallen from 200 to "a few," and "misery has replaced the relative well-being that used to exist here. At least there was work every day and the miners could satisfy their most pressing needs." [37] In his year-end summary, González Peña stressed the human misery caused by the crisis: "Both this year and last thousands have been swarming from place to place unsuccessfully looking for work, and many have had to become beggars as the only means to avoid dying of hunger." [38]

Since the onset of the crisis the strategy of the SMA, based on Llaneza's analysis of the situation of the Asturian coal industry, had been to rely on the state to help wring compromises from an ever more assertive Employers' Federation. Llaneza was prepared to negotiate wages and hours and to offer an extension of the work day and increased productivity in return for no wage cuts. Above all, he felt that it was madness to insist on high wages and short hours in the midst of a severe crisis. In short, he was prepared for the workers to make sacrifices for the health of the industry, but only if the owners did so as well.

Such an approach coincided with the labor-relations strategy of the Primo de Rivera regime as well as with its broader ambitions. The regime's labor policy was, as Tony McIvor has described it, "aggressively interventionist" [39] and formed part of an attempt to establish an antidemocratic "new state" based on corporate representation and fervent government intervention in the economy and in social relations. This new state was strongly dedicated to economic development and attempted to achieve a degree of legitimacy among the working class by integrating Socialist leaders into institutions such as the Council of Labor and the Council of State and integrating Socialist unions into the corporatist labor-relations apparatus established after 1926.[40] Certain elements within the Socialist party and the UGT, particularly Largo Caballero, were prepared to go along with the regime because they saw the new system of labor relations as strengthening their own position within the working class. In fact, the Socialists came to dominate the working-class representation on the *comités paritarios* (mixed juries) once they were established. In relying on the Socialists the regime failed to build up other labor groups, such as the Catholic unions or the Sindicatos Libres, which might have been more sympathetic to its political goals.

The week after the coup that brought Primo to power, Llaneza went to Madrid at the invitation of General Luís Bermúdez de Castro, who had been military governor of Oviedo. As Llaneza described it to the 1927 PSOE congress, the invitation for him to form part of a commission investigating recent events in the important Almadén mining region was discussed by the executive of the SMA and the National Miners' Federation, both of which authorized his accepting it.[41]

This decision was the first point of discord within the Executives of the PSOE and the UGT over the relationship of the Socialists to the regime. According to Indalecio Prieto, when Llaneza reported to the two Executives on his meetings in Madrid, a compromise was worked out to cover up the disagreements, "that Llaneza continue limiting his intervention with the government to absolutely pressing matters related to mining." By the time of the 1927 PSOE congress, this issue had led to a major split within the party. The group around Indalecio Prieto criticized the policy of collaboration, arguing that there was a qualitative difference between dictatorial and democratic systems and that Socialists should support the latter. Largo Caballero defended the need of unions to deal freely with whoever was in power, while Julián Besteiro rejected the inherent superiority of democracy per se, from the point of view of the labor left, and pointed to the persecution of the labor movement by the governments of the Restoration as proof.[42] Llaneza's decision was strongly criticized by fellow Asturian and Prieto supporter Teodomiro Menéndez, who was in turn taken to task by SMA official Amador Fernández for having gone against the opinion of the Asturian Socialist Federation, which "has agreed to accept the conduct observed since September 23 . . . to approve the continuation of this policy in the future."[43] The Asturians cast all their votes in favor of the party Executive, whose conduct was approved by 5,235 to 593.

While he was in Madrid in September 1923, Llaneza met with Bermúdez de Castro and with Primo de Rivera himself. He emphasized the need to protect both wage levels and the length of the work day and agreed to a conference with the owners. At the meetings of this joint commission the union offered to increase productivity if wages and hours were left untouched, while

General Luís Navarro proposed extending the effective work day by an hour, timing it from when the worker reached the stall and not the minehead as was the existing practice. However, with the union and the Employers' Federation unable to agree on such basic questions as productivity, investment rates, and the degree of mechanization, no progress was made. The employers claimed that the union's 20 percent wage demand was out of touch with reality.[44]

The governor of Oviedo avoided a strike by arranging a stopgap solution: an increase of 50 *céntimos* per day between April 1 and September 30, 1924, while the unions and employers worked out a final arrangement. This temporary agreement was then extended through October by all companies except the Fábrica de Mieres, which left the Employers' Federation; in November virtually all the companies suspended it, an act that forced the SMA to call a general miners' strike for November 15. According to a note sent to the government, this strike was one "of desperation." The 50 *céntimos* per day had absolutely no effect on the industry's problems, and these, especially unemployment, would continue without it. The note blamed the crisis on railway freight rates, taxes and port charges, the high cost of wood and other materials, and the commercial treaties that allowed foreign coal to undersell Asturian coal.[45]

The miners came out as ordered and, according to *El Noroeste*, supported the strike totally during the week it lasted. In the end the owners agreed to renew the payments until the end of the year while a permanent settlement was being worked out.[46] The union presented the strike as a victory: neither wages nor hours had been changed. *El Socialista* claimed that it vindicated the UGT's policy of caution. Saborit claimed, however, that the agreement was reached because of the personal intervention of Primo de Rivera, who feared a further split in the SMA and the desertion of the more militant members to the Communists and anarchosyndicalists.[47]

The holding action that the SMA was pursuing in defense of wages and hours could not be maintained indefinitely. In 1925 the government agreed to subsidize wages by 10 percent in the face of threats by Duro-Felguera, Fábrica de Mieres, and Hulleras del Turón to shut down and put 16,000 men out of work. But in the deepening crisis of 1926 and 1927 the owners were insistent upon having the seven-hour day abolished. The decision of the Consejo Superior de Combustible in May 1927 to reinstate the eight-hour day put Llaneza in a difficult position, "between his adherence to the policies of the PSOE on the one hand and confrontation with the Patronal on the other."[48] His response was to offer an extra half-hour per day in return for inspection of mine safety conditions by the workers. "We are prepared to have our work day increased by a half hour, which will leave us on a par with most British miners in this respect, but not with respect to wages."[49] The union defended this offer in a note, saying that it had been made in the name of the SMA and after a series of meetings with local delegates. The choice facing the miners was either "accept the half hour, or allow thousands of workers to be laid off." [50]

When the government officially announced the reinstatement of the eight-hour day in October, the miners showed their frustration and anger, as much with Llaneza and the union as with anything else. The congress held to debate the issue revealed the extent of disagreement between the union leadership and the rank and file. Llaneza resolutely opposed any protest. "To call a strike now would be to challenge the government, and as is natural it will use all the means at its disposal to secure our defeat." He proposed that one-half of the extra hour be paid and the other half be volunteered by the workers. If this offer were rejected after fifteen days, a general strike would be called. [51]

A number of delegates were unhappy with this, and the Executive was attacked in a long and heated debate. One delegate appealed to "the former prestige of the union, calling its present state a disgrace, especially the meager help it provided the English miners during their last strike," while another expressed his concern that "the increased work day will be the death blow to a union which in the past has been ready to fight in difficult circumstances and has won." [52] These more bellicose sentiments evoked a substantial response, and the motion rejecting a strike was approved by 787 votes after "a bitterly contested vote." [53]

Outside the congress, in the valleys, the miners were even more ready for a fight. On October 14 *Aurora Social* reported an atmosphere of "abnormality" in the mines "due to the provocation of the Patronal, which is particularly strong in some companies, and, on the other hand, to the Communist poison." In Sotrondio the miners went on strike the moment the congress was called, and in Aller there was no strike but "everyone is working unhappily and there is great discontent." [54] In Turón the Communists were able to capitalize on the discontent of local SMA militants and draw them out on strike two weeks before the general strike. [55]

The turbulence in the valleys was so great, in fact, that the union had to cancel a scheduled series of rallies. When they were eventually held the following March, *El Socialista* explained that "the Committee had not organized this series of meetings earlier as it did not feel it judicious to do so, considering the excitement, the fervor, and the passion caused by the events of last fall." [56]

Caught between the intransigence of the owners, who announced a 12.5 percent wage cut, and the open rebellion of many militants, the union had no choice but to call a general strike. Three days later it announced an agreement with the Patronal that called for increases in piece rates in proportion to the increase in the workday. This was approved in a referendum, but with all miners over the age of eighteen eligible to vote fewer than 7,000 out of a work force of 28,000 did. [57]

The union did not claim a victory. "We did not advise you to accept the formula because we thought it represented the deserved victory—far from it—but because we believed that the indefinite prolongation of the struggle would have broken our strength, which had to be saved for more opportune moments." [58] While Amador Fernández argued that the results of the referendum showed mass support for the union, *Aurora Social* recognized that this was untrue and that more than anything else the strike had illustrated that "the discontent of the miners continues against the owners and against the decisions of the Sindicato Minero." [59]

Antonio Oliveros, the editor of *El Noroeste*, called this "uprising" the first sign of the decline of the SMA. [60] Amador Fernández came to share the view that the failure to call a strike in October 1927 had led to the desertion of many miners, "some without thinking, others out of passion, others for sectarian reasons, leaving the sad impression that they were completely ignorant of the fatal reality which inevitably determined that tragic situation." [61] But rather than evidence of the beginning of this dissatisfaction, the events of the autumn of 1927 were its climax. The union had been losing support since 1920 and in 1927–28 it hit bottom (table 15).

The figures for SMA membership are not completely reliable. The union announced no official figures, and these are taken from the press accounts of the various congresses, which accounts for their volatility. Other accounts differ substantially. For example, Vigil, in his *Memorias*, credits the union with 16,000 members in 1924, while Oliveros claims that there were barely 3,000 in 1927. By using the union's own figures for payment of dues, Bernardo Diáz Nosty has calculated that in 1928 the union had only 1,260 members and that

Table 15. Membership of the SMA, 1920–30

Year	Membership	As Percentage of Work Force
1920	24,551	62.8
1921	20,000	58.0
1922	7,500	25.3
1923	9,600	32.2
1924	12,000	39.0
1925	10,832	34.9
1926	8,101	25.9
1927	9,763	34.6
1928	8,300	32.2
1929	8,870	32.8
1930	11,022	38.7

Source: *EMME; El Socialista; Aurora Social; El Noroeste,* 1920–30.

at no time before 1932 did the membership exceed 15,000.[62] In any case the trend is clear: the union that had claimed to represent 63 percent of Asturian miners in 1920 had less than 40 percent later in the same decade and on occasion as little as 25 percent. The decline in the SMA was far greater than that of the national Socialist union confederation, the UGT. Despite the loss of 5,331 members in Asturias between August 1922 and April 1928, the UGT increased its national membership during the same period. Among the national industrial federations that made up the UGT the miners were the hardest hit after the agricultural workers, but even so the National Miners' Federation lost only 3,374 members during these years, indicating that outside of Asturias its membership remained steady and even increased.[63]

The growing gap between the union and the miners was evidenced in numerous reports of apathy in various locals, especially between 1926 and 1928. In Olloniego no one paid dues and no union meetings were held, but there were three strikes in the first half of 1926 alone. "They say that the local does not bother about them and therefore they have no reason to bother about the local." *Aurora Social* reported the "great demoralization which exists among the workers there."[64] Membership in the Onedines local fell from 100 to less than sixty, the Socialist Youth chapter disappeared, and there was a notable lack of enthusiasm among those members who remained. "Before the meetings were overflowing with members, and it seemed that we competed for posts of responsibility and to do our duty. But now? . . . Just the opposite. . . . The youth is occupied with its love for football, bullfighting, and the tavern."[65]

In Aller, "the fief of Comillas," the union claimed to have gained strength until 1926, when it had 1,000 paid members and sales of *Aurora Social* had risen to 765. "Since the organization began growing, the symptoms of rebellion have appeared. First one group then another, but above all the men with the picks, have gone on strike to demand increases in the rates that would leave them better paid. . . . The cord is about to snap, and we are happy that they will not long delay a struggle that is necessary."[66] This was an exceptional tone for the Socialist press to take in 1926 and can be explained only by the special conditions in Aller: the ongoing struggle against the Sindicato Católico and the Hullera Española, which had always been a special target of the SMA. By the time of the general strike of October 1927, however, things had changed. The miners of the valley did not display much enthusiasm and even seemed confused as to what the strike was about.[67]

The decline of the union became more pronounced after the strike. As we have seen, fewer than 7,000 voted in the referendum. Membership at Trapa dropped precipitously between June 1927 and June 1928. Vegadotos, the first SMA local, once had 600 members, but by August 1928 it was reduced to only twelve dues-paying members. When the La Huería local called on hewers to join the union, no one answered the call, and workers at Coto del Musel in Laviana, "who had waited seventeen months for the results of the union's negotiations, finally lost all patience and decided unanimously to go on strike." [68] And in Turón, where the union claimed to have regained ground between 1923 and 1926—due no doubt to the persecution of the Communists by the regime—it lost it again in 1927–28. [69]

Even among those who stayed in the union there were critics. At the February 1928 congress, Llaneza's speech was met with some harsh replies. "The delegate from Coto Raso asked that the committee be deposed, and especially Llaneza. Other delegates mentioned the committee's disastrous conduct in recent months, not knowing how to respond to the increase in the work day. . . . The committee was blamed for having aborted the strike." The Executive was reelected, but by only 27 to 17, with two abstentions. [70]

Neither the fiasco of the 1927 general strike nor the subsequent falloff in union membership succeeded in making the SMA alter its policy. That it was in the middle of a crisis was recognized, but the leadership blamed the depression and the activities of the Communists. González Peña explained the problems of 1927–28 in the following terms: "To the crisis of the industry we must add the grave upsets caused by the schismatics who, taking advantage of the general malaise, tried to convince the workers that the union's lack of leadership was to blame." [71]

Throughout 1928 and 1929 the union continued to preach moderation and to rely on the state, even as at the national level the Socialists were moving away from their previous cooperation with the regime. Shortly before the March 1928 congress, *El Socialista* emphasized the importance of political influence in achieving the workers' goals and criticized "the anarchists and syndicalists who advocate a different tactic, which has greatly harmed the proletariat." [72] When in May Duro-Felguera closed two of its mines, "Historon" wrote that the union had to appeal to the government. "We have no one but the government from whom to ask for justice, bread, and work." [73]

Ramón González Peña provided the most consistent defense of this position. In his year-end summary for 1928, he pointed out how many miners had learned the hard way, not trusting the National Federation to solve their problems. At the April 1929 SMA congress, he defended the Executive in the following terms: "The committee works constantly to win all possible benefits for the miners. . . . Every intelligent engineer drives his locomotive at a moderate speed, and those who hurry and force the pace expose themselves to grave risks." [74] And at the end of 1929 he described the policy of the union as "to remain on the defensive, keeping the maximum discretion and trying to remedy as much as possible—through government action—the effects of the crisis, rejecting the use of the strike." [75]

Both the union and the UGT to which it belonged supported the *comités paritarios* (arbitration committees), which were created by Labor Minister Eduardo Aunós in August 1926. The *comités* formed part of the National Corporative Organization, which was announced three months later in November, although the elections were not held until 1929. Six months before the elections González Peña was announcing that they "will undoubtedly bring great benefits to the working class." [76] Just before the election Amador Fernández urged the miners to vote, describing the *comités* as "the little parliaments of labor." [77] The SMA swept the elections, including in Aller, where it had a 1,200 vote majority over the Sindicato Católico, and Turón, where it received all 600 votes cast. [78]

The SMA began to recover somewhat at the end of 1929. In the last four months of the year *El Socialista* reported the creation of a new local in Nembra and rapid growth in Boo, Caborana, and Olloniego. It was claimed that this new enthusiasm has been generated by the election campaign for the arbitration committees. During 1930 membership increased in Turón, where the San Andrés and Hueria de Urbies locals were reestablished, and in Aller, where there were 400 new members in October alone. [79] There is no evidence to decide either way, but it is possible that this influx of new members was made up predominantly of the younger workers who during the Republic and especially in 1934 would generate a level of militancy that the union leaders would have great difficulty in controlling.

In the meantime, the SMA was engaged in a struggle with the illegal Sindicato Unico Minero, which was supported by both the anarchosyndicalists and the Communists. Despite having been persecuted by the regime, these groups had had considerable success in gaining support among the miners. That early in 1928 the SMA undertook a propaganda campaign to counter the "disorientation" of the mine workers is evidence of their success. [80] The Chamber of Commerce of Oviedo and Gijón claimed that the "Sindicato Unico has more members every day," and Oliveros wrote that the workers who had left the SMA were going over to the Sindicato Unico. [81] This struggle for influence continued throughout 1929 and 1930, "a battle between the unions [in which] masses are rushing to join the Sindicato Unico." This assessment was basically correct. The Sindicato Unico was legalized in May 1930, and a year later, just after the declaration of the Republic, it had forty-two locals and 9,000 members. In November 1930 it led a general strike that drew 20,000 miners in sympathy with a miner dismissed by Carbones Asturianos. [82]

The Sindicato Unico was able to gain ground against the SMA, but the Communist party was unable to draw any advantage from this. In September 1929 the Asturian regional federation of the PCE was so weak and disorganized that it could not afford to hold a congress with its own funds. In December the regional union secretary proposed the creation of mine councils as a means of improving the "decayed, apathetic spirit" of the miners and of attracting "the enormous number who are neutral, disgusted by the insidious behavior of the Sindicato Minero," but soon found this "was slow going." [83] By the end of 1930 the Communists had still not created a mass movement of their own, and they admitted that many of the strikes in 1930 were controlled neither by the SMA nor by themselves. By mid-1931 Communist presence in the Sindicato Unico was said to be insignificant. The PCE national executive admitted that "if there is a delegation from the Sindicato Unico de Mineros de Asturias we will have only a very weak fragment." [84]

The continuing failure of the Communists to develop any substantial support in the coalfields was about the only solace the SMA and its leadership had as 1930 ended. The years since 1920 had been much more difficult for the union than had the first decade of its existence. Its strategy of attempting to cope with the crisis in the coal industry by relying on the state to shield the workers from the aggressiveness of the employers was a failure. Even the Primo de Rivera dictatorship, which attempted to cultivate working-class support for its new state by incorporating the Socialists into its corporatist institutions, was not prepared to force the mine owners to yield on their most pressing demands. This failure did not lead the SMA to alter its strategy, and as a result its membership fell off sharply and its rival, the Sindicato Unico, gained in strength. The collapse of the SMA would be reversed, not through any change of strategy on its part, but as a result of national political changes in 1931 that brought the period of nonconstitutional government begun in 1923 and even the monarchy itself to an end. But the more favorable political climate of the Second Republic itself contained the seeds of new and more dangerous problems.

NOTES

1. *EMME*, 1919, 31; 1921, 34; 1923, 34.
2. See ch. 2 herein.
3. *ES*, 7.III.1921.
4. Ibid., 12.III, 2.II, 24.IX.1921; García de la Fuente, *La Cuestión*, 22.
5. *ES*, 9.V.1921.
6. IRS, *Crónica acerca de los conflictos sociales en las minas de Asturias* (Madrid, 1922), 73.
7. For a general discussion of the Communist schism, see G. Meaker, *The Revolutionary Left in Spain* (Stanford, 1973), 225–312, and C. Forcadell, *Parlamentarismo y Bolchevización* (Barcelona, 1978).
8. Ruiz, *Movimiento*, 136–41; Vigil, "Memorias," 594–97. See also *AS*, 14.IX.1928.
9. *NO*, 13.XI.1920–1.I.1921.
10. *ES*, 5.I.1921.
11. Ibid., 27.V.1921. Following the November 1920 congress the union issued a

manifesto restating the role of centralization: "If we have built the Sindicato Minero with a centralized foundation it is because the system of absolute autonomy had failed." *NO*, 23.XI.1920. Llaneza was still haunted by the fiasco of the *huelgona* in 1906.

12. *ES*, 14.VI, 10.VIII.1921.

13. Ibid., 17, 29.XI, 12.XII.1921; IRS, *Crónica*, 73–87, 92–93.

14. IRS, *Crónica*, 100–101.

15. *RIMA*, 1.X.1923, 291–92.

16. IRS, *Crónica*, 101.

17. Ibid., 103–10; *ES*, 6, 12.I.1922.

18. IRS, *Crónica*, 113–25. According to a telegram from the civil governor to the minister of labor on January 19, "The formula was accepted by a very small difference of votes, indicating that although in Mieres there was a large majority in favor of returning to work, it was the reverse in the Langreo valley, where the workers favored staying on strike."

19. Ibid., 133.

20. Ibid., 140–44. Between January 1921 and May 1922 the production of saleable coal had increased by 60 kilograms per worker, the average wage had fallen by 5.17 *pesetas*, the average wage per ton by 29.55 *pesetas*, and the cost per ton in the interior by 19.55. The price advantage of Asturian over imported coal at the pithead rose by 28.55 *pesetas* per ton.

21. *NO*, 16, 23.V.1922; *ES*, 15, 18, 19, 20, 22.V.1922.

22. IRS, *Crónica*, 144–63.

23. Ibid., 163–84; *ES*, 24.V, 9.VI.1922.

24. *ES*, 18.VII.1922; IRS, *Crónica*, 198–228.

25. IRS, *Crónica*, 278–99.

26. Ibid., 201, 267–68, 286–90, 295, 301; *ES*, 31.V.1922. The union claimed the turnout was so low because many workers had left the region in search of work.

27. On the period 1918–23, see S. Ben-Ami, *Fascism from Above: The Dictatorship of Primo de Rivera in Spain, 1923–1930* (Oxford, 1983), 1–52.

28. *NO*, 3.I, 9.II.1924, 31.X, 19, 22, 25.XI.1925; *RM*, 1925, 580, 598, 673; *ES*, 19.X, 19.XI.1925.

29. *ES*, 23.XII.1922.

30. Ibid., 24.XI.1925.

31. Ibid., 31.V, 16.VI.1922; IRS, *Crónica*, 185; *AS*, 21.V.1926. Those who left the country took their political rivalries with them. At the end of 1923 a noted militant of the Sindicato Católico turned up at Valenciennes (Nord) in France, where a number of Asturians had found jobs in the mines. According to a report in *El Noroeste*, he quickly became friendly with the chief engineer and this allowed him to commit several "abuses, including having five miners, all well known in Sama and Mieres as outstanding figures in the class struggle, ejected from the country." After committing various other unpleasantries, he was found shot dead. *NO*, 6.I.1924.

32. *NO*, 4, 18.V, 30.VI.1927; *AS*, 27.V.1927; *ES*, 25.III, 22.VI.1927.

33. Civil Governor to Minister of the Interior, 21.VII.1927, Gob., Leg. 16A, Exp. 13, AHN.

34. *AS*, 1.VII., 16.XII.1925; *NO*, 2, 21, 23.VII.1927; *ES*, 17.VIII, 6, 14.X.1927.

35. Civil Governor to Minister of the Interior, 2.VIII.1927, Gob., Leg. 16A, Exp. 13, AHN.

36. *RIMA*, 1.VII.1927; *NO*, 8, 26, 28.VI, 7.VIII.1927; *AS*, 17.VIII.1927.

37. *ES*, 7.VIII.1927.

38. Ibid., 31.XII.1928.

39. A. McIvor, "Spanish Labor Policy during the Dictablanda of Primo de Rivera" (Ph.D. diss., University of California at San Diego, 1982), 37.

40. Ben-Ami, *Fascism from Above*, 283–308.

41. Partido Socialista Obrero Español, *Actas del XII Congreso del PSOE* (Madrid, 1928), 85–86.

42. Ibid., 98–168. On the divisions within the PSOE, see Preston, *Coming*, 23–24.

43. Partido Socialista, *Actas*, 350–52.

44. Saborit, *Asturias*, 213–16; *RM*, 1923, 532; *RIMA*, 1.XI.1923, 326–27, 344–48.

45. *RM*, 1924, 423, 579, 643; *RIMA*, 16.X.1924, 316; 1.XI.1924, 330–33; Ruiz, *Movimiento*, 144–45; *NO*, 6, 12, 14.XI.1924.

46. For accounts of the strike, see *NO*, 16–22.XI.1924, and *ES*, 18–25.XI.1924.

47. *ES*, 25.XII.1924; Saborit, *Asturias*, 216.

48. *ES*, 19.X., 2.XI.1925; Ruiz, *Movimiento*, 146.

49. *RM*, 1927, 325.

50. *ES*, 1, 22.VI.1927.

51. *NO*, 4.X.1927.

52. *AS*, 7, 10.X.1927.

53. *ES*, 8.X.1927.

54. *AS*, 14.X.1927; *NO*, 5, 19.X.1927.

55. *NO*, 5.X.1927; *AS*, 4.XI.1927. In March 1928 the SMA expelled four members who "took an active part in the past strike staged against the declaration of the union." *AS*, 2.III.1928; *ES*, 10.I, 1.III.1928.

56. *ES*, 15.III.1928.

57. Ibid., 19, 25.X.1927; *NO*, 16.X.1927; *RIMA*, 1.XI.1927, 334.

58. *AS*, 28.X.1927, cited in Ruiz, *Movimiento*, 149.

59. *AS*, 4.XI.1927, cited in Ruiz, *Movimiento*, 149. Amador Fernández argued that the union had to listen to the majority of those who voted, even if they were a minority of all miners.

60. Oliveros, *Asturias*, 242.

61. *AS*, 24.V.1929.

62. Vigil, "Memorias," 482; Ruiz, *Movimiento*, 149; Oliveros, *Asturias*, 285.

63. Unión General de Trabajadores, *Memoria del XVI Congreso* (Madrid, 1928), 89.

64. *AS*, 23.VII, 14.V.1926.

65. Ibid., 21.V.1926.

66. Ibid., 4.VI, 22.X.1926.

67. Ibid., 28.X.1927; *NO*, 19.X.1927; Ruiz, *Movimiento*, 148–49.

68. *AS*, 1.VI, 17.VIII, 20.I.1928.

69. Ibid., 8.X.1926, 23.XI.1928. José María Quirós wrote in both February 1927 and October 1928 to complain about growing criticism of the union in Turón. *AS*, 4.II.1927; *ES*, 9.X.1928.

70. *RIMA*, 16.III.1928. According to *El Socialista* no one spoke against Llaneza in favor of a more radical position. *ES*, 29.II.1928.

71. Ibid., 31.XII.1929; *AS*, 13.I, 24.II.1928.

72. *ES*, 6.III.1928.

73. Ibid., 20.V.1928.

74. Ibid., 31.XII.1928.

75. Ibid., 31.XII.1929; *NO*, 21.IX.1929. For his part, Llaneza insisted that the orders of the Executive be followed "with blind faith." *NO*, 1.VI.1928. A wildcat strike at the Sotón mine in November 1929 was described as an act of "disloyalty." *AS*, 1.XI.1929.

76. *AS*, 15.III.1929.

77. Ibid., 29.XI.1929; *ES*, 21.IX.1929.

78. Ibid., 3.X.1929; *NO*, 1.XI.1929. The Communist party was banned by the regime and its unions were not allowed to present candidates.

79. *ES*, 2, 26.X.1929; *AS*, 8, 22.XI.1929, 28.III, 30.V, 17.X.1930. Tudela-Veguin was the only notable exception reported. *AS*, 11.VII.1930.

80. *AS*, 9.III.1928; *ES*, 9.X.1928.

81. Cámaras Oficiales de Comercio de Oviedo y Gijón, *El comercio, la industria, y la minería de Oviedo en el año de 1929* (Oviedo, 1930), 48; Oliveros, *Asturias*, 285; Santullano, "Las organizaciones obreras en los comienzos de la IIa República," 258–59, 265–69.

82. *NO*, 11, 16.XI, 24.V.1930, 5.V.1931; Villar, *El anarquismo*, 489.

83. Central Committee to Regional Committee, 2.IX.1929; Regional Union Secretary, n.d., Microfilm 2; Minute of the Meeting of the Executive Committee, 12–14.I.1930, Microfilm 3, FIM. On September 22, 1929, the Executive Committee told the Profintern that one of its major union activities was the mobilization of the Asturian miners for immediate wage demands, taking advantage of "the discontent which has already given rise to various sporadic and partial strikes. We want to capture and organize this discontent."

84. Executive Committee to Regional Committee, 7.IX.1931, Microfilm 5, FIM.

7

The Republican Illusion, 1931–34

The declaration of the Second Republic on April 14, 1931, and the Socialists' association with it brought the SMA considerable prestige and provided a favorable context for the revival of the union under the leadership of Amador Fernández. (Llaneza had died in January 1931.) The Republic had a special meaning for the Spanish working class. As Manuel Villar wrote, "The workers and peasants attributed a mythical significance to the republican form of government. To it they attached their yearning for social justice, and they believed it to be the cornerstone of a new society based on new economic and social precepts. They trusted the Republic to rescue them from their misery."[1]

This was certainly the case in Asturias, where the Republic was greeted with "unprecedented enthusiasm . . . something extraordinary which exceeds even the possibility of describing it."[2] Leading figures of the union were identified with the new regime from its very birth: Belarmino Tomás formed part of a three-member Republican committee that assumed power in Sama de Langreo on the 14th, and in Sotrondio Amador Fernández and Graciano Antuña announced the declaration of the Republic from the town-hall balcony. SMA membership certainly seemed to respond to the new situation (table 16). Lurking behind the enthusiasm for the new regime, however, was the danger of disillusion should the Republic not meet the high expectations invested in it. A worker at Hulleras de Ríosa, José Heredia, voiced such a possibility in a letter to *Aurora Social* in September 1931: "The workers saw the newly created Republic as their savior. If these thoughts had not existed we, the workers of this town, would now be caught up in the whirlwind of a new struggle."[3]

From April 14 until June the Republic was governed by a provisional government composed of representatives of various Republican parties and three Socialists: Fernando de los Ríos as minister of justice, Indalecio Prieto as

Table 16. Membership of the SMA, 1930–33

Year	Membership	As Percentage of Work Force
1930	11,022	38.7
1931	14,960	51.1
1932	20,892	68.7
1933	19,155	69.0

Source: *EMME; El Socialista; El Noroeste; Avance.*

minister of public works, and Francisco Largo Caballero as minister of labor. Elections to a Constituent Cortes were held in June, and from then until December this parliament worked to draw up a constitution. The government continued to be a coalition of Republicans and Socialists (with Manuel Azaña as prime minister after the election of Niceto Alcalá Zamora as president of the Republic on December 16) until September 1933, when it was replaced by a cabinet headed by Radical leader Alejandro Lerroux, who called new elections for November. The policy of the SMA until the 1933 elections was essentially the same as it had been during the Primo de Rivera dictatorship—to avoid strikes whenever possible and achieve its demands through negotiation and reliance on the government.

The one major difference was that it could now support the regime unhesitatingly and condemn any attack on the Republican-Socialist coalition. In May 1931 González Peña told the union's congress that "it is necessary to trust the present government to include the workers' fundamental aspirations in the laws to be presented to the forthcoming parliament." As reported by *El Noroeste*, "He recommended calm, as impatience is a foolishness which could put the Republic in danger. He believes it is a duty to support the Republic, for although it is an error to think that the Republic will fully satisfy the demands of the workers, it is in fact a giant step forward toward their ideal that power should be in the hands of the proletariat. . . . The Republic must be consolidated." [4]

Following the abortive coup by General José Sanjurjo in August 1932, a union manifesto told the miners to stay calm and continue working, but to be ready "to throw themselves into the defense of what it has cost so much to establish in Spain." [5] Shortly thereafter *Avance* published an editorial, "The Significance of the Spanish Republic," that summarized the achievements of the regime in its first eighteen months as "profound changes in the country's political and social structures. . . . Let us remember what Spain was eighteen months ago under the Bourbons, and then consider what it is today, with democracy and freedom. The journey could not have been made more rapidly." [6]

One reader went so far as to deny the bourgeois nature of the Republic because "the Constitution leaves the road open to new advances."[7]

Following Hitler's accession to power in Germany, the Republic took on the additional attribute of the Spanish workers' only defense against "fascism." In a curiously prophetic statement, Teodomiro Menéndez claimed that "the Socialist party and the UGT are ready for the struggle. Germany and Italy provide highly tragic lessons. What has cost us so much to achieve . . . will be defended with supreme acts of heroism and passion. At the cry of 'the Republic in danger' our political and union organizations will throw themselves into a struggle that will have the makings of an epic."[8] The general strike of Asturian miners of September 1933 was identified with the defense of the Republic against "the battle being waged against it by the Right. Against them must stand the serious and intelligent strength of the working masses, tired of their submission to a heartless bourgeoisie."[9] The threat became even greater as the November 1933 elections approached. The occasion was seen as a clear choice between fascism and socialism. "Acción Popular offers a fascist regime . . . and fascism means war. Europe is on the verge of war because of German provocations, and within Spain fascism will mean civil war."[10]

The corollary of the SMA's absolute support of the Republic was its absolute refusal to blame it for the continuing—and worsening—crisis in the coal industry. The national mining conference held in August 1931 was cause for optimism. "A national conference of the various groups involved in the industry will be the point of departure for the realization of the workers' aspirations. We are on the verge of great events." The reinstatement of the seven-hour day for underground work announced by Labor Minister Largo Caballero during the conference was one positive achievement.[11]

As the depression deepened in 1932–33, with wage cuts, layoffs, and shutdowns once again becoming daily events, the SMA refused to cast the blame on the Republic. The chronic crisis of the coal industry was an inheritance from the monarchy, whose governments had done nothing to resolve the industry's basic problems. Mine closures were denounced as anti-Republican acts to be resisted. "The government must not permit monarchist elements to sabotage the new regime." Under no circumstances was the union going to criticize the government. "It is totally inadmissable for the Sindicato Minero to put itself in opposition to the government or the men who compose it, for this is what the owners want."[12]

It followed from this that the union was loath to call strikes. The first sign of the opposition to the use of the strike during the Republic was the debate at the May 1931 union congress over the article in its constitution governing the calling of strikes. Following a debate recalling that of ten years earlier over the same issue, the article was revised to give the Executive almost total control. "The locals will not call strikes without previously informing the Regional

Committees, which will in turn inform the Executive Committee, which will try to resolve the conflict through negotiation." [13]

This moderation in regard to strikes was not just the policy of the SMA, but the cornerstone of socialist conduct throughout the whole country. This was articulated by Luis Araquistáin in a series of three articles published in *El Sol* and reprinted in *El Socialista* in July 1931. He criticized the anarchists for the number of strikes they were staging, saying that this represented a danger to the Republic and was merely playing into the hands of the Right. "In the final article 'Against the Abuse of the Strike,' he affirmed that the existing mechanisms for conciliation could handle any just complaint without the need for a strike." [14]

Strikes were denounced as anti-Republican and counterproductive. Amador Fernández told a meeting at Tuilla that "they are attacks on the Republic." [15] In an article in *Avance* Graciano Antuña, another member of the SMA Executive, wrote that numerous strikes were neither wise nor revolutionary. "One must know how to choose the proper moment . . . but one must also be clear about what is being asked for. Otherwise the result will be defeat, not victory." [16]

Rather than through strikes, the union preferred to pursue its demands through negotiation and reliance on the state. On October 8, 1932, before a crowd of 3,000 in Sama, Amador Fernández defended the union's support of the mixed juries created by Largo Caballero. "Through them the general bases and minimum conditions for all labor contracts are sketched out." [17] Commenting on a strike by metalworkers in La Felguera, he urged the miners to turn to the state for remedies. The personal intervention of Manuel Azaña was received happily by *Avance*, which held out "great confidence in his intervention." [18]

The best statement of the SMA's position in this period is the following definition of the class struggle offered by *Avance* in August 1932:

> By respecting the existing work norms we will create a system of civility and mutual understanding, limiting social conflict to that natural area defined by the logical antagonism of interests. It should not be a war between slavers and Africans, a struggle between slaves and tyrants, but simply the disagreement between the worker, who aspires to a better and more humane life, and the employer, who understandably desires to obtain a reasonable return on his investment. . . . From a struggle imbued with this spirit it is always easy to reach an understanding which harms the interests of neither party. This is how we understand the class struggle and this is how we will practice it. [19]

Consistent with this declaration, the union called general strikes only when left with no alternative. In August 1932, in the face of an announced shutdown at Industrial Asturiana, the introduction of a four-day week at Hulleras del Turón, and the lowering of the piece rates at a number of mines, the SMA decided to call a general strike, but not before studying "the spirit of the workers" and finding that they were eager for one. This decision was approved unanimously at a special congress held on September 19.[20] According to the union the strike was purely defensive, "not about wage increases or improved working conditions, which must take a back seat for now. It is the determination of the workers to resolve a fundamental question, the job security of the 50,000 proletarians of the coalfields." It was also directed less at the Patronal than at "the laziness of the state."[21]

From the companies, the union demanded a steady six-day work week, and from the government, a series of measures that would increase the consumption of Asturian coal. When Hulleras del Turón offered to reorganize its work week, the union called off the strike, claiming a victory. However, following the government's refusal to accept the union's proposals, the strike was called once again, only to be canceled when the government changed its mind and promised to ensure a six-day work week.[22]

When in mid-November Fábrica de Mieres, Duro-Felguera, and Hulleras del Turón announced that they were going to close indefinitely, a general strike was called for the third time. The demand was straightforward: six days work per week. The strike lasted six days and paralyzed the coalfields, except in Turón, where the Communists did not support it. According to the civil governor's estimate, 25,000 miners were on strike, including the anarcho-syndicalists: "There are frequent debates in the streets, but there have not been any disturbances."[23] The strike ended when the government accepted a proposal based on SMA demands for the control of iron imports, tariff protection for the coke industry, and state acquisition of coal, all steps designed to increase consumption. Throughout the strike and afterward the union insisted that the strike had not been intended to harm the government, but only to hurry it along. "Now that the government has provided a solution, the job of the Sindicato Minero has finished."[24]

In January 1933 another conference among the government officials, mine owners, and union representatives was convened by the government, and this was cited by *Avance* as proof of the effectiveness of the SMA's strategy. Amador Fernández was somewhat less sanguine, calling the conference "an important first step" while not holding out much hope for a solution. To his mind what was needed was a complete overhaul of the industry: "There is no alternative to greater state intervention to set prices and organize consumption."[25] His pessimism was well founded: the owners were totally intransigent, insisting on increasing prices, lowering wages, and firing more workers, and no agreement was reached. The union responded with a referendum on the question of whether "the men prefer a strike to dismissals and wage cuts." The strike would be a head-on clash between workers and employers over the basic issues of wages and work: "The SMA has stated openly that it will cancel the strike if the owners stop firing workers. For now the government has no place here."[26] Some 70 percent of the union membership participated in the referendum and voted overwhelmingly, 15,128 to 113, in favor of a strike, and 14,293 to 392 in favor of exempting those companies that accepted a six-hour day for their workers.[27]

The strike lasted from February 6 to March 4 and paralyzed the Asturian coalfield except for Turón, Teverga, and the worker-run Campanal mine. After the first week the civil governor said that 27,500 miners were out and that the peaceful character of the strike was being lost, as "acts of sabotage have begun and coercion is increasing." On the night of the 15th five bombs went off in La Felguera, and there was a shoot-out between police and anarchists.[28] On March 4 the union called a referendum to decide on a proposal by the government—that a team of accountants and technicians examine the mining companies' books to determine whether the claims made by the Employers' Federation were justified and that during the three months this investigation was to last the government would lend 2.4 million *pesetas* to the companies. In addition, the government would create a retirement fund, to which the companies would pay 60 *céntimos* for every ton of coal produced and to which the workers would also contribute, intended to ease the unemployment problem by making possible early retirement. This was approved by 15,105 to 410.[29]

In September 1933 the companies canceled their payments to the retirement fund, and the SMA called another general strike. This time both Communists and anarchosyndicalists supported the strike. After two weeks it had spread beyond Asturias to all of the country's mining zones: 50,000 miners were on strike demanding that subsidies be offered to mines outside Asturias and that the payments to the retirement fund be continued. The SMA, and the National Miners' Federation-UGT to which it belonged, claimed a complete victory on September 28. In announcing the return to work, Amador Fernández called the outcome "completely satisfactory . . . better than magnificent."[30]

The moderation of the Socialists during the first biennium, both in Asturias and in Spain as a whole, was in direct contrast to the attitude of the Communists and anarchosyndicalists, who saw the Republic as essentially identical to the monarchy and staged three revolutionary general strikes. In the coalfields the struggle between the SMA and the Sindicato Unico (SU) continued and escalated into all-out war during the general strike called by the SU in June 1931.

At its congress in May the SU had demanded the restoration of the seven-hour day, retirement at age fifty, unemployment pay of 75 percent, elimination of piecework, and an across-the-board wage increase of two *pesetas*; it threatened a general strike if these demands were not met. The strike was not very widely supported. The Patronal estimated a turnout of 20 percent of the work force, and the Socialist press put the number of strikers at about 6,000. The center of gravity of the strikes was in Turón and Sama, although there were stoppages in some mines in Mieres. In Laviana and San Martín del Rey Aurelio virtually all the miners remained at work. The number of strikers in Aller was also very small.[31]

Although much less massive than the strikes called by the SMA, this one was unusually bitter and violent. On June 2 there was a shoot-out between groups from the two unions near the Riquela mine, and in Mieres "many miners are not going to work for fear of disagreeable encounters with those who want the strike to continue." On the 11th there was an armed attack on a train carrying workers to Turón.[32] Sabotage emerged for the first time as a part of mining strikes in the province. The power lines to Hulleras del Turón and Fábrica de Mieres were blown up, and there was an attempt to disable the aerial cable at the Corujas mine and the generator at the Barredos mine.[33]

The strike was turning into "a fierce fight between the members of the two unions" as the SMA reacted forcefully to the violence of the SU.[34] On June 3 armed militants protected Socialist miners working at the Corujas mine, and this was only part of the union's effort to guarantee "the right to work." "The Sindicato Minero has organized compact squads to guarantee the right to work, as the authorities have done nothing in this regard."[35] At the same time, Amador Fernández and Ramón González Peña joined the Chamber of Commerce in sending a telegram to the minister of the interior requesting "urgent measures to guarantee life of men and security of mines, continually threatened by minority audacious troublemakers. . . . Vast majority of men want to work."[36]

Even before the strike, Amador Fernández had complained of attacks on SMA members and "the passivity of the authorities." On June 1 he and González Peña sent a telegram to the minister of the interior denouncing the lenience of the civil governor toward Communists and anarchosyndicalists. "Passivity first authority of province, and cordial, intimate relations with Communist and syndicalist elements will be cause of tragic days in Asturias."[37] The union continued to support the authorities' use of force against its rivals. In December 1931 the police attacked workers sitting-in at the Moreda iron works, and the government sent 100 Guardia Civil to the province, fifty to the coalfields. As the civil governor told Madrid, "Agreeing with my point of view, a commission from UGT Sindicato Minero is touring the coalfield and warning against possible extremist intrigues."[38] Ironically, for all its verbal and actual violence, the SU found itself having to resort to the same methods as the SMA to resolve the strike. A delegate was sent to the national conference of the CNT, which was being held in Madrid, and the national organization took charge of the affair, negotiating a settlement with the government.

This negotiated settlement was approved by the SU in a vote of forty locals to four.[39]

The general strike of June 1931 was the high point of SU activity during the first two years of the Republic. Subsequent general strikes evoked much less response in the coalfields. According to the civil governor only the miners of Turón and La Felguera came out in December 1931,[40] and one estimate had only 3,000 of the 26,000 miners in the region supporting the strike.[41] A general strike in support of La Felguera metalworkers in December 1932 also drew little response, and where mines were totally shut down this was due more to the dynamiting of power lines—rapidly becoming a local specialty—than anything else. Likewise, the general strike of May 1933, which *Avance* called "a reactionary offensive against the Republic," was supported only in Langreo.[42]

The SU split in August 1931, as the Communists left to form their own union, the Sindicato Unico de Mineros de Asturias (SUMA), affiliated with the Communist union federation, CGTU. The SU was left with its anarcho-syndicalist supporters, who numbered a mere 1,168 in February 1932. But not all the rest of the membership, which had numbered about 9,000 in May 1931, went with the Communists. According to Villar, following the schism "disorganization spread and many miners went with neither one group nor the other."[43]

At the CGTU's National Conference for Sindical Unity held in September 1932, the SUMA claimed to have 5,000 members, all in Turón, but this was undoubtedly wishful thinking. The fourth PCE congress held nine months earlier had discussed and criticized the situation in Asturias, where the PCE was split by sectarianism and isolated from the masses. A "resolution on the immediate tasks of the SUMA" of August 1 commented on the stagnation of the union, its lack of effective leadership, and the need for structural changes to bring it into close contact with the miners. At the PCE regional conference held in Mieres in April 1933, the political secretary's report criticized the failure of the union to take the initiative in strike movements. The delegate from Figaredo described the deterioration of the SUMA following the forty-eight-hour general strike of May 1–2, 1932: "It was a real disaster . . . especially in Turón, where the best militants have been left in the street due to lack of organization."[44] By 1934 the so-called Red Turón was in a sad state. According to Manuel Grossi, "For some time before [October 1934] the workers of this valley showed great signs of confusion. The majority had abandoned the labor movement altogether, humbling themselves before the company."[45]

Under these circumstances, with the collapse of Communist and anarcho-syndicalist support among the miners in 1932 and 1933 and the increasing dominance of the SMA with its policy of moderation, one would expect the Asturian coalfields to have been relatively quiescent. But this was not the case. Asturias led all provinces in the number of strikes in 1932 and 1933. In the number of strikers it was first in 1932 and second in 1933.[46] Thus the Asturian coalfields present us with a contradiction. Unlike the years of dictatorship, when labor militancy resulted in the decline of the SMA, in the first two and a half years of the Republic militant miners remained *within* the union, even though they found themselves in conflict with its policy and its leadership.

As we have seen, the general strikes called by the union in 1932 and 1933 were purely defensive, a reaction to the deteriorating conditions of the industry that had led once again to layoffs, wage cuts, and short weeks—as short as three days in some mines. The workers responded to these assaults on their livelihood with spontaneous strikes. The union's repeated warnings of the dangers of such strikes reveal the degree to which it was losing control of its membership. As the union stumbled toward the general strike of November 1932, the civil governor expressed his doubts about the ability of the SMA to maintain control, especially in Turón. "If there is a strike it will be supported by all those miners who are on a short week, and the Sindicato will not be able to control its members." This fear was verified by Amador Fernández, when he admitted that the union had not actually organized the strike. "We did not distribute leaflets nor designate committees nor give any sort of instruction."[47] Yet 25,000 men went out.

The Socialist press reported, with concern, the growing restiveness of the miners. On January 3, 1933, *El Socialista* described the social climate in the coalfields as "charged with madness and passion, only our comrades are holding the lid on."[48] Throughout the year *Avance* reported the rising temperature. The depression was "increasing the restlessness of the workers," "adding to the miners' anguish," and creating "extraordinary enthusiasm for a strike to defend the hundreds of comrades whom the capitalists want to sacrifice altogether."[49] At Hullera Española, where the workers were owed two months' wages, 2,000 struck over the punishment of a worker in March, while in November "unrest and disgust reign."[50]

The victory of the Right in the elections of November 1933 marked the beginning of a new period. The Socialist press, which since Hitler's ascension to power in Germany had identified the Spanish Right as fascist, now declared the death of the "republican Republic," and the repressive bent of the new government would give these charges credibility, as we will see. Immediately after the election, *Avance* announced "the workers have no alternative but to take all political power for themselves."[51] Ten days later came the first outright rejection of the Republic by the Asturian socialists. "The working class has nothing to do with that democracy. The Right has triumphed with a simple aim: to make war on the working class and to destroy its organizations. They first attacked the workers' economic interests . . . to get the unions to rise to the defense. Now they will try to destroy everything. . . . The workers are tired of partial victories and are ready to carry the fight beyond the defense of their material interests. They will arrive at the conquest of absolute power . . . to establish Socialism in the country." [52]

The government's suspension of the CNT following the attempted insurrection of December 1933 was viewed as the first step in this war on the labor movement. "It shows the fascist character of the right's program: a state without unions. . . . There is nothing but revolution or ignominy." [53] In a speech to the Juventudes Socialistas (Socialist Youth), Amador Fernández analyzed the history of the Republic and the course of the rightist offensive, comparing the situation in Spain with that of Russia in 1917. "We must echo the shout that Lenin gave and that brought victory, 'Now or never.' The Spanish working class is ready to take power and realize the full Socialist program." [54] Following the events in Austria in February 1934, Graciano Antuña likened that country to Spain. "Those who liquidated our Austrian comrades are the same people who want to smash the working class here." [55]

By the summer of 1934 the Socialist swing to the left was complete and irreversible. In August *Avance* proclaimed that "the working class is not interested in the Republic in its original state. . . . It only wants to finish with it." [56] González Peña told the Centro Obrero in Oviedo that "music won't tame the fascist beast. He can only be tamed by force. . . . We must prepare ourselves as does the hunter. We must get ready for the hunt." At the same time the union continued to warn its members against going on strike without orders, but the reason now given was that frequent strikes would dissipate the strength of the working class before the final struggle. [57] As Graciano Antuña wrote in July, "Now, more than ever, discipline." [58]

The civil war rhetoric of the Socialist party press was given credence by the increasing repression directed at the workers and their trade union and political organizations by the Lerroux and Ricardo Samper governments. Searches of the Casas del Pueblo for arms began in February, following the approval of a law requiring all privately owned guns to be turned in to the authorities. The searches continued, reaching a peak in September, when Casas del Pueblo, Centros Obreros, the offices of *Avance*, and the Teatro Llaneza in Sama were searched. The Sama Casa del Pueblo was searched three times in seven months. No guns were found, and as Civil Governor José Pérez de Pozas told the Madrid press after the October revolution, "far from being useful and positive for the public peace the searches were almost counterproductive." [59] In March the government made public the draft of an antistrike bill, and the Guardia Civil and Guardia de Asalto were increasingly used to break up strikes and meetings. In May and September the Guardia Civil was called in during strikes at Duro-Felguera, and on September 1 police attacked a rally of Socialist women's organizations in Sama, killing six people. [60]

Perhaps the aspect of this repression that evoked most response was the war declared by the civil governor against *Avance*, the daily paper financed by the SMA. Javier Bueno, who took over the editorship in July 1933, turned what had been a tame and undistinguished newspaper into the militant mouthpiece of the Asturian working class. He established a network of correspondents throughout the coalfields and a marvelous distribution system that took the paper to the farthest reaches of the coalfield, to the factory gates of Mieres, Gijón, and Avilés, and out into the countryside. It had a daily run of almost 25,000 copies, and was so popular that miners would refuse to enter the mine until the day's issue had arrived.[61]

In the course of 186 days beginning in March 1934, the paper was banned ninety-four times and fined 25,000 *pesetas*, and Javier Bueno was jailed three times. Its presses were attacked, and its street vendors were harassed. The union kept the paper going despite the great financial drain this represented. The money to pay the fines was raised by public subscription, and mass visits of thousands of people to Javier Bueno while he was in prison in Oviedo became a regular feature of Sunday life.[62]

The radicalization of the Asturian socialists was less a direct response to the political course the country was taking than to the militancy of its own rank and file. The SMA had had difficulty in controlling its members before the election of November 1933, and it would have even more afterward. The beginning of direct state repression and the consequent shattering of the Republican illusion provided the bridge between the purely economic demands of the miners and the political sphere. The Republic had been greeted as a savior by the working class in Asturias and elsewhere, but the savior had clearly failed—and not only failed, but had turned from savior into scourge. At the same time it was clearer than ever that the miners' well-being was dependent on the nature of the state, and this gave their economic aspirations a revolutionary edge. The course of the strike movement after November 1933 shows the miners' rejection of Republican legitimacy and the increasing politicization of their actions. Moreover, this was a process that was taking place outside the control of the SMA leadership.

The degree of discontent was well illustrated in the strike at the Sotón mine in May. It began on the 12th over a relatively trivial incident—the refusal of a supervisor to credit one of the hewers with his full day's advance. After two days the strike had spread to all the other mines belonging to Duro-Felguera and involved some 3,000 men. When the management called in the Guardia Civil and declared a lockout, the strike spread to the municipalities of Siero, Laviana, and San Martín del Rey Aurelio. An agreement that called for the supervisor in question to be moved to another of the company's mines was quickly reached, but when he reported for work at the María Luisa mine on June 5, the workers went on strike. By the 15th some 15,000 men were participating in a strike that was both unanimous and spontaneous. "The order did not come from any union organization, but still they went on strike like a single man." Although the SMA criticized the strike as a waste of energy, *Avance* praised "the spontaneous fighting spirit of the working class." [63]

The politicization of the miners is particularly apparent. In the first *bienio* of the Republic there was only one strike that could be called political, in the sense of challenging or protesting the actions of the state or its agents, but in the first nine months of 1934, of thirty-two mining strikes mentioned in *Avance*, eight can be considered political, and of those three were general strikes. [64]

The first was a twenty-four-hour strike in solidarity with the Austrian socialists, which effectively closed down all mining operations in the province. [65] With the exception of the construction workers of Oviedo and "some isolated cases in other towns," it was exclusively a miners' strike. Although the civil governor said that the strike was "called by elements of the UGT and the Communists," it did not draw a response from all Socialist and Communist party workers. As the civil governor himself remarked, "It is strange that in many places where they have an organization the workers have not gone on strike." [66] Certainly the Socialists and Communists never claimed to have organized it.

Five of the political strikes were in protest against police actions. In March miners in Langreo, San Martín del Rey Aurelio, Tudela-Veguin, Laviana, and Siero staged a spontaneous strike to protest arms searches in the Casas del Pueblo and the frisking of men as they left the mines. [67] On April 2, 1,500 men at the Mariana mine struck to protest the arrest of five militants, and the next day there were 15,000 on strike in Mieres, Aller, and Lena, in what the civil governor called "a total general strike." [68] The prisoners were freed when a crowd of 3,000 demanding their release surrounded the Mieres jail. [69] In July all the men at the Barredos mine struck to protest the confiscation of an issue of *Avance*, and in September there was a general strike in Langreo, Laviana, and San Martín del Rey Aurelio to protest the police attack on a rally in Sama in which six people were killed. "In Sama the stores did not open, nor the bars, nor the cafés, nor the banks, nor the bakeries. Everything was shut tight as a drum." [70] Finally, on September 27, miners at Boo stayed away from work to be present while police searched their homes for arms. [71]

The other two political strikes were in protest against rallies organized by the CEDA. In April the PCE called a twenty-four-hour general strike against the rally scheduled at El Escorial. Despite the opposition of the SMA, 4,000 came out in Aller, 1,000 in Sama, 250 in Quiros, and "plenty" in Mieres, Moreda, and Turón. [72] The most impressive of all these strikes was that of September 8–9 against the CEDA rally at Covadonga, the shrine of the Reconquest in Asturias itself. The entire central part of the province was shut down—stores closed, train services stopped, phone lines were cut, and groups of armed workers patrolled some of the highways to turn back cars.[73]

September 1934 was the "climax of social tension" in the Asturian coalfield. In addition to the two general strikes already mentioned, there was a strike at the Fondón mine that by the end of the month was on the point of spreading to other mines. In this last month before the revolution the Asturian miners were openly contesting the legitimacy of the Republic, and the Socialist leadership found itself caught in a contradiction: "On the one hand to maintain the pressure and respond to government provocation; on the other to rein in the movement and try to prevent the revolutionary crisis from breaking before the arrival of word from Madrid which would start the insurrection. This tactic had to be applied to an ever more irritable and touchy mass movement which was increasingly opting for the street, the strike, and often for guns."[74]

The role of youth in this process of radicalization was particularly important. One of the striking features of Asturian labor militancy in the period before the revolution, and during the revolution itself, was the active support of the younger workers in the Socialist Youth (*Juventudes Socialistas*). As Bernardo Díaz Nosty has observed, "The youth were the real base of the armed movement, the vanguard. Their role was so decisive that it is difficult to imagine the Asturian Commune without them."[75] It is not possible to gauge the weight of the younger miners in the work force as a whole, but it appears that much of the growth of the UGT, and the SMA in particular, came from this sector.[76]

The centrality of such generational shifts in the development of labor militancy has been stressed by both James Cronin and Richard Geary. "The structural transformation, or reconstruction, of the working class that involved both a new type of industry and a new social environment" during World War I was the basis for the "explosion of activism" between 1917 and 1920. This young working class was "far more volatile in its industrial and political behavior" than the older generation.[77] In Asturias the process came about a decade later and was not as sweeping as in the countries that had participated in World War I, but it was taking place. Likewise, the Asturian "explosion of activism" came about a decade later, coinciding with the Second Republic.

As we saw in Chapter 3, SMA officials and militants had complained constantly about the apathy of the young miners, claiming that their sole concern was "vice." This changed during the Republic, as the union establishment began to complain for very different reasons. At the SMA congress in May 1931, Amador Fernández expressed satisfaction at the "many young people" in attendance, and, according to *Aurora Social*, most of the miners who joined the union in the second half of the year came from this group.[78]

Yet it was precisely the younger miners who were least susceptible to the authority of the union leadership and repeatedly had to be called to order by it. In March 1932 the union claimed that an unauthorized strike at Fábrica de Mieres was the work of the youth element, "comic opera radicalism." [79] Following the general strike of September 1933, there were complaints about the attitude of the younger miners to the retirement scheme. One veteran wrote to *Avance* criticizing their readiness to go on strike instead of making use of the government's arbitration mechanism: "In this way they want to destroy the organization which cost so much to create. These young people worry about only vice and diversion and dare to say that the union does not take care of them. Wretches! They should have known the times when we had to work 12 and 14 hours a day for our miserable wage." [80]

In July 1934 an article by Graciano Antuña called on young miners not to be pushed into action by the stimulus of political events: "From our youth we need not only enthusiasm, strength, and determination but also something much more important, absolutely indispensable for effective action in these difficult times, discipline." [81] The same month Ramón González Peña warned against youthful revolutionary enthusiasms. "We cannot," he said, "allow our young comrades to monopolize the revolution." [82]

Immediately following the election of November 1933, the PSOE and UGT Executives began to discuss the possibility of an armed insurrection against the government, and by February 3, 1934, they had named a committee to oversee the preparations. However, the Socialists were not alone in thinking about revolution in the winter of 1933. Earlier that year Joaquín Maurín, leader of the dissident Communist organization the Bloque Obrero y Campesino (BOC), had developed the idea of the Alianza Obrera (Workers' Alliance) as a means of fighting fascism and advancing the social revolution.

Maurín had begun his career in the CNT. In 1921 he attended the third congress of the Comintern as a CNT delegate and supported the creation of ties between the two organizations. By 1924 he saw that his ideas had no future in the CNT, so he left to join the Catalan Federation of the Communist party. In 1930 he was expelled from the PCE for dissenting from Comintern policy, and the next year his faction merged with another group to create the BOC, which remained a harsh critic of "official" Communism.

During the 1930s Maurín earned a reputation as the most sophisticated Marxist theoretician whom Spain had produced. This reputation was based on his analyses of Spanish history and contemporary politics that formed the basis of his political strategy. The first of these works, *La Revolución Española*, published in 1932, dealt with the first year of the Republic. The fall of Primo de Rivera, he argued, had initiated a revolutionary situation, but the Republic had failed to capitalize and complete the bourgeois revolution by liquidating the large landed estates. In order to prevent a military coup it was necessary to create a united movement of the working class, the peasantry, and the Catalan regionalists, "the movement of national emancipation." When the democratic revolution was complete, the workers and peasants would go on to make the socialist revolution.

Maurín's calls for the unity of the country's progressive forces took on much greater urgency once Hitler had come to power in Germany. Antifascism now became the immediate goal of this interclass alliance. Maurín saw fascism as a product of the international economic crisis. With its economic hegemony threatened, the bourgeoisie formed a united front with a sector of the petit bourgeoisie and abandoned political power to a group of "mercenaries" who would defend their economic position by destroying democracy. The lesson he drew from Germany and Italy was that neither democracy nor culture, unions nor political parties could stop fascism. The working class could only defend itself by answering the bourgeois "fascist front" with a united front of its own. Even in Germany a well-organized but divided working class had been defeated. But this united front, which Maurín called the Alianza Obrera, would not be just a defensive measure. Like the soviets, it would also be a tool of revolution. Once the battle had been won, the various working-class organizations could go their own way, although Maurín did not think this likely.[83]

At its second congress, held in June 1933, the BOC voted to create an Antifascist Workers' Alliance in Catalonia. In July all worker organizations in the region were invited to attend a meeting to discuss the alliance, and all except the PCE and the CNT sent delegates. The election of November 1933 made the threat of fascism in Spain appear imminent, and the Alianza was finally launched on December 16. The manifesto was signed by the BOC and a number of small working-class organizations, but the most important organization in the region, the CNT, refused to join.[84]

Maurín wanted to extend the Alianza throughout the country, which meant interesting the socialists, but their initial response was not encouraging. An article in *El Socialista* listed five conditions for acceptance: "First, that all hostilities cease; second, that all past injuries be forgotten; third, that the alliance be made from above, not below; fourth, that all sides truly want a united front; and fifth, that all are prepared to make major concessions to the others."[85]

In February 1934 Largo Caballero went to Barcelona and met with Maurín, and although he praised the Alianza as a form of worker unity, he showed little interest in committing the Socialist party to building a nationwide alliance. The reticence of the Socialist leadership in Madrid appears to have been due primarily to a fear that the Alianza would usurp their position as revolutionary leaders. The PSOE-UGT-FJS revolutionary committee authorized its regional and provincial committees to join local alliances but "only so long as the party never lost control of the insurrectionary movement."[86] According to Largo Caballero, the revolutionary committee was forced to "tolerate" the Alianza

Obrera: "As it was not possible to dissolve them and very difficult to submit them to a rigorous discipline, we tolerated them in the hope that reality would impose itself on everyone." [87]

The first alliance was created in Catalonia, but the Catalan experience was fundamentally flawed, as the hegemonic working-class organization, the CNT, refused to have anything to do with it or with any of the parties that adhered to it. Committed to its view of the state as despotic, there was no room in the CNT's analysis for distinguishing fascism from other political forms. Yet the CNT was not a monolith, and at least one significant regional organization was prepared to dissent from the sectarianism emanating from Barcelona. In the past the Asturian federation, a minority in a region in which the labor movement was clearly dominated by the socialists, had shown itself more willing to cooperate with them than had the national organization, and it did so once again in 1934.

On February 10, 1934, a plenum of regional federations called on the UGT to join in making the libertarian revolution. In other words, the Socialist union was being invited to abandon its ideas and organization and join the CNT. This resolution was a defeat for the Asturian anarchosyndicalists, who in December 1933 had written to the CNT National Committee expressing the need for genuine cooperation with the socialists if any effective revolutionary activity were to take place. On March 4 the Asturian federation held a regional plenum in which it rejected the decision taken in February and approved a motion to the effect that "we are not disposed to follow the suicidal path imposed by the Regional Confederations which prefer, or so it seems, to destroy the CNT rather than admit their mistakes. . . . This region will ignore the decision of the National Plenum . . . and will therefore be free of the responsibility which may one day fall on the CNT for the failure of the revolution in Spain or the coming of fascism." [88] Five days later, on March 9, the regional plenum agreed to open negotiations for an Alianza Obrera with the UGT. The participation of the Communist CGTU was specifically ruled out because of the "campaign of defamation" it had launched against the Asturian CNT. [89]

The first meeting between representatives of the UGT and CNT was held in Oviedo on March 11. The three CNT delegates said that their organization was impressed with the revolutionary statements of the Socialist party press and the UGT Executive and that it was prepared to form a revolutionary alliance with the Socialist union if it, in turn, would change its attitude to the CNT. The Socialists replied that they were willing to forget the past if the CNT agreed to forget the repression that it had suffered at the hands of the Republican-Socialist government. After these initial remarks, it was agreed that the Socialists would prepare a draft program to be submitted to the CNT Regional Committee before the next meeting, which was to be in Gijón a week later. The anarchosyndicalists left the meeting "happily impressed by the attitude of the UGT delegation . . . and with the conviction that the preparations made by the UGT and Socialist party were being so seriously attended to that the revolutionary movement, supported by the CNT, . . . could not fail." [90]

After the Oviedo meeting, the Asturian regional committee received a letter from the CNT National Committee responding to its decision to go ahead with the Alianza. The National Committee warned the Asturians not to distribute the report to other regional organizations, as it was likely to create further conflicts, but the Asturians replied that they stood behind the document.

Meanwhile, the Socialists delivered their draft program as promised. At the next meeting of the two delegations, on March 18, the anarchosyndicalists presented their own proposal, which had four main points: that the Alianza Obrera was to be between the CNT and UGT—the Socialist party was not to be signatory; that revolutionary working-class political parties could participate in the movement if they accepted the alliance program without question; that the goal of the movement was the creation of a "federalist, socialist regime"; and that after the revolution the workers would be free to choose the bases of the new social system. When the regional committee had been assured that the Socialist proposal was consistent with these points and did not violate any of the CNT's fundamental principles, it authorized its representatives to sign the pact. [91]

The signing took place at a meeting in Gijón on March 31. The delegates also drafted a note to be published the next day that, "to allow us to continue working without arousing the suspicion of the authorities," stated only that the Alianza had been created to fight against war and fascism. [92] That same day the two delegations, which now were called the Alliance Commission, began to draw up a list of the forces of each organization in each town in the province; they agreed to appoint a delegation for each organization "so that together they could establish the necessary working relationship." [93]

The decision to cooperate with the Socialists was not unanimous. The number of local organizations that opposed the Alianza was "very reduced," but among the opposition was the important La Felguera organization. [94] (Presumably it was La Felguera that refused to name a local delegation for the alliance.) [95] At a regional plenum held in May the question of cooperating with political parties occasioned a "vigorous debate," with many of the delegates "unable to understand why they had to allow any politicians in a movement which should have consisted solely of the working class." [96] At another plenum in September the conduct of the regional committee was approved by a vote of 30 to 6, although the alliance itself received much less support, 39 to 35. [97]

The opponents of the Alianza within the Asturian CNT charged that the regional leadership had taken the decision without consulting the local organizations. Had the Alianza merely been a pact between two union leaderships made behind the backs of the workers, as was charged, it would have been worthless. Given the long history of antagonism between the two organizations, no treaty was going to create overnight confidence. As José María Martínez said in defending the regional committee from these charges, "The openly pro-alliance attitude which exists among the workers means that the alliance will exist anyway, for that is what the workers want." [98]

The Alianza Obrera was, in reality, a reflection of the sense of solidarity that had been developing among the workers of the province in a slow and piecemeal manner for over a year before it was formally created. During the February 1933 general strike, Socialist and anarchosyndicalist miners at Santa Cruz de Mieres formed a single strike committee composed of two members of each union. At Carbones de la Nueva members of the SU accepted SMA leadership in a strike in August 1933, but the Communists stayed apart. [99] Calls for a united front began in January 1934. The Langreo Committee for a United Front sent a note to *Avance* urging "the various workers' parties to establish liaison committees to make the desired united front a reality." [100]

When Amador Fernández publicly criticized the holding of two meetings in February at which both Socialists and Communists spoke, he was answered immediately by a militant from Figaredo who described the sympathy for a workers' alliance among Socialist miners there. Certainly there was sympathy in Sama, where the meeting drew so many people that they could not all squeeze into the Teatro Llaneza. In March, before the creation of the Alianza Obrera, there existed a Comité pro Paro Forzoso, with representatives from the PSOE, CNT, UGT, CGTU, and the BOC, whose goal was to raise funds for the unemployed. [101]

On the other hand, where the struggle between Socialists and anarchosyndicalists had remained bitter, as in La Felguera, there was little support for the alliance. The CNT was dominant in this area, and in 1932–33 had staged a nine-month general strike against Duro-Felguera. The SMA had nothing to do with this strike until it led to closures that created hardship for Socialist miners. The union then began to collect and distribute relief, but only to Socialist workers. This "longest strike" created an irradicable fund of bitterness, which helps explain the opposition of the La Felguera CNT to the Alianza Obrera. [102]

By the end of September the coalfields were a powder keg ready to explode at any moment. The ministerial crisis that was provoked by José María Gil Robles's demand that his party form part of the cabinet and that ended on October 3 with the appointment of three ministers from the CEDA provided the spark. The revolutionary committee in Madrid gave the word for the insurrection that it had been planning for almost a year and sent an unhappy Teodomiro Menéndez to carry it to Asturias. When the signal was given late on the night of October 4, the coalfields exploded with the revolutionary force of the miners' anger.

NOTES

1. Villar, *El anarquismo*, 19–20.
2. *NO*, 15, 16, 19.IV.1931.
3. *AS*, 11.IX.1931.
4. *ES*, 28.V.1931; *NO*, 26.V.1931.
5. *Avance*, 11.VIII.1932.
6. Ibid., 30.VIII.1932.
7. Ibid., 29.XII.1932. See also 17.III, 15.IV, and 11.VI.1933.
8. Ibid., 14.III.1933.
9. Ibid., 10.IX, 18.X.1933.
10. Ibid., 24.X, 18.XI.1933.
11. *AS*, 7.VIII.1931; *ES*, 19–20.VIII.1931. Before the conference the SMA demanded that its members maintain the "most absolute discipline."
12. *AV*, 6.I, 2, 7.II.1933.
13. *NO*, 26.V.1931. An amendment allowing the regional committees to call strikes if necessary was passed over the initial opposition of Amador Fernández. The March 1932 congress passed a motion that "in the future neither the locals nor the regional committees will declare strikes that do not conform to our statutes." *AV*, 21.III.1932.
14. Preston, *Coming*, 63.
15. *AV*, 8.XII.1931.
16. Ibid., 24.IX.1932, 6.IV.1933. See also 25.XI.1931, *ES*, 1.IX.1932, and *AS*, 6.XI, 19.XII.1931.
17. *ES*, 9.X.1932.
18. *AV*, 26.XI.1932, 8.I, 29.VIII.1933.
19. Ibid., 2.VIII.1932.
20. Ibid., 19.VIII, 6, 8, 11, 13.IX.1932; *ES*, 3, 6, 13.IX.1932. On August 8 the union issued a manifesto in which it said that a vigorous response was required. The owners, it said, had never accepted the Republic or its reforms, and the time had come to defend "a minimum of existence, of life. . . . We are not after new gains which might appear excessive. We are only defending our present positions." The union agreed that it had to respect economic realities, but only after all miners were assured work. *AV*, 9.VIII.1932.
21. *ES*, 15.IX.1933.
22. *AV*, 13, 18.IX, 18, 23.I.1933.
23. *ES*, 15, 20.XI.1932.
24. *AV*, 14, 22.XI.1932. The civil governor reported that support for the strike in Turón was barely 30 percent.
25. Ibid., 11, 15, 23.I.1933.
26. Ibid., 26.I.1933.
27. Ibid., 26–31.I.1933; *ES*, 31.I.1933.
28. *ES*, 7.II–1.III.1933; *AV*, 7.II–1.III.1933.
29. *AV*, 1–9.III.1933; *ES*, 1–5.III.1933. The retirement plan provided 5 *pesetas* per day for miners over fifty-five, 125 per month for married men or heads of families under fifty-five and 100 per month for single men. Miners under twenty received 90 *pesetas* per month, and women, regardless of age, 60.

30. *ES*, 2–7, 20, 23, 30.IX.1933; *AV*, 24, 29, 30.VIII. 2–30.IX.1933.

31. *NO*, 2–6.V.1931; *ES*, 2.VI.1931; *AS*, 12, 19.VI.1931; *EMME*, 1931, II, 303.

32. *NO*, 3, 11, 12.VI.1931.

33. Civil Governor to Minister of the Interior, 6.VI.1931, Gob., Leg. 7A, Exp. 8, AHN; *NO*, 7–10.VI.1931; *ES*, 11.VI.1931.

34. *ES*, 11.VI.1931.

35. *NO*, 3.VII, 4.VI.1931.

36. Civil Governor to Minister of the Interior, 1.VI.1931, Gob., Leg. 7A, Exp. 8, AHN.

37. *NO*, 31.V.1931; Fernández and González Peña to Minister of the Interior, 1.VI.1931, Gob., Leg. 7A, Exp. 8, AHN.

38. Civil Governor to Minister of the Interior, 10.XII.1931, Gob., Leg. 7A, Exp. 8, AHN.

39. *NO*, 12, 16.VI.1931. According to Benjamín Escobar, the union ended up accepting in Madrid what it had turned down in Oviedo.

40. Civil Governor to Minister of the Interior, 15.XII.1931, Gob., Leg. 7A, Exp. 8, AHN.

41. *ES*, 15, 18.XII.1932, 10–11.V.1933; *AV*, 16.XII.1931, 10–13.XII.1932.

42. *AV*, 9–10.V.1933.

43. Oliveros, *Asturias*, 320; Villar, *El anarquismo*, 51–52.

44. Section 81, Microfilm 5; Actas de las Sesiones de la Conferencia Regional, Section 88, Microfilm 6, FIM. According to the report of one Communist delegate to the seventh Comintern Congress, in the spring of 1935 the party had 300 members in Asturias and the Communist Youth had 500. Legajo H15, Gijón, AHA-GC.

45. Grossi, *La insurrección*, 30.

46. M. Tuñón de Lara, *El movimiento obrero en la historia de España* (Barcelona, 1977), 903.

47. Civil Governor to Minister of the Interior, 4.IX.1932, Gob., Leg. 6A, Exp. 50, AHN; *AV*, 15.XI.1932.

48. *ES*, 3.I.1933.

49. *AV*, 11, 19.I, 4.II, 12.VIII, 26, 28.IX.1933.

50. Ibid., 7.XI.1933.

51. Ibid., 29.XI.1933.

52. Ibid., 9.XII.1933. On December 12 *Avance* called the outcome of the election "the definitive discrediting of democracy" among the workers.

53. Ibid., 26.XII.1933.

54. Ibid., 28.I.1934.

55. Ibid., 26.II.1934.

56. Ibid., 19.VIII.1934.

57. Ibid., 5.IX.1934.

58. Ibid., 29.VII.1934.

59. Ibid., 13.II, 28, 30, 31.III, 16, 22.IX, 2.X.1934; *ES*, 23, 25.IX.1934; *NO*, 30.IX.1934.

60. *AV*, 17.V, 2, 4, 8.IX.1934.

61. *Historia General de Asturias*, VII, 35–40.

62. Ibid., 33–41; *AV*, 19, 23.V, 29.VI, 11, 17, 18, 29.VII, 11.VIII.1934.

63. Ibid., 13–26.V, 6–26.VI.1934; *NO*, 13–26.V, 6–26.VI.1934.

64. This definition of political strike is taken from Tuñón de Lara, *Metodología de la Historia Social de España* (Madrid, 1979), 138–43.

65. *AV*, 14–20.II.1934; *NO*, 20.II.1934.

66. *NO*, 20.II.1934.

67. *AV*, 25.III.1934.

68. Ibid., 3, 4.IV.1934.

69. *Historia General de Asturias*, VII, 29. On March 15, 3,000 people had gathered outside the jail where two socialists were being held on charges of burning bundles of the Catholic paper *El Debate*.

70. *AV*, 2, 4.IX.1934.

71. Ibid., 28.IX.1934.

72. *Historia General de Asturias*, VII, 28; *NO*, 30.IX.1934.

73. *ES*, 9.IX.1934; Díaz Nosty, *La Comuna*, 123.

74. *Historia General de Asturias*, VII, 97.

75. Díaz Nosty, *La Comuna*, 151.

76. *Historia General de Asturias*, VII, 161.

77. J. Cronin, "Labor Insurgency and Class Formation," *Social Science History*, Feb. 1980, 137–40; R. Geary, "Radicalism and the Worker: Metalworkers and Revolution," in R. J. Evans, ed., *Society and Politics in Whilhelmine Germany* (London, 1978), 277–79.

78. *AS*, 29.V, 2.X.1931.

79. *AV*, 7.V.1932.

80. Ibid., 9.XI.1933.

81. Ibid., 11.VII.1934.

82. Ibid., 29.VII.1934.

83. This summary is based on handwritten drafts for articles on fascism held in the Maurín Papers, Box 11, Archive of the Hoover Institution, Stanford, Calif.

84. V. Alba, *El Frente Popular* (Barcelona, 1976), 257–58.

85. *ES*, 29.XII.1933.

86. Vidarte, *Bienio*, 186.

87. Largo Caballero, "Notas históricas," 115.

88. *Solidaridad Obrera*, 13.III.1936; "Gestiones para la Alianza Obrera Revolucionaria en Asturias," Gijón, Serie J, Carpeta 12, AHN-GC, Salamanca.

89. The following account is based on this document.

90. Ibid., f. 10.

91. Ibid., f. 11–12.

92. Ibid., f. 12–13.

93. Ibid., f. 13.

94. Ibid., f. 5.

95. Ibid., f. 13.

96. Ibid., f. 25–27.

97. Ibid., f. 30–31.

98. *AV*, 11.V.1934. According to Avelino Entrialgo, author of the "Informe," there

was "an atmosphere for an alliance which one could feel among the working people of our province."

99. *ES*, 10.II.1933; *AV*, 17.VIII.1933.

100. *AV*, 26.I.1934.

101. Ibid., 6, 7, 15.II, 9.III.1934.

102. *Historia de Asturias*, VIII, 225–29.

8

Asturias, October 1934
The Anteroom of the Civil War

The Asturian revolution lasted only two weeks, and its defeat was followed by a savage repression in which some 30,000 people were imprisoned and many tortured. The defeat is neither surprising nor difficult to explain. The insurrection was not preceded by a crisis of the state, merely by a cabinet crisis that was settled before the rising began. The army and police were both reliable, unaffected by revolutionary propaganda and free from serious discontent. There was no chance of their refusing to fight against the Asturian workers. Had the government had to disperse its forces against a number of revolutionary foci, it is possible that the movement could have succeeded, but this was not the case. The Asturian workers found themselves alone against the entire military apparatus of the Spanish state. The outcome was a foregone conclusion.

The two available explanations of why the insurrection did materialize in Asturias are both inadequate. One, which makes the organizational role of the socialists the focus of analysis, ignores the question of why the working class responded to Socialist organization only in Asturias. The other, which says that it did so because the Asturian workers were much more militant and radicalized than other sectors of the Spanish working class, begs the question: Why was this so?

The high degree of radicalization of the Asturian coal miners cannot be explained by invoking general theories about the alleged greater radicalism of miners in general. These theories are all based on static models of the mining community that stress its homogeneity and uniformity. This description did not at all fit the coal miners in Asturias. They were not an isolated, homogeneous, undifferentiated block. Instead, within the mine work force there existed multiple lines of cleavage that served to shatter any natural solidarity that the mining experience might have produced.

First, the miners were divided by geographic origin, between Asturians, most of them natives of the coalfield municipalities; mixed workers, who combined work in the mines with work in the lands they owned or rented; and the immigrant fulltime miners. Second, the social life of the miners reinforced this basic difference and created new ones. Miners were never ghettoized in large homogeneous settlements that restricted their range of social contacts, but they were widely dispersed, usually in centers of fewer than 500 people, always in close contact with other social groups, and often at some distance from the colliery. Regional rivalries were rampant, and the visceral hatred of the Gallegans was especially intense. There were informal networks among immigrants from a region, a province, or even a village that further solidified this division. In addition, there was a generational split that separated those men who entered the mines during the wartime expansion from the older men, and a second such split that made the young radicals who entered the work force and the union during the Republic the target of criticism of the older, more cautious union officials.

Third, the miners' working lives did not inevitably contribute to overcoming these divisions. The work itself was essentially individual, and teamwork was rare. In very few cases did one miner's wages depend on the work of another. The differing prospects of mobility between native and immigrant miners reinforced differences based on regional origin, while the distinction between outside workers and inside workers—the "real miners"—and within this group between the hewers and the rest were other points of cleavage.

The effect these divisions was reflected in the slowness with which the organized labor movement took root in the coalfields despite the preexisting labor protest. The SMA, which was to be the main vehicle of class struggle in the coalfields, was not founded until 1910. It never represented the entire mine work force and was engaged in constant and bitter—and sometimes violent—struggle with Catholic, anarchosyndicalist, and Communist rivals. In its first decade the SMA won important gains for the mine workers and established itself as one of the strongest unions in Spain, but this initial success was largely based on the favorable conditions generated by Spanish neutrality during World War I. The end of the wartime boom was a watershed. Both the Asturian coal mining industry and the SMA entered a long period of crisis, and it is here that the roots of the Asturian revolution are to be found.

The mine owners responded to the crisis by cutting the work force, lowering wages, and intensifying production through mechanization, lowered piecework rates, the reimposition of indirect methods of labor discipline, and the extension of the work day. At the same time, the social conditions in the coalfields, already horrendous, deteriorated even further, and the inconsistent prewar attempts to use the provision of social services to create a docile work force were abandoned, as mine owners were no longer faced with a chronic labor shortage.

The SMA responded to the crisis with a policy of increasing moderation and dependence on the state, which did not succeed in protecting its members from the effects of the depression. The union itself went into crisis, symptomized by growing internal dissent and the challenge to the traditional leadership, the large number of unauthorized strikes, the massive desertion by the rank and file, the apathy of those who remained, and the indifference of the younger miners. By 1927–28 the union was on the verge of disappearing.

The prestige gained by the Socialists from their role in the creation of the Second Republic and the hopes that the new regime inspired among the miners, together with the influx of a new, more militant generation of workers, allowed the SMA to recover. However, when neither the Republic nor the union's continued moderation succeeded in resolving the miners' problems, the SMA once again began to lose control. The victory of the Right in the elections of November 1933 and the subsequent repression irreparably shattered the Republican illusion and led to the definitive radicalization of the mine workers. Both the swing to the left of the Socialist leadership and the creation of the Alianza Obrera were reflections of this radicalization and of the leadership's response to the growing militance of the rank and file.

The insurrection was neither spontaneous nor unplanned. Rather, it had been conceived as part of a national movement planned by the Socialist party and its union affiliates to topple the right-wing government of the Republic and replace it with a left-wing government that would implement a number of reforms. However, the insurrection received the massive support of the working class only in Asturias, and here events went much further than the Madrid revolutionary committee had expected.

In Asturias socialist planning put a match to the powder keg of unrest and rebelliousness that had been building up among the miners for years. The revolution was the expression of that unrest. Within Spain, and particularly for the labor movement, the Asturian Commune has had a symbolic importance similar to that of the Paris Commune for the European labor movement. As Raymond Carr and Juan Pablo Fusi have written, it has become the almost "mythical" point of reference in the history of the Spanish working class.[1] But the interest and importance of the Asturian revolution of October 1934 are not limited to this local symbolic role, for in many important ways this insurrection foreshadowed the Spanish Civil War that was less than two years in the future.

The military aspects of the Civil War in Asturias resembled those of the events of October 1934. In 1934 the workers concentrated all their efforts on taking Oviedo, ignoring other more important objectives, especially Gijón.

During the Civil War the value of the Asturian working class to the Republican cause was seriously undercut by the deceitful seizure of Oviedo by Colonel Antonio Aranda, which made necessary another siege of the city, this time lasting until the northern front fell to the Franco forces in November 1937. There was also an important resemblance to one of the military features of the Civil War as a whole: the use of aerial bombardments of cities, while not massive by the standards of later conflicts, was the forerunner of this terror tactic of which the most notorious example was Guernica.

At another level, the political aspects of the two conflicts have important similarities. The Alianza Obrera of 1934 presaged the close wartime cooperation of the UGT and CNT in Asturias. Likewise, the reticence of the Communists to participate and their attempt to convert the workers' militias into a regular army anticipate one of the central conflicts within the Republican camp. The determination of the Communist leaders to defend Oviedo to the end and not move into the coalfields with the rest of the provincial committee was paralleled during the Civil War by their determination to defend Madrid and their resistance to the National Defense Council when it decided to negotiate with Franco in March 1939.

During the revolution there was a pronounced tendency toward the disintegration of all central authority, which was embodied in the predominance of the local committees over the provincial committee. During the Civil War mines and factories were run by individual councils, but political authority was retained by the Republican government as represented, at least in theory, by the Council of Asturias. The fracturing of political authority did take place, but at the level of the regions, not of the towns. With the military rebellion of July 18, 1936, the authority of the central government disintegrated and was replaced by regional political institutions, the *concejos* (councils). The Council of Asturias theoretically represented the central government, but in fact it acted as an independent entity and, unlike the Council of Aragon, for example, was never brought under the control of Madrid (or Valencia), and in the last days of the war in the north actually declared itself independent.

Finally, the Asturian revolution signaled the failure of the Second Republic to resolve its central dilemma: the threat of social conflict if it did not provide meaningful social change. With the first lay the continued support of millions of working-class Spaniards; with the second, failure and ultimately civil conflict. In Asturias, as elsewhere in Spain, the Second Republic was received by the working class as its salvation, but it did not take long for it to realize that if social reform were to come it would have to be fought for. In Asturias, where the coal miners had been fighting a defensive battle against the mine owners since 1919, this realization came earlier than in other parts of the country. So, too, did the violent conflict it engendered. Both the Asturian revolution and the Spanish Civil War were social conflicts fed by the disappointment of the hopes for a better life that the Republic had kindled in the Spanish working class.

NOTE

1. R. Carr and J.P. Fusi, *Spain: Dictatorship to Democracy* (London, 1979), 141.

Bibliography

Archives

Archivo de la Hullera Española, Ujo. Incomplete company archive in the attic of a building belonging to the state coal company, HUNOSA.

Archivo del Partido Comunista de España, Fundación de Investigaciones Marxistas, Madrid. Microfilms of internal party documents relevant to Asturias, 1927–34.

Archivo Histórico del PSOE, Fundación Pablo Iglesias, Madrid. Typescript memoirs of Francisco Largo Caballero, "Notas históricas de la guerra en España, 1917–1940." Typescript memoirs of Manuel Vigil, "Memorias de un octogenario." Minute Books of the Executive Committee, 1933–34. Correspondence.

Archivo Histórico del SMA, Fundación Francisco Largo Caballero, Madrid. A very small number of assorted documents.

Archivo Histórico Nacional, Madrid.

Archivo Histórico Nacional—Sección de la Guerra Civil, Salamanca. Gijón, Serie J, Carpeta 12; Madrid, Carpeta 721.

Archivo Municipal, Mieres. Municipal Census, 1910. Various files on social conditions.

Archivo Municipal, Pola de Laviana. Municipal Census, 1930. Strikes of 1902, 1911.

Archivos Pasivos de HUNOSA, Mieres and Ciaño. Personnel registers of former companies incorporated into HUNOSA.

Hoover Institution Archives, Stanford, California. Joaquín Maurín Papers.

Newspapers and Periodicals

Anales de Minas. Madrid, 1833–46.

Aurora Social. Oviedo, 1900–1904, 1908–9, 1926–32.

Avance. Oviedo, 1931–34.

Boletín de la Cámara Oficial de Comercio, Industria y Navegación de Oviedo. Oviedo, 1906–9.

Boletín Oficial de Minería y Metalúrgia. Madrid, 1917–30.

Boletín Oficial de Ministerio de Fomento. Madrid, 1861–62.
Estadística Minera y Metalúrgica de España. Madrid, 1861–1934.
Minero de la Hulla. Mieres, 1914–17, April 1929.
El Noroeste. Gijón, 1906–34.
Revista Industrial Minera Asturiana. Oviedo, 1915–34.
Revista Minera. Madrid, 1858–1934.
Revista Nacional de Economía. Madrid, 1917–21.
Revista Socialista. Madrid, 1903–6.
Semana Popular Ilustrada. Barcelona, 1890–92.
El Socialista. Madrid, 1886–1934.

Books, Articles, and Theses

Acevedo, I. *Los topos.* Madrid, 1930.
Adaro, L. *Los carbónes nacionales y la marina de guerra.* Madrid, 1911.
———. *La cuenca carbónifera de Asturias.* Madrid, 1914.
Aldana, L. *Consideraciones generales sobre la industria Hullera de España.* Madrid, 1862.
Aldecoa, M., et al. *Dictamen oficial sobre la industria hullera en Asturias.* Madrid, 1926.
Alvarez Buylla, R. *Observaciones prácticas sobre la minería carbonera de Asturias.* Oviedo, 1861.
Alvear, F. de. *Informe al ayuntamiento de Aller sobre la necesidad de proteger a la industria hullera nacional.* Oviedo, 1925.
Andrade, J. *La burocracia reformista en el movimiento obrero.* Madrid, 1935.
Arboleya, M. *El caso de Asturias.* Barcelona, 1918.
Asociación de la Industria Hullera de Asturias. *Los carbónes asturianos.* Gijón, 1879.
Asociación Patronal de Mineros Asturianos. *Reglamento del trabajo y del salario mínimo.* Oviedo, 1920.
Bailen, J. *Principaux traits du developpement économique de l'Espagne de 1914 à l'avenement du Directoire Militaire.* Paris, 1924.
Barrera Ibarreche, A. "Sociedad Carbónes de la Nueva." Thesis, Escuela Superior de Ingenieros de Minas, 1920.
Barthe y Barthe, A. *El aumento de riqueza de España desde 1795.* Madrid, 1907.
Becerro de Bengoa, R. *De Palencia a Oviedo.* Palencia, 1884.
Bello, L. *Viaje por las escuelas de España.* Madrid, 1926–29.
Benavides, D. *Democracia y Cristianismo en la España de la Restauración, 1875–1931.* Madrid, 1970.
———. *El Fracaso Social del Catolicismo Español: Arboleya Martínez, 1870–1951.* Madrid, 1975.
Benavides, M. *La revolución fue así.* Barcelona, 1935.
Bizcarrondo, M., *Octubre del '34.* Madrid, 1977.
Buckley, H. *Life and Death of the Spanish Republic.* London, 1940.
Bulmer, M. "Sociological Models of the Mining Community." *Sociological Review* 23 (February 1975), 61–92.

Buxton, N. K. *The Economic Development of the British Coal Industry*. London, 1978.

Cabrera Calvo-Sotelo, M. "La Estrategia Patronal en la IIa República." *Estudios de Historia Social* 7 (1978), 7–162.

Cámaras Oficiales de Comercio, Industria y Navegación de Oviedo y Gijón. *El comercio, la industria, y la minería de Oviedo en el año 1929*. Oviedo, 1930.

Cambon, P. *Les conditions du travail en Espagne*. Paris, 1890.

Canals, S. *Asturias—su presente estado*. Madrid, 1900.

Canella Secades, F. *La emigración asturiana*. Oviedo, 1881.

———. *Representación asturiana administrativa y política desde 1808 a 1915*. Oviedo, 1915.

Casariego, F. *Saneamiento de Sama y Langreo*. Madrid, 1918.

Casariego, J. E. *El Marqués de Sargadelos*. Madrid, 1950.

Castaño Sanjuan, V. *El estado actual económico-social de las industrias mineras de hulla en España*. Madrid, 1933.

Castelain, L. *L'Espagne: ses terrains houlliers*. Brussels, 1864.

Castillo, J. J. *El Sindicalismo amarillo en España*. Madrid, 1977.

Chastagnaret, G. "Contributions à l'étude de la production et des producteurs de houille des Asturies de 1861 à 1914." *Mélanges de la Casa de Velásquez*, 1973, 582–631.

———. "Speculation et exploitation minière en Espagne au milieu de XIX siècle." *Mélanges de la Casa de Velásquez*, 1974, 357–85; 1975, 281–307.

Ciges Aparicio, M. *Los vencedores*. Madrid, 1910.

Collado y Ardanuy. *Apuntes para la historia contemporánea de la minería española en los años 1825 a 1849*. Madrid, 1865.

Comisión de Estudio de la Riqueza Hullera Nacional. *Información pública efectuada en 1906*. Madrid, 1909.

———. *Información relativa a la crisis del mercado hullero en España*. Madrid, 1915.

La Compagnie Royale Asturienne des Mines, 1853–1953. Paris, 1954.

Crew, D. *A Town in the Ruhr: Social History of Bochum, 1860–1914*. New York, 1980.

Criado Hernández, C. M. *La Población de Asturias, 1875–1970*. Oviedo, 1975.

Denis de Lagarde, L. *De la richesse minerale de l'Espagne*. Paris, 1872.

"Descripción general del principado de Asturias." *Mercurio de España* 3 (1821), 158–92, 246–87.

Díaz Faes-Intriago, M. *La Minería de la Hulla en Asturias*. Oviedo, 1979.

Díaz Nosty, B., *La Comuna Asturiana*. Bilbao, 1974.

Duro-Felguera, S. M. *Memoria*. Madrid, 1901–4, 1920, 1927.

Edwards, P. K. "A Critique of the Kerr-Siegel Hypothesis of Strikes and the Isolated Mass: A Study of the Falsification of Sociological Knowledge." *Sociological Review*, 1977, 551–74.

Elhuyar, F. de. *Memoria sobre el influjo de la minería en la agricultura y la industria*. Madrid, 1825.

Erice, F. *La Burguesía Industrial Asturiana, 1885–1920*. Gijón, 1980.

Escalera, E. *Recuerdos de Asturias*. Madrid, 1886.

Ezquerra del Bayo, J. *Minas de carbón de piedra de Asturias*. Madrid, 1831.

―――. *Datos y observaciones sobre la industria minera*. Madrid, 1844.

Fábrica de Mieres S.A. *Memoria*. Oviedo, 1926–31, 1938.

Fernández, J. *Distrito minero de Oviedo*. Madrid, 1933.

Fernández Cabeza, L. *Proceso de la Economía Mierense en los Tres Cuartos del Siglo Ultimo*. Mieres, 1977.

Fernández Cuesta, N. *La vida del obrero en España desde el punto de vista higiénico*. Madrid, 1909.

Fernández Díaz-Faes, J. M. *Lo social en la Asturias del siglo XX*. Oviedo, 1966.

Fernández Flores, W. *Los que no fuimos a la guerra*. Madrid, 1941.

Fernández García, A. *Langreo: De la Industrialización a la Crisis Actual*. Gijón, 1983.

Fernández García, D. *La Sociedad Hullera y yo*. Barcelona, 1933.

Fernández Hernández, J. "Memoria de prácticas en las minas de la Sociedad Felgueroso Hermanos." Thesis, Escuela Superior de Ingenieros de Minas, 1915.

Fernández Zapico, B. *En el ocaso: experiencias de un minero*. N.p., n.d.

Fontana, J. "Nacimiento del proletariado industrial y primeras etapas del movimiento obrero." *Cambio Económico y Actitudes Políticas de la España del Siglo XX*. Barcelona, 1973.

Forcadell, C. *Parlamentarismo y Bolchevización*. Barcelona, 1978.

Fuerte Arias, R. *Asturias industrial*. Gijón, 1902.

García, J. L. *Antropología del Territorio*. Madrid, 1976.

García Arenal, F. *Datos para el estudio de la cuestión social*. Gijón, 1980.

García de la Fuente, E. *El problema hullero*. Mieres, 1921.

García Díaz Peyroux, C. *Teverga: Historia y Vida de un Concejo*. Oviedo, 1978.

García Fernández, J. *Sociedad y Organización Tradicional del Espacio en Asturias*. Oviedo, 1976.

García San Miguel, L. *De la sociedad Aristocrática a la Sociedad Industrial en la España del Siglo XIX*. Madrid, 1973.

Gascue, F. *Industria carbonera asturiana*. Gijón, 1888.

Geary, R. *European Labour Protest*. London, 1981.

―――. "Radicalism and the Worker: Metalworkers and Revolution, 1914–1923." In R. Evans, ed., *Society and Politics in Wilhelmine Germany*. London, 1978.

Gimeno y Azcárate, M. *La criminalidad en Asturias*. Oviedo, 1900.

González García, I. "Las inversiones y los inversores en Asturias, 1885–1900." *Studium Ovetense*, 1975.

González Lasala, J. "Memoria sobre las minas de carbón de piedra de Arnao." Manuscript, Instituto Geológico Minero, Madrid, 1847.

González, Valdés, F. *Topografía médica del consejo de Oviedo*. Oviedo, 1911.

Grand, A. *Étude sur le bassin houllier des Asturies*. Paris, 1874.

Grossi, M. *La insurrección de Asturias*. Gijón, 1978.

Gutiérrez, M. M. "Carbón de Piedra." *Cartas Españolas*, 1831, 290–327; 1832, 1–8.

Halleck, H. W. *A Collection of Mining Laws of Spain and Mexico*. San Francisco, 1859.

Harrison, J. *An Economic History of Modern Spain.* Manchester, 1978.

Harrison, R., ed. *The Independent Collier: The Miner as Archetypical Proletarian Reconsidered.* Hassocks, 1978.

Herrero Garraldo, I. *La política del carbón en España.* Madrid, 1944.

Higgin, G. *Commercial and Industrial Spain.* London, 1886.

Historia de Asturias: Economía y Sociedad, Siglos XIX y XX. Salinas, 1981.

Historia General de Asturias: Octubre 1934. El Ascenso. Gijón, 1979.

Holynski, A. J. J. *Coup d'oeil sur les Asturies.* Paris, 1843.

La Huelga de Laviana. Pravia, 1902.

Hulleras del Turón S.A. *Memorias.* Bilbao, 1892–1935.

Información sobre el derecho diferencial de bandera: carbónes. Madrid, 1866.

Instituto de Reformas Sociales. *Crónica acerca de los conflictos en las minas de carbón de Asturias desde diciembre de 1921.* Madrid, 1922.

———. *El Trabajo en las Minas.* Madrid, 1970.

———. *Informe acerca de la fábrica y obreros de Mieres.* Madrid, 1907.

———. *Informes de los inspectores del trabajo.* Madrid, 1915–19.

———. *Información sobre la emigración española a los paises de Europa durante la guerra.* Madrid, 1919.

International Labour Office. *The World Coal Mining Industry.* Geneva, 1938.

Jiménez de Saavedra, F. "Asturias." *El Comercio de Ambos Mundos*, July 21, 25, 28, 1826.

Jové y Canella, J.M. *Topografía médica de Langreo.* Madrid, 1925.

———. *Topografía médica de Laviana.* Madrid, 1927.

———. *Topografía médica de San Martín del Rey Aurelio.* Madrid, 1923.

Juliá, S. *Madrid, 1931–1934.* Madrid, 1984.

Kerr, C., and A. Siegel. "The Interindustry Propensity to Strike: An International Comparison." In A. Kornhauser, ed., *Industrial Conflict.* New York, 1954.

Laborde, A. *A View of Spain.* London, 1809.

Labra, R. M. de *De Madrid a Oviedo. Notas de viaje.* Madrid, 1881.

Lacomba, J. A. *La Crisis Española de 1917.* Madrid, 1970.

Lamberet, R. *Mouvements ouvriers et socialistes: l'Espagne.* Paris, 1953.

Largo Caballero, F. *Mis recuerdos.* Mexico City, 1954.

Laslett, J. M. H. "Why Some Do and Why Some Don't: Some Determinants of Radicalism among British and American Coalminers, 1872–1924." *Bulletin of the Society for the Study of Labour History*, 1974, 6–9.

Latorre, C. *Nomenclator general de la provincia de Oviedo.* Oviedo, 1889.

Lecciónes de laboreo de minas. Oviedo, 1866.

LePlay, F. "Itinéraire d'un voyage en Espagne." *Annales des Mines.* 30 Ser., V, 1834, 175–236.

Llaneza, M. *Estudio de la industria hullera española y la necesidad de su nacionalización.* Oviedo, 1921.

Llano, A. de. *Hogar y Patria: Estudio de casas para obreros.* Oviedo, 1906.

Lockwood, D. "Sources of Variation in Working Class Images of Society." *Sociological Review*, 1966, 249–67.

Louis, H. "Coal Mining in Asturias, Spain." *Transactions of the Institution of Mining Engineers* (Newcastle), 1904, 420–33.

Luxán, F. de. "Viaje científico a Asturias." *Memorias de la Real Academia de Ciencias de Madrid*, 1861, 105–92.

McIvor, A. "Spanish Labor Policy during the Dictablanda of Primo de Rivera." Ph.D. diss., University of California at San Diego, 1982.

Madoz, P. *Diccionario geográfico-estadístico-histórico de España*. Madrid, 1848–50.

Malo de Molina, M. *Manual del minero español*. Madrid, 1863.

Martínez Cachero, L. M. "Historia económica de la emigración asturiana." *Conferencias sobre economía asturiana*, III. Oviedo, 1959.

Marvaud, A. *La cuestión social en España*. Madrid, 1975.

Mesa y Alvarez, P. *La riqueza minera y metalúrgica de España*. Madrid, 1899.

Miguel, A. de. *El potencial económico de España*. Madrid, 1945.

Ministerio de Industria. *Monografía de la minería de carbón*. Madrid, 1960.

Ministerio de Industria, Dirección General de Agricultura, Minas y Montes. *Informe relativo al estado ecconómico y situación de los obreros de las minas de España*. Madrid, 1911.

Ministerio de Trabajo. *Estadística de salarios y jornadas de trabajo, 1919–1930*. Madrid, 1931.

Molíns i Fábrega, N. *UHP: La insurrección proletaria de Asturias*. Gijón, 1977.

Moreau de Jonnes, A. *Estadística de España*. Valencia, 1835.

Moro, J. M. "La Desamortización en Asturias en el Siglo XIX." Ph.D. diss., University of Oviedo, 1978.

Muniz, J. G. *La industria hullera*. Sama de Langreo, n.d.

Muniz García, J. "Minería y Capital Extranjero en la Articulación del Modelo de Desarrollo Subordinado y Dependiente de la Economía Española en la Segunda Mitad del Siglo XIX." *Información Comercial Española*, 1976, 514.

Muniz Prada, N. *Apuntes para la topografía médica del concejo de Mieres*. Oviedo, 1885.

———. *Nociones del higiene*. Oviedo, 1886.

Muniz y Vigo. *Asturias*. Oviedo, 1900.

Nadal, J. *El Fracaso de la Revolución Industrial en España, 1814–1913*. Barcelona, 1975.

Nevares, S. *El patrono ejemplar*. Madrid, 1936.

Nicou, P. "L'industrie minière et métallurgique dans les Asturies." *Annales des Mines, Memoires*, 1905, 203–57.

Nomenclator de las ciudades, villas, lugares, aldeas de España. Provincia de Oviedo. Madrid, 1922, 1933.

Nuevo nomenclator de España. Madrid, 1876.

Núñez, I. *La revolución de octubre de 1934*. Barcelona, 1935.

Olariaga, L. *La crisis hullera en España*. Madrid, 1925.

Oliveros, A. *Asturias en el resurgimiento español*. Madrid, 1935.

Oriol y Vidal, R. *Carbones minerales de España*. Madrid, 1873.

Palacio Valdés, A. *La aldea perdida*. Madrid, 1963.

Partido Socialista Obrero Español. *Actas del XII Congreso del PSOE*. Madrid, 1928.

Pastor, M. "Memoria del Grupo Sama." Thesis, Escuela Superior de Ingenieros de Minas, 1926.

Pereda, J. V. *Memoria sobre el carbón fosil*. Oviedo, 1814.

Pérez González, R. "Industria, Población y Desarrollo Urbano en la Cuenca Central Hullera Asturiana." Ph.D. diss., University of Oviedo, 1980.

Perpiñá Grau, R. *Memorandum sobre la política del carbón*. Valencia, 1935.

Pla, J. *El carbón en España*. Madrid, 1904.

Pollard, S. *The Genesis of Modern Management*. London, 1965.

Preston, P. *The Coming of the Spanish Civil War*. London, 1983.

Quirós Linares, F. "El Puerto de Gijón." *Eria*, 1980, 179–221.

Ramos Oliveira, A. *La revolución española de octubre*. Madrid, 1935.

Reseña sobre las minas de hulla de Aller (Asturias). Madrid, 1887.

Riego, R. de. *La mecanización de los servicios en las minas*. Oviedo, 1929.

Rimlinger, G. V. "International Differences in the Strike Propensity of Coal Miners in Four Countries." *Industrial and Labor Relations Review*, 1959, 389–405.

Roldán, S., and J. L. García Delgado. *La Formación de la Sociedad Capitalista en España, 1914–1920*. Madrid, 1973.

Rosal, A. del. *1934: El Movimiento Revolucionario de Octubre*. Madrid, 1984.

Ruiz, D. *El Movimiento Obrero en Asturias*. Gijón, 1980.

Saborit, A. *Asturias y sus hombres*. Toulouse, 1964.

———. *La huelga de agosto de 1917*. Mexico City, 1964.

Saco y Breig, E. *La emigración de Asturias*. Madrid, 1881.

Sánchez García-Sauco, J. A. *La Revolución de 1934 en Asturias*. Madrid, 1974.

Santullano, G. *Historia de la Minería Asturiana*. Salinas, 1978.

———. "Las Organizaciones Obreras en los Comienzos de la IIa República." In M. Tuñón de Lara, *Sociedad, Política y Cultura*. Madrid, 1973.

Saus, T., "Prácticas de residencia en la mina Mariana de la Fábrica de Mieres." Thesis, Escuela Superior de Ingenieros de Minas, 1924.

Solís, P. G. *Memorias asturianas*. Madrid, 1890.

Suárez, J. *El problema social minero*. Oviedo, 1896.

Suárez, S. *El caso de la Fábrica de Mieres*. Mieres, 1934.

———. *Mineros de España*. Oviedo, 1958.

Los sucesos de agosto ante el parlamento. Madrid, 1918.

Taylor, A. J. "The Coal Industry." In D. H. Aldcroft, ed., *The Development of British Industry and Foreign Competition*. London, 1968.

Townsend, J. *A Journey through Spain in the Years 1786 and 1787*. London, 1792.

Trempé, R. *Les Mineurs de Carmaux*. Paris, 1971.

Vasconi, A. *Sobre el régimen de trabajo en las minas españolas*. Madrid, 1910.

Vigil, M. *Los mineros asturianos*. Oviedo, 1900.

Villar, M. *El anarquismo en la insurrección de Asturias*. Barcelona, 1935.

Widdrington, S. E. *Sketches in Spain during the Years 1830, 1831 and 1832*. London, 1833.

———. *Spain and the Spaniards in 1843*. London, 1844.

Index

Note on the Author

Adrian Shubert is a member of the Department of History, York University, Toronto. His B.A. degree is from the University of Toronto (1975); he has two M.A. degrees, from the University of New Mexico (1976) and the University of Warwick, England (1978); and his Ph.D. is from Queen Mary College, University of London. He is the author of *Spain, 1808–1982: A Social History* (forthcoming) and numerous articles in such journals as the *International Labor and Working Class History, Social History, European Studies Review*, and *Sistema*.